RADICAL
TRADITIONS

THEOLOGY IN A POSTCRITICAL KEY

SERIES EDITORS

Stanley M. Hauerwas, Duke University,
and Peter Ochs, University of Virginia

RADICAL TRADITIONS cuts new lines of inquiry across a confused array of debates concerning the place of theology in modernity and, more generally, the status and role of scriptural faith in contemporary life. Charged with a rejuvenated confidence, spawned in part by the rediscovery of reason as inescapably tradition constituted, a new generation of theologians and religious scholars is returning to scriptural traditions with the hope of retrieving resources long ignored, depreciated, and in many cases ideologically suppressed by modern habits of thought. RADICAL TRADITIONS assembles a promising matrix of strategies, disciplines, and lines of thought that invites Jewish, Christian, and Islamic theologians back to the word, recovering and articulating modes of scriptural reasoning as that which always underlies modernist reasoning and therefore has the capacity — and authority — to correct it.

Far from despairing over modernity's failings, postcritical theologies rediscover resources for renewal and self-correction within the disciplines of academic study themselves. Postcritical theologies open up the possibility of participating once again in the living relationship that binds together God, text, and community of interpretation. RADICAL TRADITIONS thus advocates a "return to the text," which means a commitment to displaying the richness and wisdom of traditions that are at once text based, hermeneutical, and oriented to communal practice.

Books in this series offer the opportunity to speak openly with practitioners of other faiths or even with those who profess no (or limited) faith, both academics and nonacademics, about the ways religious traditions address pivotal issues of the day. Unfettered by foundationalist preoccupations, these books represent a call for new paradigms of reason — a thinking and rationality that are more responsive than originative. By embracing a postcritical posture, they are able to speak unapologetically out of scriptural traditions manifest in the practices of believing communities (Jewish, Christian, and others); articulate those practices through disciplines of philosophic, textual, and cultural criticism; and engage intellectual, social, and political practices that for too long have been insulated from theological evaluation. RADICAL TRADITIONS is radical not only in its confidence in non-apologetic theological speech but also in how the practice of such speech challenges the current social and political arrangements of modernity.

RADICAL TRADITIONS

Published Volumes

James J. Buckley and George A. Lindbeck, eds.,
The Church in a Postliberal Age

Peter M. Candler Jr.,
*Theology, Rhetoric, Manuduction,
or Reading Scripture Together on the Path to God*

David Weiss Halivni,
Revelation Restored: Divine Writ and Critical Responses

Stanley M. Hauerwas, *Wilderness Wanderings*

P. Travis Kroeker and Bruce K. Ward,
Remembering the End: Dostoevsky as Prophet to Modernity

David Novak, *Talking with Christians: Musings of a Jewish Theologian*

Peter Ochs and Nancy Levene, eds., *Textual Reasonings:
Jewish Philosophy and Text Study at the End of the Twentieth Century*

Randi Rashkover and C. C. Pecknold, eds.,
Liturgy, Time, and the Politics of Redemption

Eugene F. Rogers, Jr., *After the Spirit:
A Constructive Pneumatology from Resources outside the Modern West*

David Toole, *Waiting for Godot in Sarajevo*

Michael Wyschogrod,
Abraham's Promise: Judaism and Jewish-Christian Relations

John Howard Yoder, *The Jewish-Christian Schism Revisited*

Liturgy, Time, and the Politics of Redemption

Edited by

Randi Rashkover and C. C. Pecknold

WILLIAM B. EERDMANS PUBLISHING COMPANY
GRAND RAPIDS, MICHIGAN / CAMBRIDGE, U.K.

Wm. B. Eerdmans Publishing Co.
2140 Oak Industrial Drive, N.E., Grand Rapids, Michigan 49505 /
P.O. Box 163, Cambridge CB3 9PU U.K.

Printed in the United States of America

11 10 09 08 07 06   7 6 5 4 3 2 1

Library of Congress Cataloging-in-Publication Data

Liturgy, time, and the politics of redemption / edited by Randi Rashkover and C. C. Pecknold.
        p.   cm.   — (Radical traditions)
    ISBN-10: 0-8028-3052-8 / ISBN-13: 978-0-8028-3052-4 (pbk.: alk. paper)
    1. Episcopal Church — United States — Liturgy.   2. Public worship — Episcopal Church.
    I. Rashkover, Randi.   II. Pecknold, C. C.   III. Series.

BX5940.L58   2006
264 — dc22

                                                                2006011721

www.eerdmans.com

Contents

Acknowledgments   ix

Introduction: The Future of the Word and the Liturgical Turn   1
Randi Rashkover

PART I: LITURGICAL ACTION

A Christian Act: Politics and Liturgical Practice   29
Graham Ward

Morning Prayer as Redemptive Thinking   50
Peter Ochs

PART II: LITURGICAL TIME

Figuring Time: Providence and Politics   91
Scott Bader-Saye

Rosenzweig's Liturgical Reasoning as Response
to Augustine's Temporal Aporias   112
Steven Kepnes

PART III: LITURGICAL SCROLLING

Eternity in History: Rolling the Scroll   127
    Robert Gibbs

Holy Seeds: The *Trisagion* and the Liturgical Untilling of Time   141
    Ben Quash

PART IV: LITURGICAL IMPROVISATION

For Such a Time as This: Esther and the Practices
of Improvisation   167
    Samuel Wells

The Ritual Is Not the Hunt: The Seven Wedding Blessings,
Redemption, and Jewish Ritual as Fantasy   188
    Shaul Magid

PART V: LITURGICAL SILENCE

Cosmic Speech and the Liturgy of Silence   215
    Oliver Davies

CONCLUSION

Liturgy, Time, and the Politics of Redemption:
Concluding Unscientific Postscript   229
    C. C. Pecknold

Contributors   245

Index   247

Acknowledgments

Thanks go to York College of Pennsylvania for a Faculty Enhancement Grant, to the Cambridge Interfaith Programme in the University of Cambridge, and to the Episcopal Church Foundation for vital research funding, all of which greatly supported and enhanced the work of this volume. We have to thank our families for making it more enjoyable, if not easier, to work on the volume. We would like to dedicate this book to our teachers: David Ford, Robert Gibbs, George Lindbeck, David Novak, and Peter Ochs. They have sharpened our vision and have taught us that in the face of the world's suffering, a robust politics of redemption will depend on Jewish and Christian communities laboring together in the time God has given us.

INTRODUCTION:

The Future of the Word
and the Liturgical Turn

Randi Rashkover

Patmos

The occasion for this volume is a unique and historically significant convergence of Jewish and Christian theologians who share a confidence and sense
of urgency surrounding the theological and theopolitical import of liturgical
texts and performance. At the heart of the convergence is the claim that the
distress characteristic of contemporary Western society requires not only a
deeper commitment to a theology centered around the Word of God, but also
a commitment that appreciates how the Jewish and Christian liturgical traditions uniquely link the Word of God to the human encounter with the world,
all the while offering the possibility of a transformation of human life in the
world via the Word. The volume is premised upon the notion that parallel
Jewish and Christian inquiries into the character of liturgical life unveil the
unique contours of a theological realism in both traditions that challenges
and provides an alternative to modernist categories of history, sociality, politics, economics, and ethics. The recovery of a liturgically funded thick description sheds new light on Judaism and Christianity as effective agents of
redemptive repair in the world now rather than as prophetic anticipations of
a "not-yet" messianic fulfillment. The recourse to the theo-cosmological perspectives of Jewish and Christian liturgical performances represented in this
volume raises the possibility of a new chapter in Jewish-Christian relations. If
liturgical life mediates the Word of God with the world and the world with
the Word of God, Jews and Christians may locate new resources for their mutual engagement via their lives of redemptive praxis.

The roots of this contemporary convergence extend all the way back to an
earlier and equally groundbreaking convergence of Jewish and Christian

theologians known as the Patmos[1] Group, whose members included (at vary-
ing times) Franz Rosenzweig, Eugen Rosenstock-Huessy, Rudolph Ehrenberg,
and Karl Barth. Unprecedented in Jewish-Christian relations, the Patmos
Group brought together Jewish and Christian theologians whose work over-
lapped less because of a conscious effort to locate conceptual similarities and
more because of a shared sense that recent events in history, i.e., World War I
and its aftermath, laid bare the final failure of eighteenth- and nineteenth-
century humanism to live up to its promise of progress and called out instead
for a return to the resources of the revelatory traditions and their texts. This
remarkable convergence of Jewish and Christian theologians produced the
basis for what can be called a "Word of God theology" in both traditions. As is
well documented,[2] the Word of God theology presented by Rosenzweig,
Rosenstock-Huessy, and Barth offered believers more than a new chapter in
theological development. Rather, the Patmos Group members radically altered the mandate and character of both Jewish and Christian theology away
from an indebtedness to fashionable currents in secular and philosophical
thought and back into the biblical resources of their own traditions. This
side-by-side recovery of a theological realism happened not a moment too
soon and would shortly thereafter be tested, as the years after World War I set
the stage for World War II and its devastating challenges to both the Jewish
and Christian communities. Noteworthy among the Christian believers who,
during the Nazi reign of power, armed themselves with a theology of the
Word as their response to the violence of the day were Barth, Rosenstock-
Huessy, and Dietrich Bonhoeffer. While of course it was Franz Rosenzweig
who suggested that "God must redeem man, not through history, but —
there is no alternative — through religion,"[3] it was Barth, Bonhoeffer, and
Rosenstock-Huessy who were challenged to apply the theology of the Word
to their political response to the Nazi regime. Undoubtedly, much respect is
due their efforts via the Confessing Church and its bold resistance to the Nazi
war machine. Driven, however, by the immediacy of the crisis facing Jews and
Christians, neither Bonhoeffer nor Barth could fully investigate the theo-

---

1. The name seems to derive from reference to the place, Patmos, sometimes referred to as
"Jerusalem of the Aegean," where St. John the Theologian was exiled between 95 and 97 A.D. and
was inspired to write the Book of Revelation.

2. David Myers, *Resisting History: Historicism and Its Discontents in German-Jewish Thought*
(Princeton: Princeton University Press, 2003), pp. 94-103.

3. Alexander Altmann, "Franz Rosenzweig and Eugen Rosenstock-Huessy: An Introduction
to Their 'Letters on Judaism & Christianity'" in *Judaism Despite Christianity: The 'Letters on
Christianity and Judaism' between Eugen Rosenstock-Huessy and Franz Rosenzweig*, ed. Eugen
Rosenstock-Huessy (New York: Schocken Books, 1971), p. 29.

political possibilities characteristic of their own liturgical practices. Dire circumstances dictated that Bonhoeffer, for one, remain politically active through his alliance with the Kreisau Circle — a largely nonreligious community whose language of resistance assumed the rhetoric of a secular political underground movement. This translation of the Word of God into the language of political resistance was, Bonhoeffer held, the "cost of discipleship" during a time of few other options. Yet Bonhoeffer held out the hope for a day when the Word of God would be fully active in the world — the full breadth of its mediating possibilities realized, so that at once time would make a difference to the church and the church would make a difference in time. "The church," Bonhoeffer said,

> must come out of its stagnation. We must risk saying controversial things. Our church, which in these years has fought only for its self-preservation, as if it were an end in itself, is incapable of being the bearer of the personal and redeeming word for mankind. . . . The day will come in which people will again be called upon to pronounce the word of God in such a way that the world will be changed by it. . . . Until then the concern of a Christian will be a quiet and hidden one. [And yet] there will be people who pray and do what is righteous and await God's time.[4]

Bonhoeffer's comments earmark the limits of the Jewish-Christian convergence occasioned by the era of the two World Wars — limits that we must and can exceed in our present times.

After Patmos: The Questions of Our Time

In his essay "Barth, Barmen, and the Confessing Church Today," George Hunsinger challenges readers by asking whether there ought and can be a Confessing Church in America today. If in the term "Confessing Church" we include not only a church of Christian witness but also a Jewish community of prophetic praise,[5] then the essential contention of this volume is Yes, with some clarification. In his essay, Hunsinger goes to some lengths to defend the need for a Confessing Church. Today, twenty years after his article was pub-

---

4. Harold Stahmer, "Introduction," in Rosenstock-Huessy, ed., *Judaism Despite Christianity*, p. 18.

5. For a detailed analysis of how Jewish religious life parallels Barth's Confessing Church see Randi Rashkover, *Revelation and Theopolitics: Barth, Rosenzweig, and the Politics of Praise* (London: T&T Clark, 2005).

lished, the need for a Confessing Church is even clearer. Daily we experience the violent failures of modern nationalism's strategies for political peace and worldwide economic equilibrium. Moreover, unlike Nazi Germany during the War period, America today offers religion an unprecedented opportunity for participation in the public sphere so far as there is increasing recognition among philosophers and political theorists that we live in a post-secular age.[6] The question at hand is not whether we need a Confessing Church — that is, whether we need Christian and Jewish communities to enlist the resources of their traditions as their central languages and guides for political response. The question is how we need them to do so. In Hunsinger's terms, how do we relate the center of the Word of God and our testimony to God to the details of the periphery and our particular encounters with the world?

The need to link explicitly and describe the Word in the world — that is, to permit one's testimony and witness to divine revelation to incorporate and assume one's encounter with the world, is part and parcel of the unique demands of our particular *kairos*. There is little doubt that the *teshuvah* inspired by the work of Rosenzweig, Barth, and others dramatically reoriented the character of religious life in wartime and during the postwar era. Jews and Christians alike benefited from the recovery of their traditions out from under the limits of modernity. Our times demand that we press this recovery of the Word of God theology to demonstrate its ability to lend discourse to all spheres of human life. Our times demand that we recognize the reach of the Word of God in the service of the full range of human experiences — not only experiences that lend themselves to the obedience of witness or praise in the face of challenge but experiences of suffering, failure, limit and need. We must, as Robert Gibbs has argued elsewhere, "reclaim the interrogative"[7] mood within theology.

In his classic review of Rosenzweig's *Star of Redemption,* entitled *Correlations in Rosenzweig and Lévinas,* Gibbs insightfully notes that for all of Rosenzweig's careful excavation of the grammar of the Word of God, missing from his account is an analysis of the "question." While clearly poised to bypass the thorns of traditional apologetics, Rosenzweig's theology of the Word stakes its philosophical plausibility on the theological indeterminancy of the world coupled with the verifiability of the theological worldview.[8] A

---

6. Jeffrey Stout's *Democracy and Tradition* (Princeton: Princeton University Press, 2004) is the most well-known example of the claim that contemporary America is best described as post-secular.

7. Robert Gibbs, *Correlations in Rosenzweig and Lévinas* (Princeton: Princeton University Press, 1992), p. 101.

8. For a discussion of Rosenzweig's position on the relation between philosophy and a the-

valiant philosophical defense, Rosenzweig's theology of the Word nonetheless falls short of accounting for the troubling encounter between the believer and the limits and obstacles both within herself and her world. It is true, as Gibbs points out, that the believer's dialogue with God ends in a "cry" — but Rosenzweig's believer has quick recourse to verification of or testimony to the God who loves, and such recourse fuels both her individual and her community's labor of redemption. Surprisingly, it is the neo-Kantian Hermann Cohen whose account of the ethical striving of the believer more poignantly portrays the dimensions of both human suffering and guilt that are inevitable features of the believer's religious life. Gibbs echoes this concern and says, "Our question, beyond the . . . romantic hymns of love in love, our question comes from across the abyss of the Holocaust. Where is God? And why was God silent, absent, impotent, anything but loving, in the atrocities of this century? . . . Can we ask God a question?"[9] Believers need to be able to have a discourse for a host of questions, including but not limited to those concerning divine presence. Believers need to be able to lend language to a range of human needs — their own and those of others as they arise in the particularities of the political, economic and social lives. We must ask, can the Word engage the world qua Word? Need a commitment to the Word sacrifice itself to a language of realpolitik, secular historicism, and market capitalism as the "cost of discipleship," or might the Jewish and Christian traditions offer resources for an accurate and powerful engagement with these realities now? The Word of God theology faces nothing less than the philosophical challenge of coming to terms with the not yet fully redeemed world.

In a now famous essay, "Redemption, Prayer, and Talmud Torah" Rabbi Joseph Soloveitchik wrote, "Judaism . . . wants man to cry out aloud . . . to react indignantly to all kinds of injustice or unfairness . . . whoever permits his legitimate needs to go unsatisfied will never be sympathetic to the crying needs of others . . . need awareness constitutes part of the definition of human existence. . . ."[10] Elsewhere in the same essay he wrote,

> [R]edemption . . . is identical with communing, or with the revelation of the word, i.e., the emergence of speech. When a people leaves a mute world and enters a world of sound, speech and song, it becomes a redeemed peo-

---

ology of verification see Gibbs, *Correlations in Rosenzweig and Lévinas,* and Rashkover, *Revelation and Theopolitics.*

9. Gibbs, *Correlations,* p. 101.

10. Joseph Soloveitchik, "Redemption, Prayer, and Talmud Torah," *Tradition* 17:2 (Spring, 1978): 55-72.

ple, a free people. In other words, a mute life is identical with bondage; a speech-endowed life is a free life.[11]

But the speech of redemption, Soloveitchik clarifies, is not strictly the language of song and praise but includes as well the language of complaint, of protest, of question and suffering. In the essay Soloveitchik recounts a passage from the Zohar that details Moses' acquisition of language from out of the event of the theophany of Sinai, and Soloveitchik notes that as important as Moses' ability to praise or testify to the God of Sinai was his subsequent ability to give language to suffering — his own and that of others. Bequeathed to Moses and the Jewish people was a revelation of justice — but a revelation whose Word did not nullify but rather gave rise to the utterance of suffering; "in short — the dead silence of non-existence was gone; the voice of human existence was now heard."[12] The language of redemption, Soloveitchik tells us, is the language of human need as much as it is the language of worship and praise.

Soloveitchik's work lends poignant expression to the link in Judaism between the Word of God and the human discourse of need, petition, wonder and doubt. Of even greater significance here is Soloveitchik's appreciation for prayer as the discourse of human need. Prayer in Judaism, he reminds us,

> is bound up with the human needs, wants, drives and urges which make man suffer. Prayer is the doctrine of human needs . . . of the nineteen benedictions in our *Amidah*, thirteen are concerned with basic human needs, individual as well as social. . . . Even two of the last three benedictions *ritzeh* and *s'im shalom* are of a petitional nature.[13]

Echoing the position of Moses Maimonides, Soloveitchik proclaims, "The person in need is summoned to pray. . . ."[14] *Halakha*, he tells us, views "prayer and redemption as two inseparable ideas . . . the *halakha* requires that the Silent Prayer be preceded, without a break, by the benediction of *go'al* Israel which proclaims God as the redeemer of Israel."[15] Redemption, in other words, transpires not after or despite our needs but here in the midst of them and through our articulation of them. Prayer, Soloveitchik understood, is the human face of the Word of God.

11. Soloveitchik, "Redemption, Prayer, and Talmud Torah," p. 56.
12. Soloveitchik, "Redemption, Prayer, and Talmud Torah," p. 59.
13. Soloveitchik, "Redemption, Prayer, and Talmud Torah," p. 65.
14. Soloveitchik, "Redemption, Prayer, and Talmud Torah," p. 65.
15. Soloveitchik, "Redemption, Prayer, and Talmud Torah," p. 55.

Soloveitchik's deep appreciation for the discourse of petitionary prayer as an expression of the redemptive Word — his refusal to see a conflict between the praise of God and the human account of suffering — is a testament both to the tradition's resources for linking the Word to the world and to Soloveitchik's own rich articulation of it. Soloveitchik helps extend the reach of a Word of God theology into the recesses and language of human existence. Soloveitchik's attention to petitionary prayer in particular has the overall effect of bolstering the philosophical value of a Jewish Word of God theology. Contrary to what the late Gillian Rose labeled the utopian messianism of post-modern Jewish thought, Soloveitchik's theology demonstrates how time makes a difference within the Jewish labor of redemption.

There are, however, limits to Soloveitchik's account of the nexus between the revelatory word and the needs of the created environment. Simply said, Soloveitchik cannot make sense of the prayer of Hannah. It is common knowledge among Jews that the rabbis see Hannah's prayer as described in 1 Samuel 1 as a standard for Jewish *tefillah*.[16] At first, Hannah's situation resembles Sarah's situation in Genesis 16. Both women are barren and both want to have a child. Still, it is important to note the difference between the two. Sarah desires a child who is already promised ("I will make of you a great nation" [Genesis 12:2]), whereas Hannah's petition is not contextualized within the narrative of the divine promise. Hers is not a prayer of destiny — a prayer for what God has already willed. Rather, Hannah's prayer is outside the context of a covenantal circumscription. Hannah's prayer is a bold announcement of her own personal need before a God who she believes will listen. Independently she discerns both her need and the terms within which she believes it is right for this need to be met. She forges her own covenantal exchange with God — "If thou wilt indeed look on the affliction of thy maidservant, and remember me, and not forget thy maidservant, but wilt give to thy maidservant a son, then I will give him to the Lord all the days of his life" (1 Samuel 1:11). Worth noting is the fact that Hannah's prayer to God is quiet and private. "Hannah was speaking in her heart; only her lips moved, and her voice was not heard" (1:13). Nonetheless, the individuality of Hannah's need does not render it incommunicable to others, as shortly after Eli's initial failure to understand her act she explains to him the content of her petition and

---

16. The rabbis learn many *halakhot* from Hannah. Hannah, for example, teaches us, as she taught the uncomprehending Eli who thought her drunk, that prayer should not be audible to others. The Talmud teaches that audible prayer is wrong: "He who makes heard his voice in his prayer is one of little faith; he who raises his voice in his prayer is a false prophet." This is because such behavior reflects depraved theological concepts. *Berakhot* 31a and Rashi to Samuel 11:13.

he understands. "Then Eli answered, 'Go in peace, and the God of Israel grant your petition which you have made to him'" (1:17). Moreover, Hannah's prayer, while voluntaristically scripted and performed, is not strictly an example of autonomous decision-making. Hannah articulates her need in the context of her confidence in God's willingness to entertain and aid her in its realization. Hannah's prayer links autonomous discernment with a faith in divine aid, and the biblical text endorses this petitionary formula as a foundation for a theopolitical society insofar as the account of the rise of the Davidic dynasty that follows 1 and 2 Samuel has its basis in Hannah's petitionary discernment.

Oddly enough, Soloveitchik's account leaves no room for Hannah's prayer. While it is the case that Soloveitchik appears to recommend a human discourse of need, his endorsement of a petitionary discourse of changing needs gets drowned out by what he calls the *logos* of need — the logic of need diagrammed by Torah and *halakha*. There is technically, according to Soloveitchik, a dynamic relationship between the language of need *(tzi'ahkah)* and the *logos* of need *(tefillah)* offered by the study of Torah. With my personal desires announced, I approach Torah and in my study gain an authentic discernment of which of my needs count as teleologically appropriate and which do not. Guided by *halakha,* I learn, he says, "to pray for the gratification of some needs since I consider them worthy of being gratified. I refrain from petitioning God for the satisfaction of other wants because it will not enhance my dignity."[17] Is, however, the language of need retained in this encounter with *halakha* as Soloveitchik describes it? In this account, would women, for example, have the regular opportunity to express their needs in *halakhic tefillah?* Does *halakha* circumscribe which needs women ought to seek to gratify and which are inappropriate? If so, wouldn't *halakha* so perceived undermine the free discernment of need represented by Hannah in 1 Samuel 1? Soloveitchik's perception of the Toraitic logic of need silences the very nature of petitionary prayer he earlier linked to redemption.

What results from Soloveitchik's failure to understand the autonomous discernment and temporality linked to petitionary prayer is a view of *halakhic* life that is frozen in time and painfully dissociated from the range of human experiences that constitute our responses to the covenantal God — a life more characterized by absolute sacrifice than by the confidence in the divine nearness presupposed by a discourse of prayer. "*Halakhic* man is not a man of words," Soloveitchik tells us in his classic work, *Halakhic Man.* "The

17. Soloveitchik, "Redemption, Prayer, and Talmud Torah," p. 66.

thinking *logos* precedes the speaking *logos.* . . ."[18] He then proceeds to tell the following story:

> Once my father entered the synagogue on Rosh Hashanah, late in the afternoon, after the regular prayers were over and found me reciting Psalms with the congregation. He took away my Psalm book and handed me a copy of the tractate Rosh Hashanah. 'If you wish to serve the Creator at this moment, better study the laws pertaining to the festival.' While the congregation would recite *piyyutim* on the days of Awe, R. Hayyim would study Torah.[19]

What a far cry this account is from Soloveitchik's earlier claims linking redemption to prayer. The loss of the discourse of prayer in Soloveitchik's work guarantees a tragic slippage between his portrait of the lonely man of faith who prayerfully articulates his loneliness before the covenantal God who promises hope and comfort and the *halakhic* man whose commitment to a transcendent God requires the forfeiture of the human experience for the sake of the divine rational ideal. In the end, the price for this unwillingness to pay homage to the discourse of prayer is the dissolution of the vitality and relevancy of the Jewish life. Soloveitchik's "*halakhic* man" is an ideal image of a Jew who cannot exist in his own skin here in the world of the divine creation. Missing from his Judaism is Hannah's bold announcement of need and the vital relation between the discernment of need and the social, economic, and political reality of the Jewish people as described by 1 and 2 Samuel. Needed is the recuperation of the discourse of prayer to mediate the Word of God with the demands of the world, thereby permitting the Word to make a difference in and to time.

The challenge to extend the Word of God theology into the recesses of our encounter with our world faces Christian theology just as much as it confronts Jewish thought. Barth's theology of the Word has frequently been charged with a neglect of an anthropological-ethical account that details the human experience of witness in the time of the unredeemed world. Below I will enter into a more sustained analysis of Barth's theology and its relation to liturgical life. Suffice it to say here that Barth's Christocentric theological realism appears to limit the range of human witness to praise of God.[20] The ques-

---

18. Joseph B. Soloveitchik, *Halakhic Man,* trans. Lawrence Kaplan (Philadelphia: The Jewish Publication Society of America, 1983), p. 86.

19. Soloveitchik, *Halakhic Man,* p. 87.

20. For a lucid analysis of Barth's ability to contend with religious deviations from the norm see Susannah Ticciati, *Job and the Disruption of Identity: Reading Beyond Barth* (London: T&T Clark, 2005).

tion concerning the freedom to engage in prayer that lends voice to our encounter with the world is related to the question concerning the moral agency and freedom of the human person as addressed by John Webster in his *Karl Barth's Ethics of Reconciliation*. Here Webster poses the question whether, for all the benefits of Barth's theological realism, it is nonetheless the case that "if good human action is only an endorsement of these [theological] states of affairs, does not the moral agent vanish, resolved into the prior divine decision. . . .?"[21] Does Barth's theological realism guarantee a theological determinism that forecloses the believer's right to speak from out of the depths of her experience as an extension or contributing aspect of her witness to God? Can the Word of God permit a human proclamation that details the travails and particularities of the encounter with the unredeemed world? If so, what might constitute the unique features of this discourse?

The Word of God and the Theo-logic of Prayer

While the exact semantics of the word *tefillah* are unclear, the term is frequently translated as "service of the heart" — with *"lev"* as the organ not uniquely of feeling, but rather reflection or discernment. The term "liturgy" has its origins in the Greek *leitourgia,* or public service. Together, these Jewish and Christian terms invite theologians to consider the performance of religious life as public service rooted in the praxis of reflection and discernment. Does a Word of God theology harbor a space for this religious performance as lived by Jews and Christians? Is there a theological basis for the liturgical turn?

The Discourse of the Question and the Outer Sanctuary

Any consideration concerning the extent to which Word of God theology can include and express itself in a discourse of prayer that mediates between the believer's witness and her encounters with the world requires a deeper description of the character of this discourse of prayer. We may find such a description in a classic piece written by Jacques Derrida entitled "How to Avoid Speaking," in which he makes an insightful linkage between the discourse of interrogation or the question and the language and performance of prayer.

21. John Webster, *Karl Barth's Ethics of Reconciliation* (Cambridge: Cambridge University Press, 1995), p. 53.

Derrida's work demonstrates how language houses the possibility of an extended openness to the "question," or, what is the possibility of either my or an other's future encounters with the world, what Derrida elsewhere calls the "promise." By promise, Derrida means the unique coupling of language's iterability and thereby extendibility into re-contextualizations that promise a neverending horizon of new meaning. His account of human language as promise is philosophically potent so far as it demonstrates how language invites an extended openness to the possibility of another one's voice or of a recontextualization of the set of signs. As John Caputo has said, "language is the event of the coming of the other."[22] Language at once becomes the site for exercising the drive towards theoretical transformation (a new truth is always just on the horizon) as well as the environs for moral rationality (my position is always tensed by the promise of a different voice that re-contextualizes). Derridean rationality bears the mark of an openness and demand for questioning reminiscent of radical skepticism softened however with a sense of responsibility and promise — what Derrida has referred to as the "yes" of language's ability to house the possibility of extended truth. If the challenge facing Word of God theologies has to do with their ability to reach into the discourse of the human encounter with the world, then Derrida's account of discourse offers a useful description of the human language with which the Word of God must negotiate.

In "How to Avoid Speaking," Derrida flirts with the linkage between the discourse of prayer and the language of promise. Commonly appreciated as a telling exposure of the speech implicit within negative theology, "How to Avoid Speaking" also inscribes an elegant description of prayer as a discourse that guides one through the response to that which is elevated in the negative. There are, Derrida claims, two traits worth distinguishing with respect to prayer: prayer is always an address to the other as other and prayer is a celebration of the One to whom it is addressed. Derrida stakes a lot on the claim (important to us), however, that the two features are, though inseparable, nonetheless different. As an address, prayer, he says is not constative and it is not, noteworthily, "about" God. Rather, as address, prayer is a movement that speaks to God and not of God. As an address to God, prayer is the human side of the Word of God, the discourse of "asking, supplicating, searching out . . . to the other. . . ."[23] Prayer in this account traverses and marks the landscape of

---

22. John Caputo, "What Do I Love When I Love My God?" in *Questioning God*, ed. John Caputo, Mark Dooley, & Michael J. Scanlon (Bloomington: Indiana University Press, 2001), pp. 300-301.

23. Jacques Derrida, "How to Avoid Speaking," in Graham Ward, ed., *The Postmodern God* (Oxford: Blackwell Publishers Ltd., 2002), p. 170.

persons' response to God. It is close to the ground and picks up the particularities of the current asking, the current supplicating and the immediate searching out.

However, commenting on the opening passage of *The Mystical Theology* by Dionysius the Areopagite, Derrida reminds us that as discourse prayer is also always an event of promise. "After having prayed," Derrida recounts, "Dionysius presents his prayer. . . . He quotes it in what is properly an apostrophe to its addressee, Timothy. . . . The one who asks to be led by God turns for an instant toward another addressee, in order to lead him in truth."[24] Prayer passes itself on to the next one whose unique supplication, searching out, and asking will comment upon and supplement my own prayer. Of course, as discourse and as promise, my own prayer already includes the passing on to the other's language of need. Language's alter-ability and public nature inscribes this communal possibility.

In this context, prayer is an anthropo-theological language that permits time to make a difference and, consequently, makes a difference in time. An on-the-ground account of my searching out before God, prayer marks my time and takes up this announcement before the God whom I naturally address and presuppose in his nearness. Prayer challenges the Word to greet me in my time and space. It performs the philosophical imperative. Prayer announces that this time and this place are sacred. It invites the divine nearness. "This apophasis belongs to a history; or rather it opens up a history and an anthropo-theological dimension. . . . *This* place itself is assigned by the event of the promise and the revelation of Scripture. . . . The situation of *this* speech situates a place. . . ."[25]

As the human face of the Word of God drawing near our world, prayer not only invites the divine descent but transforms our environs as well. Responsive to, in search of, and attentive to God, prayer transforms our world into what Derrida calls the "outer sanctuary." It primes our world to host sacred space and in so doing transforms it — shapes it and readies it for this cultic responsibility. It initiates the presence of the Word in our world and unleashes its potential for re-describing and re-telling its character. Still, Derrida's work is self-consciously atheological. Is there room within the Word of God theologies for the above-described language and performance of prayer?

---

24. Derrida, "How to Avoid Speaking," p. 174.
25. Derrida, "How to Avoid Speaking," p. 175. Italics mine.

The Need to Pray

It is the essential contention of this volume that not only can a Word of God theology extend into a language of prayer as it marks persons' encounter with their world, but also that only a Word of God theology can render this encounter with the world possible. If theological realism requires contact with the world as we know it, it is also true that the human experience of the world needs theological realism, or the Word of God. Ultimately, it is the unique character of divine freedom that gives rise to and supports the performance of prayer as the praxis of reflecting upon and transforming the world with the Word.

Derrida's description of prayer as the bearer of needs defines the character of the discourse that Word of God theologies need to assume. Prayer, in this account, permits both the extension into the promise of the next one's needs and the current articulation of my own standing before God. Derrida's rendezvous with prayer permits him to stumble upon the nexus between liturgy and redemption that is at the heart of this volume. As testimony, memory, hope, and petition, the life of prayer presupposes that God's promise is available to us in the past, the present and the future. Prayer is the sine qua non for the correlation between the Word of God and the repair of our current situation. Elsewhere, however, Derrida argues that I cannot open myself to the other without ultimately sacrificing myself, substituting the language of sacrifice for prayer. When he does so he undermines his own notion of the promise or the messianic.

According to Derrida's account, language is the site of the discourse of the other only in the future. The voice of the other is not yet spoken — it is the *différance* between my voice, my account, my language, and what exceeds the bounds of my account or my voice. I cannot, Derrida says, invite the other and await her visitation at the same time. The moment I prepare a culture of hospitality, I have foreclosed the possibility of the voice of the other — save as the future not-yet interrogation of my own linguistic horizon. My failure to extend hospitality to you except at the expense of myself and my worldview means that my recognition of the promise of language mires me in an experience of infinite guilt from which I cannot free myself. Neither can I behave hospitably towards you (save with my ultimate sacrifice) nor can I free myself from my own guilt for failing to do so. The life of the outer sanctuary above described is silenced by my inability to hear you and my inability to ask for help. What was once the promise of an opening to my need and the needs of others has devolved into an economy of mourning over my failure to sacrifice my life for you. I mourn my own survival.

Derrida's thought devolves into nihilism because it assumes that language cannot host *différance* except as a future negation of its current form (or the memory of its past negation). Like Soloveitchik before, Derrida cannot explain Hannah. If Soloveitchik's *logos* of need overdetermines Hannah's needs, Derrida's sacrifice of death renders them incompatible with responsibility to the other. From a Derridean perspective, Hannah's announcement of personal need is unethical — a brash neglect of the imperative of the promise. Both instances nullify the particularity of the human experience of the world and cannot offer antidotes for its transformation. We might then ask what permits Hannah to petition God as she does. The answer, of course, is her faith in God and, more specifically, her faith in a God who loves and draws near her in his freedom, her faith that "God is with us." Fueled by this faith, Hannah rests assured in the knowledge that God can answer her prayers and the prayers of others and in the hope that he will lovingly exercise his freedom to do so.

The Structure of Creation and the Liturgical Life

That a Word of God theology harbors a space for a liturgical praxis of petition, discernment and public service is already evident in Genesis 1. In his book *Covenantal Rights,* David Novak articulates how the theology of divine command implicit in Genesis 1 provides the basis and mandate for prayer. The central feature of the commanding God of the biblical account is transcendence. Novak highlights the biblical concern to mark the difference between creator and creature — we are mortal; God is at once coeval with and transcendent to time. The God of Genesis displays absolute power and engenders terror in the hearts of those who know him. Our lives are in his hands. However, God's power is not a sufficient basis for divine right. There is, Novak argues, a correlation between rights and duties. Persons have rights only when those rights can be met through the dutiful behavior of another. Consequently, obligations presuppose that the one to whom I am obligated has a right to obligate me (i.e., there's a good reason for my duty), but for the case at hand, rights presuppose that others who are so obligated have an ability to enact or fulfill their obligation. One does not have a "right" to command another who is powerless.

Consequently, Novak says, "in order for God's power to be understood as a right, it must be seen as a claim on somebody else, who himself or herself is able to freely respond to that claim."[26] To command, a transcendent God must

---

26. David Novak, *Covenantal Rights: A Study in Jewish Political Theory* (Princeton: Princeton University Press, 2000), p. 40.

forfeit some of his exclusive power and transfer it to those who are expected to dutifully carry out divine commands. God may be powerful without humankind, but God has a right to exert that power as a command only if and when he creates persons who have the ability to respond freely to it. Transcendence must become relational in order to be recognized as transcendence. Transcendence requires that God divest himself of some of his freedom for the sake of our freedom. "God is *for us* through his commandments."[27]

Of course, once granted, human freedom not only enables us to obey divine commands, but provides the basis for our dignity or our rights as well. That is, human life (i.e., I have a right to live or others have an obligation not to murder me) is valuable for the sake of and because of the character of divine transcendence. "Being commanded is itself what lies at the very core of human existence and thought. . . ."[28] It is what provides the very basis for our independent humanity. Human worth is a sign of a gift from an absolutely free and transcendent God. It signifies or is the location for the correlation between divine transcendence and divine nearness or relationality. Human rights derive from the other slope of transcendence — the slope of relationality that is a necessary aspect of any authentic manifestation of transcendence as command. The wholly other God is the God of absolute freedom who forfeits his freedom as a way of expressing his freedom.

This analysis of the correlation between divine right and human right discloses the theological basis of a liturgical life of praise, repentance, hope and petition. As transcendent and free, the God of the creation account commands persons to acknowledge this transcendence and obey (and repent when necessary) divine authority. At the same time however, the transcendent God draws near in his transcendence. A theology of divine command permits the full retrieval of need as a condition of the possibility of any acknowledgement of the transcendence. The logic of divine command renders prayer a mode of rational discourse. "What we . . . learn from scripture and the rabbis is how humans have the right to cry to God, thus believing that God will listen to our cry, even though we do not have the right to determine what God will actually do to us or for us in response."[29] If God is transcendent, then God is free. If God is free, he argues, then God is free to answer my needs. To deny that God can answer my needs is to challenge the notion of divine freedom and transcendence. Prayer is a testament to the fact that the ex-

27. Novak, *Covenantal Rights*, p. 41.
28. Novak, *Covenantal Rights*, p. 42.
29. Novak, *Covenantal Rights*, p. 58.

posture of divine transcendence is "for us" and that we have a right to hope that it is for us in the ways that we need. "Prayer is the most personal approach to God possible from the human side. It is the overcoming of our lack of certitude about anything God will do to us by our hope that he will act for us in a way that we can understand and appreciate."[30]

When we recognize the liturgical posture implicit in the structure of creation we open up the transformative capacity of the Word of God in the world. This reading of Genesis 1 helps us appreciate how the human responsibility to be guardian over God's created order presupposes and is guided by this liturgical relationship to God. God says, "Have dominion over the fish of the sea and over the birds of the air and over every living thing that moves upon the earth" (Gen. 1:28). We are commanded, it seems, without instruction, without guidance. This is, however, not the case. Built into the very structure of our created status is the liturgical posture that provides and performs the purpose for the task (praise to God), the confidence that we can perform the task (gratitude to God for our abilities), the ability to discern what we need (the freedom to cry out) and the hope that we will be granted it (petition). There is no separation between ourselves as masters of nature and as creatures of God. We cannot be the one without the other and it is the liturgical life that mediates between the two as the service of the heart *(tefillah)* that translates into public service *(leitourgia).*

The Order of Praise and the Liturgy of Repair

Of course, the link between divine freedom, divine nearness, and liturgical mediation with the world is not unique to a Jewish reading of Genesis, but can be discerned out of a Christian account of the Word as well. It is well documented that Barth's theological realism is rooted in his understanding of the freedom of the God who loves. While Barth's theology has raised eyebrows concerning its ability to permit and/or shed light on the range of human experiences and actions in the unredeemed world, Barth's theology of divine freedom does give rise to a complex account of liturgical life as not only praise, memory and anticipation but as petition and the reflective discernment of persons' on-going encounter with the world.

Who or what is God?, Barth asks in the *Church Dogmatics.* God is the one revealed through the biblical word, and as such, God is the being who acts or loves in freedom. By freedom, Barth means not only the freedom from de-

---

30. Novak, *Covenantal Rights,* p. 58.

pendence on anything exterior but also the positive freedom to absolute creativity and activity.

> The biblical witness to God sees His transcendence in the fact that without sacrificing His distinction and freedom, but in the exercise of them, He . . . maintains communion with this reality other than Himself in His activity as Creator, Reconciler and Redeemer. . . .[31]

The God of the biblical text freely acts to limit his freedom via his communion to that which is other than himself. God has "the prerogative to be free without being limited by His freedom."[32]

With respect to humanity, this means that the transcendent God may draw near to persons in the particularities of their existence. Technically, there is no limit to the reach of the Word of God in its immanent relation to the human experience. The Word of God need not be removed from the reality of human life but may, in its freedom,

> ally [itself] within creation. . . . God is free to be wholly inward to the creature and at the same time as Himself wholly outward. . . . His revelation in Jesus Christ embraces all these apparently so diverse and contradictory possibilities. . . . If we deny Him any one of them we are denying Jesus Christ and God Himself.[33]

If, however, there is no limit to the reach of the Word of God in its immanent relation to human experience, this means that the believer is always in a position to petition God for the fulfillment of her needs and the needs of others (even if she is not in a position to expect that God will always meet them). Divine freedom legitimizes the believer in her navigation between her life in the unredeemed world and her praise of the Word. God is near in her praise and in her repentance but also in her difficulties, in her distance from God, in her efforts to contend with the range of problems present in all spheres of worldly and embodied behaviors and experiences, e.g., political, economic, legal, moral, medical. God's freedom means that the divine promise to commune with humanity can transpire here in the unredeemed world. To deny this possibility is to deny the character of divine sovereignty. As command, God's revelation in Jesus Christ summons persons to a liturgy of testimony

---

31. Karl Barth, *Church Dogmatics*, II.I., ed. G. W. Bromiley and T. F. Torrance, trans. T. H. L. Parker et al. (Edinburgh: T&T Clark, 1992), p. 303.

32. Barth, *Church Dogmatics*, II.I., p. 274.

33. Barth, *Church Dogmatics*, II.I., p. 315.

that helps to build the order of praise here and now. As loving freedom, God's revelation in Jesus Christ legitimizes and warrants a liturgy of petition and discernment that is at once public service and redemptive repair.

Barth's analysis of the love of the neighbor confirms the extension of the Word of God into the liturgy of public service and redemptive repair. The love of the neighbor is the form that the witness to God assumes in the unredeemed world and time, and therefore it is the "concrete shape which corresponds to the world which now is and passes."[34] Love of the neighbor is a liturgical posture that mediates between the repetition of the praise of God and the demands and needs of the neighbor in all of her particularity as the one or ones for whom I must pray for God's help. As such, the love of the neighbor will extend the Word of God into the discourse and events of our immediate world.

The neighbor is a sign of Jesus Christ, that is, one who testifies to the reality of God's compassionate revelation in Christ, e.g., the Good Samaritan and the apostles. To love the neighbor in this case means to act like the neighbor and praise God. The neighbor, however, need not be an apostle or even a Christian. A neighbor can be anyone who in his humanity functions as a testimony to Christ in his humanity. The neighbor's suffering and sin offer testimony to Christ as the one who greets us in our sin and elects us into communion with God. In both instances however, the neighbor testifies to the gospel and summons me to the same. My relation to the neighbor generates only a posture of witness. Love of the neighbor, Barth insists, does not first and foremost mean my assistance to the particular needs of the one who suffers. Such a reading of the love of the neighbor elevates law over gospel and neglects the theological realism that determines God's unique sovereignty and compassion as the unique source of redemptive healing. Nonetheless, Barth claims, to say that love of the neighbor equals the praise of God and not ethics is not the same as saying that the praise of God cannot lead to or generate a behavior and language of aid. The gospel is not the law but the gospel generates and creates the conditions of the possibility for law. Said in terms relevant to this volume, witness becomes the law for Barth through the language of prayer or *leitourgia*.

I have, according to Barth, an obligation to the neighbor rooted in the possibility that while he may be a sign of Christ's humanity, he himself may not be privy to the Word of God. I must, therefore, say something to him about the other side of human need — namely, God. I must, in other words,

---

34. Karl Barth, *Church Dogmatics*, I.II., trans. G. T. Thomson and Harold Knight (Edinburgh: T&T Clark, 1994), p. 411.

say something to him about the possibility of announcing his need to God in prayer. Of course, my telling the neighbor about the God to whom we may pray is nothing other than my act of taking up his need in the content of my prayer. My testimony to God before him is occasioned by and directly related to the particularities of his need. Through my encounter with the neighbor, the Word of God has descended into the particularities of his encounter with the world. The Word of God has been invited into the outer sanctuary and herein the order of redemption partakes in the reality of the current situation, all the while the current situation is transformed into the Word of God. Of course, Barth says, I must translate and manifest my prayer for the next one in and through concrete actions. My effort to lend her assistance takes on the form of actions in the world whether these actions be political, economic, medical, legal, or moral. The Word of God extends into and changes the shape of these concrete worldly behaviors. The believer both builds the order of praise and redeems the world through the very activities that constitute its reality. Rooted in praise for God and extended into the prayer for the neighbor, these concrete forms of assistance are liturgical, through and through. "To lay hold of that assurance and put it into action," Barth says, "means calling upon God in prayer."[35] To do so, however, is to act in the faith that the divine promise for redemption draws near us even now and even through our worldly practices.

> The promise given to the Church has still to be received again and again by each of its members. The Church with its commission and promise lives in its sinful members. . . . Prayer is the subjective determination of the assurance that we can love our neighbor . . . praying is the decisive thing . . . the casting of our care upon God; our care about ourselves — how it is with our loving; and our care about the other. . . . In the last resort we can only love the neighbor by praying for ourselves and for him. . . .[36]

Public Service and the Service of the Heart Performed

The claim that theology is liturgically inscribed is not new. Catherine Pickstock and John Milbank have done a great deal to demonstrate the link between theology and doxological practice on the one hand, and thinkers as diverse as Georges Bataille and Pierre Bourdieu have helped recuperate the

---

35. Barth, *Church Dogmatics*, I.II., p. 453.
36. Barth, *Church Dogmatics*, I.II., p. 454.

temporality, spatiality, and meaning of religious practice from out of the objectivizing grasp of nineteenth-century cultural anthropology.

Unique to this volume is the detailed account of how the theo-anthropological space for which we have now accounted impacts on and opens up a consideration of the Word liturgically performed and interpreted and the extent to which this liturgical interpretation of the Word transforms our current historical, political and economic orders and behaviors. On the one hand, then, it is the charge of this volume to describe the mutual impact of scriptural hermeneutics and liturgical life as an interpretative praxis. Liturgical postures will be discovered both within and supplementary to scriptural texts as the lived practices that perform and interpret the Word in time. On the other hand, the volume purports to show how the hermeneutical link between scriptural Word and liturgical practice mediates the Word with what Sam Wells refers to as the "givens" of our world. The volume explores how this mediation affects our understandings and performances of history, politics, economics, and ethics. The order of the essays is governed not by a linear account of the traditions but by pairing a Jewish and Christian inquiry under categories emergent from the analyses of liturgical practice, e.g., action, time, scrolling, improvisation and silence, with the expressed purpose of facilitating conversation between the essays.

In his essay, "A Christian Act: Politics and Liturgical Practice," Graham Ward offers an inquiry into the Christian liturgical act as "a *praxis* that participates in a divine *poiēsis*" grounded in his reading of "Abide in me, and I in you" (John 15:4). Shaped always by the co-abiding with and of Christ, the Christian liturgical act transforms Western notions of the agency, relationality, object, purpose and effect of action. "The asymmetry [of the co-abiding] is the index of living by grace, of being maintained by that which is within and beyond me. The chiasmus is the congress, then, of two mysteries — the incomprehensible depths of God and the mystery that is being human itself" (p. 35). Performed and negotiated in our world, Christian action is, Ward argues, redemptive not strictly as doxological performance, but as political, ethical, and aesthetic performance as well.

Peter Ochs's "Morning Prayer as Redemptive Thinking" examines how the liturgical practice of performing the morning prayer "trains participants in making judgments" about our world. Ochs demonstrates how a certain reading of the Morning Prayer sequence disarms participants of a single-minded indebtedness to the "logic of propositions" which lends itself to over-generalizations or "isms" that have dominated the Western social, political, and economic imagination. Read this way, prayer becomes redemptive by providing a template for an epistemological reordering and positions those who participate in it to stand before God in the world via the multiplicity of relations (I-God; I-you; we) and the mutuality and process orientation of judgment formation (before God, with others, and into the future).

Liturgy's impact on politics and sociality is directly linked to its unique temporality. In their essays, both Scott Bader-Saye and Steven Kepnes address this feature of liturgical practice. Commenting on modernity's commodification of time and postmodernity's dissolution of narrative time, Bader-Saye reminds readers how the Christian liturgical calendar constitutes community. "The reading of Scripture, the celebration of Eucharist, and the marking of saints' days serve to create an imagined contemporaneity among God's people stretching from the biblical world to the present, from the living to the dead" (p. 96). Participation in the liturgical calendar inculcates Christians into the temporality of the providential narrative — at once linking them to the narrative of God's relation to the Jews as well as to their own knowledge of God's presence in history. In a similar vein, Steven Kepnes' "Rosenzweig's Liturgical Reasoning" offers a close reading of Genesis 1 in collaboration with Franz Rosenzweig's hermeneutics of liturgical practice in order to demonstrate how Jewish liturgy in general and both the Shabbat service and the Hallel prayer in particular narrate a mode of temporality that bridges between natural, social and celestial time. Communally performed, these liturgical occasions offer the Jewish people access to a temporality that glimpses "the unity of the human soul and world under God that will occur in the future redemption."

In "Eternity in History: Rolling the Scroll," Robert Gibbs considers how eternity enters into time through the scrolling of the biblical text. Truth, that is to say, eternity, Gibbs argues, takes time, time that is structured into units (hours, e.g.) that have a beginning, middle, and end and whose units repeat themselves. Weekly, we see this in the Sabbath. As a day of rest, the Sabbath marks a liturgically commemorated time to reflect upon our freedom to invite and receive eternity into our social practices. The practice of scrolling the Torah embodies the Jewish awareness of the year as the occasion for eternity and also opens the community to the particular historicity of the Torah portion reminding listeners that eternity enters into time amidst the contingencies and particularities with which we live. The Torah becomes the Word of God so far as it is liturgically performed, and the liturgical performance gains its particularity by reading the weekly portions.

Ben Quash's "Holy Seeds: The *Trisagion* and the Liturgical Untilling of Time," examines the role of the *Trisagion* in the eucharistic prayer and discovers the prayer's political value through a close reading of its scriptural origins in the Book of Revelation and the Book of Isaiah. Liturgically wedged between accounts of God's creation and the night of the final supper, the Sanctus, Quash argues, announces concurrently the glory of the divine presence in its fullness (Book of Revelation) along with the divine long suffering before humanity's choice for emptiness and self-mastery (Isaiah). So read, the Sanctus refers us to the temporality of the scriptural text when "what is said at one point will often, in the purposes of God, be heard later" (p. 158). Like Gibbs's account of how the weekly Torah reading negotiates between eschatological universality and historical particularity, the *Trisagion* guides participants through the complexities and the choices of our time illuminating the value in the "delay" that is sacramentalized as the occasion for "discerning, struggling, and coming to terms with God's instruction."

In their essays, both Sam Wells and Shaul Magid illuminate a theatrical component to liturgical practice which allows participants to wed theological imagination to a reading of the times through religious performance. Like Gibbs and Quash, Wells appreciates the hermeneutical value of liturgical performance as well as the performative value of the scriptural text and characterizes both via the dramatic category of improvisation. A category that fuses together narrative, creativity, imaginative reversal and what Wells refers to as "over-acceptance" — the placement of givens "into a much larger story — the story of God's ongoing relationship with his people" (p. 171), the improvisation of the Word of God offers "training" in how to act as a Christian in the world without falling prey to the assumed conditions of the world. Wells presents an improvisational reading of the Book of Esther which he argues offers specific "training in a politics of redemption." In stark contrast to either a politics of power or historical necessity, a politics of redemption "over-accepts" the contemporary environment and imaginatively scripts the Word of God within it in ways that resonate with Ward's account of the Christian act as the praxis that participates in the divine *poiēsis*.

In a careful reading of the Seven Blessings as interpreted by Hasidic Rebbe Shneur Zalman, Shaul Magid's "The Ritual Is Not the Hunt: The Seven Wedding Blessings" details how ritual "has an inverse relation to reality" not only because it represents an ideal not herein achievable but rather "because the ritual is constructed with deep contradictions that we, as humans, are constitutionally unable to resolve" (p. 204). Rituals appropriate tensions present in our social and political environs and create imaginary solutions to these particular problems. Liturgy anticipates redemption not by profiling an unreachable ideal but rather by positing variant solutions to current problems in the world.

The collection of essays closes with a piece by Oliver Davies, "Cosmic Speech and the Liturgy of Silence." Davies' exploration into the "silence of the Cross" reveals the reparative value of Jesus' own sacrificial silence as the liturgical announcement of the divine silence long hidden in the textuality of the created order. By extension, Jesus' own liturgical sacrifice makes possible the eucharistically performed silence of all. Eucharistic silence restores the intimacy between God's creative word and the world he has created and becomes therefore an essential feature in healing the variant instances of alienation and isolation in our midst.

Together the essays profile how the liturgical turn challenges modernist notions of history that stress linearity and produce the politics of isolationism, fragmentation, and determinism and poses instead alternative models of liturgical temporality that have the capacity to redefine sociality and choreograph a new politics of redemption.

New Convergences?

In 1913, Franz Rosenzweig, a student studying law at Leipzig, met Eugen Rosenstock-Huessy, then twenty-five, a lecturer at Leipzig and a devoted Christian. According to Rosenstock-Huessy's own account, one summer evening that year he, Rosenzweig, and Rudolf Ehrenberg (Rosenzweig's cousin) gathered together for a conversation during which, Rosenstock-Huessy recalled,

> Franz, a student of philosophy and history for eight years by that time, defended the prevailing philosophical relativism of the day, whereas [I] Eugen bore witness to prayer and worship as [my] his prime guides to action. . . . The three men separated very late that night, never to touch on the subject of religion again until 1916.[37]

Three years later Rosenzweig wrote to Rosenstock-Huessy,

> Now that I want to continue, I find that everything that I want to write is something which I can't express to you. For now I would have to show you Judaism from within, that is be able to show it to you in a hymn, just as you are able to show me, the outsider, Christianity.[38]

By 1916, Rosenzweig's response to Rosenstock-Huessy mirrored Rosenstock-Huessy's own account of his exchange with Rosenzweig on that first summer

---

37. Eugen Rosenstock-Huessy, ed., *Judaism Despite Christianity: The 'Letters on Christianity and Judaism' between Eugen Rosenstock-Huessy and Franz Rosenzweig* (New York: Schocken Books, 1971), p. 73.

38. Rosenstock-Huessy, *Judaism Despite Christianity*, p. 62.

evening in 1913. How to explain the change in Rosenzweig's position? As has been well documented, Rosenzweig's transformation from a student of Hegel to a religious thinker had already been brewing with his critique of Hegelian historicism.[39] Nonetheless, it was not until his encounter with Rosenstock-Huessy's liturgically focused theology of the Word that Rosenzweig began his return to life as a practicing Jew. At first, a philosophico-theological defense of his own position in the face of a pointed challenge, Rosenstock-Huessy's July 1913 remarks on the orientation of history and politics within the calculus of the Word prayed to and worshipped, guided Rosenzweig into both a deep engagement with the liturgical life of the Jewish people and a now published correspondence, *Judaism Despite Christianity*, with his friend Eugen Rosenstock-Huessy, devoted largely to their reflections on the parallels and divergences between Judaism and Christianity as practiced in the context of World War I–era Europe. Rosenstock-Huessy's and Rosenzweig's correspondence testifies to the inestimable value linked to a Jewish-Christian exchange premised not on an effort to discern commonalities but rather rooted in the willingness of each to publicize to the other the details and character of their lived practice. The basis for each thinker's articulation of a post-secular (Johannine) politics, Rosenzweig and Rosenstock-Huessy's correspondence ended not only because of Rosenzweig's ailing health but as well because of the rise of Nazi Germany and the blow it issued to religious thought.

Today we live separated from their correspondence both by the Holocaust and as well by the rising possibility of a post-secular era in politics. Jews and Christians face a greater need and a better opportunity for conversation than that presented to Rosenzweig and Rosenstock-Huessy. We may, however, still learn from the structure of their conversation as the mutually edifying exposure of Judaism's and Christianity's liturgical lives. The liturgical turn taken up in this volume follows after and has the potential to deepen their experiment in Jewish-Christian relations by introducing a sustained conversation between Jewish and Christian theologians based in the similarities and differences in their conceptions of time, eternality and socio-political change — similarities and differences which identify why Jewish and Christian theologians need each other as they seek to be socially, ethically and politically responsible in the world.

Certainly Judaism and Christianity have much to learn from one another. As the essays in this volume will, I believe, demonstrate, Judaism may learn from Christianity's practiced application of liturgical life into the political realm and Christianity may learn from Judaism's careful investigation into

39. See Myers, *Resisting History*, pp. 69-105.

the reasoning structures of its scriptural texts and liturgical performance. Whether Judaism's and Christianity's respective liturgical orderings bring them closer together or farther away from each other remains to be answered by the reader. It is, however, our hope that the essays in this volume stage the possibility for Christians and Jews to inspire each other in the common work of repairing our shared world.

PART I

LITURGICAL ACTION

A Christian Act: Politics and Liturgical Practice

Graham Ward

In the opening passages of his *Nicomachean Ethics,* Aristotle deliberates about an investigation into the ethics and ends of any action *(praxis).* He determines that the science that most adequately addresses "what people shall do and what things they shall refrain from doing," the realization of the Good that is not secured from one person only but for the wider community, is political science. He concludes that "our investigation [into the ethics and ends of any action] is in a sense the study of Politics."[1] We might note here that the Good is *kalon* — which is also the Beautiful. Praxes, therefore, have to be examined ethically, aesthetically, and politically. They have also, for Aristotle, to be examined theologically — though he himself does not undertake such an examination. But he recognizes that the securing of the Good is also a divine achievement *(theioteron).*

In his *Politics,* in a discussion concerning the actions that maintain a democracy, Aristotle advises that "it is a good thing to prevent wealthy citizens, even if they are willing, from undertaking expensive and useless public services *(leitourgein),* such as the giving of choruses, torch-races, and the like."[2] The Greek *leitourgia,* from which we derive our "liturgy", was a technical political term for a service rendered to the city or state. It was a service that might be laid down by the law; it was conducted with honor, if not solemnity. It is a work or a labor *(ergon)* with respect to a people or community *(leitos).* And so elsewhere in *Politics, leitourgia* can be used nontechnically to refer to any act of service.[3] It would seem, though nowhere as far I am aware does Aristotle ex-

---

1. Book I.ii.
2. Book V.8 (1309a).
3. Book III.5 (1278a).

plicitly say this, that *praxis* stands to *leitourgia* as genus to species — in other words, all specific acts of service concretize the universal form of action.

It is this relationship between the politics, ethics, and aesthetics of praxes as they relate to *leitourgia* that I wish to explore in this essay. St. Paul brings these two uses of *leitourgia* together in a verse at the end of his great chapter on kenosis in the Letter to the Philippians. Having outlined the nature of Christ the servant in the *carmen Christi* (Phil. 2:5-11) and the nature of faithful, sacrificial obedience (2:12-18), he refers to two of his close friends, Timothy (2:19-24) and Epaphroditus (2:25-30). Of Epaphroditus he writes, "He nearly died for the work of Christ, risking his life to complete *(anaplērōsē)* your service to me *(tēs pros me leitourgias)*" (2:30). While commentators view Paul as employing *leitourgia* as a service related to a gift of money (see 4:15), all of them concur that he is using the word to indicate something of the priesthood of all believers. This is a cultic service, a "priestly service";[4] Epaphroditus is "performing the duties of a priest."[5] This may be so, but there is more than this. The service for the community is a political act, in the sense Aristotle maintained that political action concerned the building up and maintenance of the community. The service is also theological. For *anaplērōsē* is related to Paul's extensive use of the noun *plērōma* with respect to the operations of the Spirit in the world — the filling up, the plenitude, the bringing to completion — and the verb *plēroō*.[6] In Philippians 2:17, with reference to cultic sacrifice, he speaks of himself as "to be poured as a libation upon the sacrificial offering of your faith" *(epi tē thusia kai leitourgia tēs pisteōs humōn)*.

Having outlined the subject of my investigation, let me introduce the theological framework within which I will situate the examination of a Christian act. It can be summed up in a verse from St. Paul's Letter to the Colossians (3:3): "Your life is hid with Christ in God."[7] I am not going to ex-

---

4. Moises Silva, *Philippians* (Chicago: Moody Press, 1988), p. 161.

5. Gordon D. Fee, *Paul's Letter to the Philippians* (Grand Rapids: Eerdmans, 1995), p. 284. See also J. B. Lightfoot, *Epistle to the Philippians* (London: Macmillan and Co., 1879), p. 119.

6. See my *Christ and Culture* (Oxford: Blackwell, 2005) for an exposition of *plēroō* and its relationship to *kenoō* in Pauline teaching. The cultic use of *leitourgia* is later than Aristotle. It is thought to have developed in Hellenistic Egypt and becomes prominent in its employment in the LXX to translate Hebrew cultic terms. See Strathmann on *leitourgeō* and *leitourgia* in *The Theological Dictionary of the New Testament*, Volume V, ed. G. Kittel, tr. Geoffrey W. Bromiley (Grand Rapids: Eerdmans, 1967), pp. 221-22.

7. I might have used here Psalm 139, in which the life of the faithful one is also conceived as hidden in God. I would then have read this psalm from the perspective of Christianity. There are also Jewish readings of this psalm that might open up a conversation across faith traditions. To invite such readings to contribute to and question my own renders the politics of redemption that I am arguing for in this essay to become explicit.

amine the framework itself. I am aware that various interpretations might be made of that verse. But I am reading it in terms of the Church's doctrine of participation. That is, the Christian's life is a participation in Christ and the operations of the triune God within realms created in and through Christ as God's Word. As such, discipleship is not simply following the example of Christ; it is formation within Christ such that we become Christ-like.

Within the context of Aristotle's understanding of the politics of any action and liturgy as an overt act of public service, and within the Pauline framework of a life hidden in Christ, I want to ask: What kind of act is a Christian act? To clarify what is at stake by explicitly working within what, after Balthasar, I would call a theo-logic[8] — a form of reasoning operating upon the basis of a grammar of the Christian faith — we might consider that various elements compose an act in general. I suggest six key elements, an examination of which might enable us to ask the most fundamental question of all — what does it mean to act? These six elements constitute the poetics of action, and they are: an agent (that which is doing the action); the nature of the action done by that agent; the evaluation of the action done by the agent; the object with respect to which the action is taking place; the effect (both upon the agent and the object of the action); and finally the inner intellectual and/or affective workings such that there was any action at all (variously considered as intention, desire, hope, and judgment with respect to both the act and/or the object of the action). We can call these workings "disposition" or even, after Davidson, "pro-attitudes."[9] On the basis of examining these six elements, I will argue that we need to revisit an old Aristotelian question concerning the difference between *poiēsis* and *praxis*.

Agent

I will not be able to treat each of these elements in the detail they require. So this is only a sketch. Nevertheless, let us proceed with an examination of that first element, the agent, from a Christian theological perspective — that is, on the basis of that framework of Christian participation in the operations of God in the world. We can begin by acknowledging that "participation" implicates any agent in a relational ontology. We might sum this up in terms of the

8. *Theo-Drama: Theological Dramatic Theory*, IV, tr. Graham Harrison (San Francisco: Ignatius Press, 1994), p. 76.

9. See Donald Davidson, *Essays on Actions and Events* (Oxford: Oxford University Press, 1980), p. 4.

statement of Christ to his disciples in John's Gospel: "Abide in me, and I in you" (John 15:4). In what follows I am going to take this statement as axiomatic for an account of a Christian act. As such, in this act we are not, therefore, treating an autonomous subject who, in full knowledge of the facts of any situation, acts consciously, in and for herself. There is no room in the conception of a Christian praxis for self-sufficiency. This already implicates us in a different construal of "freedom" than that operating in notions of the liberal secular subject. In fact, what characterizes this Christian agent is the surrender, the sacrifice, noted by Paul, such that he or she is bound by what Augustine called a *vinculum caritatis* — a bond of love. De Lubac clarifies the operation of this love within the Christian, when he writes: "The relationship between man and God can never be conceived as being fundamentally governed by any natural law, or any necessity of any kind interior or exterior. In the gift of himself that God wills to make, everything is explained — in so far as it can be explained — by love, everything, hence including the consequent 'desire' in our nature, in whatever way we understand that desire."[10] God's love *pro nobis* awakens a God-given natural desire *in nobis*, that leads Christian persons beyond that which is natural into that which is constituted by grace.

We need to take this much further, for I do not wish to suggest that Christians have no sense of their singularity, their uniqueness — no self-identity. The Christian agent is neither a cipher nor absorbed into God. Frequently it is assumed that theologians like myself who find resources for creative theological thinking in poststructuralist authors work uncritically with these resources. That is certainly not always the case. Of course, a number of these authors, influenced by Spinoza, would wish to espouse a very weak sense of the subject; and some of them seem to leave little or no room for agency because the self is reduced to a nodal point in an extensive and extending grid of forces. I am thinking here of figures like Deleuze, Foucault, and Derrida. In speaking, then, of a relational ontology in a Christian act in which the subject is always participating in that which transcends him or her — in fact, not only transcends but grounds any sense of there being a him or a her — I do not wish to implode notions of selfhood, but rather refigure them.

Most significantly, in a Christian act identity is not dissolved into the anonymity of an economy of knowledge/power (Foucault);[11] an economy of semiotic, libidinal, and social flows (Deleuze); or an economy of *différance*

---

10. *Le mystère du surnaturel* (Paris: Les Editions du Cerf, 2000), p. 281; *The Mystery of the Supernatural*, tr. Rosemary Sheed (New York: Herder and Herder, 1998), p. 229.

11. For a more detailed account of Foucault's problems with agency, see my *Religion and Cultural Transformation* (Cambridge: Cambridge University Press, 2004).

(Derrida).[12] All of these operate solely on a plane of immanence;[13] though we might learn something of the nature of economy itself from each of these three thinkers. Nevertheless, the Christian acts in Christ — and the Christic operation while working within the world (immanently) also works beyond it, external to it (transcendently). Furthermore, it is not anonymous. We have to tread cautiously here, bearing in mind that with respect to God, as the apophatic theologians have taught us, we can only stare into unsayable glory. Aquinas will also emphasize that our knowledge is not of God in God's self but of the effects of the operations of God in the world. But there is a world of difference between the anonymity of differentiating power, semiosis and *différance* and "ineffability." Derrida confuses the two in his essay "How to Avoid Speaking: Denegations" and his interpretation of pseudo-Dionysius,[14] but one cannot worship the passage of deferral, nor can one receive grace from it.[15] Furthermore, while recognizing the incomprehensibility of the divine, the Christ is not without identifying markers. For God in Christ is Jesus of Nazareth. The Christian act then can be identified by its conformity to a

12. For a more detailed account of Derrida's problems with handling the subject, see my *Christ and Culture*, pp. 251-54.

13. Admittedly, Derrida does deal with what he calls a "quasi-transcendental" and this has exercised the minds of numerous scholars who argue about the extent to which Derrida is constructing a transcendental argument in a Kantian fashion. We have at best, with Derrida, an *effect* of transcendence that language cannot erase. The *effect* is and, for Derrida, can only be examined immanently.

14. See Graham Ward, ed., *The Postmodern God* (Oxford: Blackwell, 1997), pp. 167-90, and Kevin Hart's excellent introduction to the text. While pseudo-Dionysius's writings employ an apophatic mode of discourse that makes clearly manifest the operation of *différance*, the ineffability of the divine is not reducible to God making himself "present" or even God absenting himself. All "ineffability" is circumscribed by Christ; as all creation (language included) has its existence in Christ. And Christ as the incarnation of God does not leave Christians without something to say or pointing to an empty tomb. It is the depths of the mystery about what is said that announces the ineffable. What is said is not something to be leaped over, like Lessing's ugly ditch, to reach some pure silence of God's self-presence. What is said is to be endlessly meditated upon, supplemented (in Derrida's language), that the ineffable Word might open up the depths of the mystery. In brief, Derrida conflates a Hellenic notion of *Logos* with a Christian one, and has no understanding of sacramentality.

15. Not that Derrida himself conflated God and *différance*. In fact, he insisted they were not the same. Whatever "God" named was transcendent; *différance*, on the other hand, marked the condition for the possibility of any naming whatsoever. The point here is that Derrida can deconstruct the writings of pseudo-Dionysius in terms of the metaphysics of presence they play with but fails to understand the doctrine of analogy that is ultimately related to Christ as the incarnation of God, that allows pseudo-Dionysius to speak at all. In other words, there is a mediation in these writings, and an acceptance of the writings themselves as mediatory, that situate the operation of *différance* within a soteriological economy.

Christ-likeness; it will in some sense be an *imitatio Christi*. I say "in some sense" not to introduce a vagueness, but a complexity. What we treat in the Gospels are testimonies to the life, work and person of Jesus of Nazareth; depiction and descriptions that are also interpretations which hand themselves over to us who also interpret them. Nevertheless, what characterizes a Christian action indexes something of that historical person, the gendered Palestinian Jew, who was God incarnate. For those who "follow after" will act in accordance with what the American philosophical theologian Robert Scharlemann calls an "acolouthetic reason";[16] the "disciples'" actions can only be parsed according to the grammar of a life hidden in Christ.

Let me return to the statement in John's Gospel, "Abide in me, and I in you," and relate the chiasmic structure of this relationship both to the notions of freedom through servitude and also self-identity. There is a paradox at the heart of the word "subject." For, on the one hand, it reflects subordination *sub-jectum*, while, on the other, it invokes sovereignty, the one in control. This paradox is circumscribed in the Johannine formula, "Abide in me, and I in you." There is an "abiding" *in* Christ, but there is also an abiding *of* Christ. There is an abiding *in* me, but also an abiding *of* me. This co-abiding is complex and richly suggestive. It is the chiasmic heart of an *ekklēsia*. Why chiasmic? Because observe the curious manner of the reciprocal relation with respect to the Eucharistic body, the liturgy of incorporation and incarnation itself. By the act of receiving the Eucharist I place myself *in* Christ — rather than simply placing Christ within me. I consume, but I do not absorb Christ without also being absorbed into Christ.[17] Only in this complex co-abiding is there life, nourishment, nurture: because or through or by means of this feeding there are both participation of human life in God's life and participation of God's life in human life. Something comes into its own in this relationality. The incarnation is fully realized only by the participation of God in human life and the participation of human life in God. Two points proceed from this before we start to consider the implications here for determining the nature of a Christian act. First, Jesus is the Christ only in relation to other human beings; the act of redemption is a relational act; Christology concerns not the identity of this one subject but it concerns an operation effected in and through this complex co-abiding. Second, though I would insist on a profound difference between the human and the divine, there must exist within

16. *The Reason of Following: Christology and the Ecstatic I* (Chicago: University of Chicago Press, 1991), p. 124.

17. For a more detailed account of the chiasmic relation with respect to the Eucharist see *Christ and Culture*, pp. 92-110.

the nature and self-understanding of the Trinity a quality that has affinity with what it is to be human. To create human beings there must abide in God an image and likeness of what it is to be human. This image of what it is to be human is hypostasized in Christ and the redemptive operation with respect to the Word and the world. "He who eats *(trōgōn)* of my flesh and drinks of my blood abides *(menei)* in me, and I in him. As the living Father sent me, and I live because *(dia)* of the Father, so he who eats *(trōgōn)* me will live because *(di')* of me" (John 6:56-57).[18] We can observe the operation of the chiasmus here. For while there is an abiding *(menō* — to stay), *dia* can be used causatively ("because of this . . . that) or as a word implying transit "through" something.

Let us consider further three characteristics of this spiritual embodiment. First, with respect to the individual: I embody Christ's body and this body embodies mine. In the Eucharist the bodies are emphatically carnal and carnally relating, but their co-location is unthinkable. We continually return to that chiasmus, "Abide in me, and I in you." The coming together of the two bodies does not create a third body whose location can be determined. It is exactly the opposite: the coming together of the two bodies effects a reciprocal dislocation of both bodies. There is an abiding, but it takes place in this complex space whose boundaries are folded back upon themselves. One body relates to the other, but each is relocated with respect to a co-abiding.

There is, then, in being human, an eternal incompleteness; eternal because in the chiasmic displacement of my body by Christ's there is a fundamental asymmetry. One might take, for example, the "I in you and you in me" as the condition of true earthly partnership in which two become one flesh. For the structure of such partnership is also chiasmic and therefore displacing. But with Christ, even when, as 1 John 3:2 puts it, we shall see him as he is, and "I shall know even as I am known," I come most into myself only by being hidden in him. Finitude endlessly discovers itself in infinitude. The asymmetry is the index of living by grace, of being maintained by that which is within and beyond me. The chiasmus is the congress, then, of two mysteries — the incomprehensible depths of God and the mystery that is being human itself:

18. Bultmann in his *The Gospel of John: A Commentary*, tr. G. R. Beasley-Murray (Oxford: Blackwell, 1971), notes, "The offense [of this saying to the disciples] is heightened in v. 54 by the substitution of the stronger *trōgein* for *phagein*. It is a matter of real eating and not simply of some sort of spiritual participation" (p. 236). Brown in his commentary (*The Gospel According to John* [London: Geoffrey Chapman, 1971]) agrees and sees the change as part of John's attempt to "emphasize the realism" (p. 283). For a longer examination of the issue, which still has not convinced all the scholars, see Ceslas Spicq, "*Trōgein*. Est-il synonyme de *phagein* et *d'esthien* dans le Nouveau Testament?" *New Testament Studies* 26 (1979-1980): 414-19.

"Although no man knows the things of a man, save the spirit of the man which is in him, yet there is something of man which the inner spirit of man itself does not know."[19] My acts take place within the sphere of faith as liturgical service. This is obedience not necessarily to a set of injunctions, but to that which leads and draws me after.

Later, I will speak more about desire as the dynamic for this leading. Here it is a matter of recognizing that the completeness that is desired is understood as not being within one's own abilities to fulfill. A way is opened up of responding to each situation encountered with more than oneself and of recognizing also that the situation encountered is not all of one's making. There is a leading, a providence, and the leading is a teaching — and what is taught is discernment, faith, and listening. A communication, a communing, is learned that affects every action surrendered in Christ. Practices issue from an ongoing prayerful attentiveness. Claudel in his essay *"La Sensation du Divin"* speaks of "our entire religious life [a]s our *attention* to the particular *intention* God had when he called us into existence."[20] The Christian agent is constituted in this incompleteness and conformed to Christ through the practises of hope, vision and expectation that govern his or her relations to the world. The agent works here within and for what Augustine called the "heavenly city." And the agent is sojourner, for there is no place of permanent abiding. Gregory of Nyssa, in his *Homilies on the Song of Songs*, describes how "the Word says once again to the bride whom he has awakened: 'Arise.' And when she has come to him, he says, 'Come.' For one who has been called to rise in this way can always rise further, and one who runs to the Lord will always have wide open spaces before him. And so we must constantly rise and never cease drawing close."[21] The Christic agent is always a migrant. The Letter to the Hebrews describes this migration thus: "Not having received the promises, but having seen them afar off, they were assured of them, embraced

19. Augustine, *Confessions*, Book 10. c.5. See also Karl Rahner, *Theological Investigations* 3, "Thoughts on the Theology of Christmas," tr. Karl-H. and Boniface Kruger (London: Darton, Longman, and Todd, 1967), pp. 24-34. Rahner: "[M]an is precisely in this way open, one who does not possess within himself what he essentially needs to be himself. . . . Man can be expressed only by talking about something else: about God, and who he is not" (pp. 30-31).

20. In *Nos sens et Dieu: Etudes Carmelitaine XXXIII* (Bruges, 1954), p. 97.

21. *Commentary on the Song of Songs*, tr. Casimir McCambley (Brookline, Mass.: Hellenic College Press, 1987), homily five, pp. 109-24, esp. p. 119. There are some who view Gregory of Nyssa's neverending journeying as implying that we never reach the place where we see God in Christ face to face. Others have emphasized how this journeying is always in Christ and to Christ and not articulating some bad infinite. For a good résumé of the issues involved and an answer to them see Henri de Lubac, *Le mystère du surnaturel* (Paris: Les Editions du Cerf, 2000), pp. 249-55.

them, and confessed themselves strangers and pilgrims [*xenoi kai parepidēmoi*] on the earth. For those who say such things declare plainly that they seek a homeland . . . that is, a heavenly country. Therefore God is not ashamed to be called their God; for he has prepared a city for them" (11:13-16). *Xenoi* and *parepidēmoi* are complex Greek words. *Xenoi* can mean both "to be in a foreign country" and "to be a guest." *Parepidēmoi* is a combination of *para* and *epidēmeō* — where *epidēmeō* can describe either "the one who stays at home" (and is non-migratory) or "the one who is residing in a place as an alien" (the migrant). The agent of the Christian act, eternally incomplete, journeys on.

The second observation concerning this spiritual embodiment is with respect to the faith community. For, in this realm that exceeds any limitations of place, the mutual indwelling which characterizes what St. Paul calls *koinōnia* announces the presence of an *ekklēsia* always living beyond itself. As with the individual, so with the church — it is always interpenetrated by that which refigures its boundaries. Several bodies map onto and dislocate each other (the body of Christ, the individual body, the social body of the church feeding off the Eucharistic body). As such, the *ekklēsia* is much less the institution and much more the history of a body that is continually overreaching itself. We might employ here Gregory of Nyssa's term *skopos*.[22] The *skopos* is the whole trajectory of an object's development in and through time. Nyssa's example is that of Rome — the *skopos* of Rome refers to all that Rome was, is or will be. The *skopos* of the church is its tradition.[23] It is the history of its co-relation, its indwelling and being indwelt. As such, the church has a history, a temporality. It is not that location is eclipsed. A location remains: the body or collected bodies of believers, which are material and particular. Such bodies constitute and context social and political meaning and institutional and behavioral norms with respect to their dwelling in Christ and Christ in them. They do this because their complex embodiment maps onto and contexts other social bodies (the family, the nation-state, the bodies of believers belonging to other faiths, for example). But the co-abiding is not reducible to the particular and material location or the social, cultural, and political meanings embedded in them. The *ekklēsia* is a location of liminality, a co-relation that lives always on the edge of both itself and what is other.

We might see this liminality in action through a peripatetic teacher like St.

22. The Greek word frequently employed by Gregory in describing teleological movement toward perfection is often translated "goal" or "aim."

23. For an account of "tradition" see my essay "Tradition and Traditions: Scripture, Christian Praxes, and Politics" in *Christian Theologies of Scripture: A Comparative Introduction*, ed. Justin Holcomb (New York: New York University Press, 2006).

Paul, moving from one ecclesial community to another, from one *koinōnia* to another, not simply relating these nodal points but involving them with issues beyond their own frontiers, persuading them to participate in community-life in other terrestrial centres. This is the effect, for example, of his plea for money for famine relief. So the churches of Macedonia are related to Corinth and both to Jerusalem, and greetings are exchanged and hospitality offered.[24]

To take this further (and this is the third characteristic of spiritual embodiment), we might consider the liminality of this complex co-abiding in Christ with respect to always opening any Christian to new social encounters. As I said above, any encountered situation involves acting and responding, but also leading. Increasingly, the cultural and historical contexts in which the Christian lives involve encounters not just with non-believers but also with other believers. But if we understand that the act of encounter cannot be reduced to any single agent's will, then we have to recognize an act of God's leading in every encounter. We are led into conversation with Jewish people, Muslims, Hindus, Sikhs, and so forth. This is theological challenge that is lived out continually today: that a Christian acts only minimally within a Christian conclave. There are, then, cultural negotiations made, conversations, communications that also involve this complex co-abiding and others also abiding in complex, theologically determined spaces. We will pursue this further. For the moment it is important that any notion of the Christian as agent is not reducible to an account of the will and the act, and that the interrelationality within which the subject comes to an understanding of himself or herself cannot be separated from the practices in which this interrelationality takes place. Such practices resist totally the privatization and atomism of the individual; and radically denounce spiritualities that reinforce such privatization and atomism. This is both within the church and outside in the wider cultural market-place for spiritualities.[25] It is this which renders all specifically religious practices with respect to the Christ being in me and I being in the Christ (such as prayer, confessions, praise, participation in ecclesial liturgies) highly political. For they participate in interrelational economies that move beyond the ecclesial and sacramental bodies of Christian living to the civic, national and international bodies in which they are implicated, and the bodies of believers that form other faith communities.

---

24. See here Rowan Williams's essay "Does It Make Sense to Speak of a Pre-Nicene Orthodoxy?" and the role played in the early church by the epistolary form in *On Christian Doctrine* (Oxford: Blackwell, 2001), pp. 11-15.

25. See Jeremy Carrette and Richard King, *Selling Spirituality* (London: Routledge, 2004).

I say "interrelationality" here rather than "intersubjectivity" for two reasons. First, relations are far larger than the two consciousnesses involved in evaluating it can measure — relations by nature exceed subjects. Secondly, intersubjectivity assumes already the independence and atomisation of subjects. Returning to these interrelational practices, it would seem that each practice embodies a process of subjectification. That is, the subject undergoes a certain formation or production of himself in and through the practice. Theologically, this is conceived of as "vocation" — of being formed in Christ. And this formation has a teleology. In the words of the writer of the Book of Revelation (who picks up a reference to a suggestion in the Book of Deuteronomy): "To the one who overcomes I will give . . . a white stone, with a new name written on the stone which no one knows except him who receives it" (2:17) — and, presumably, the one who wrote it, the Son of God. In a number of biographical sketches of Christian saints, von Balthasar takes up this idea in terms of a lifetime living out a certain statement about the nature of God; a divine name, if you will, carved out of the lives of each of those who serve him.[26] Again this supports that what we are treating here in terms of the Christian as agent is not a figure consumed by the divine but a person actually particularized by being divinized; not a subject without a sense of self nor a subject in full conscious possession of herself — but a subject on the way to a final recognition of who she is in Christ. The acts they are involved in, participate in, co-operate within (I view those descriptions as synonymous) form the particularity of the agent they are.

Governing agency, then, are the principles of interrelationality and subjectification. These render the body of any agent always living beyond himself or herself in and towards other bodies (the Eucharistic body, the ecclesial body, the social body and the body of Christ).

The Nature of the Action

Let us now consider the second of our elements of action: the nature of the action done by the agent. For it would follow from what we have just investigated about selfhood and participation that the orientation and interpretation of any action would constitute not just an anthropology but a Christology. We might indeed attempt to catalog various types of action — teaching,

---

26. See his books *Elizabeth of Dijon: An Interpretation of Her Spiritual Mission*, tr. A. V. Littledale (New York: Pantheon, 1956) and *Thérèse de Lisieux: A Story of a Mission*, tr. D. Nicholl (London, 1953).

commanding, obeying, entertaining, and so forth. But insofar as all Christian action participates in the economy of love, all action is service and therefore liturgical. For the final determination of an act in Christ is doxological. Of course this appears an easy set of inferences to make, but to be more clear about what is philosophically involved here we can go further. For to ask about the nature of an action seems to drive us towards the isolation of an act and how that act is named, as if the single act is the most basic element in action. This is far from certain. As a number of language philosophies of the twentieth century have shown us, the word is not the most basic element of meaning. Meaning emerges at the level of the sentence and even then, as thinkers as diverse as Wittgenstein and Stanley Fish have taught us, the meaning of the sentence cannot be divorced from the context within which that sentence is cited.

Similarly, the nature of a single act — "he mowed the lawn," for example — cannot be determined in isolation from the relationship of the agent to gardening as a whole, the household context circumscribing both agent and action, and the social mores that encourage such an action. For the act of mowing the lawn may be an act of relaxation, an act of pleasure, an act of obedience (having been told to do it), a means of apologizing, a means of making someone else feel guilty, and so on. In other words, the nature of the action can only be determined at the level of practices with respect to a certain social, cultural, and historical context. To take an example: Judas's kiss can only be understood in terms of the gospel narratives as a whole. I say "as a whole" and immediately we are aware that no narrative is a self-contained whole; it is forever generating new readings when situated in new contexts. But at least when we read Judas's kiss in the context of the passion narratives we have we can name it as an "act of betrayal." The point here is that an act cannot be "read" outside the larger practices of which it is a part.

But if the nature of an act cannot be determined apart from an appreciation of the practices that situate that act, where does this "situating" process end such that the nature of the act can be named? His mowing the lawn was *an act of charity* for an elderly neighbor. Judas's kiss was an *act of betrayal.* To equate this examination of naming or judging an act with an inquiry into the sixth of our key elements — the inner intellectual and/or affective workings such that there was any action; to equate this judging with an enquiry into intention, motivation, desire, willing and wishing — is premature. It is premature because it resolves the problematic of naming the nature of the act at the level of the subject. At the level of the subject, taking into consideration various textual clues and postulated reconstructions of Judas's discipleship, his kiss was an act of exposure: exposing a messianic impostor. But as we have seen above, the chiasmic Christian subjects not only come to an understanding of themselves interrelationally — that is, in and through encounters with the other-than-him/herself — the subjects also come to an understanding of themselves through the practices in which they participate, the practices of subjectification. In other words the act takes its nature and naming from the practice of which it is a part. The practice operates as a hermeneutical framework that governs the interpretation of acts.

What does this mean in terms of a Christian act? Well, it situates even the smallest and most local of actions — mowing the lawn — within an economy of divine action governed by both a soteriology and an eschatology. We note how such a framework takes us far beyond conscious willing and intending. That is why Nyssa and Augustine accord desire the primary animator of the ensouled flesh. As we have seen, our desire for God participates in God's utterly unconditional desire for us — and not only us but also for the redemption of creation. There is in the Christian act, then, not only a telos, but also a utopic moment. The act is both now and proleptic. It reaches towards a future fulfillment. As such, the act is always an operation not just of love (towards God), but of faith and hope. The French writer and philosopher Maurice Blanchot once wrote, "Hope bespeaks the possibility of what escapes the realm of the possible; at the limit, it is relation recaptured where relation is lost."[27] We can see from the trajectory of this examination of the act that while each agent will have some local knowledge of what the act engaged in is, that knowledge quickly sheers off into mystery. We simply cannot name the nature of our act. For its nature concerns what role the act plays in the divine economy, the theo-drama (to use von Balthasar's term).[28]

The Evaluation of the Action

With this last observation we move from the second key element to the third — the evaluation of the action done by the agent. For to name the act would be to give it its meaning, and to give it its meaning we would have to be able to evaluate it in terms of its final end. The naming is already an act of judgment. But again let me be as clear as possible here. I am not claiming that Christians are like somnambulists or puppets. When they act they will no doubt name

27. *The Infinite Conversation,* tr. S. Hanson (Minneapolis: University of Minnesota Press, 1993), p. 41.

28. See the five volumes of *Theo-Drama: Theological Dramatic Theory* (San Francisco: Ignatius Press, 1988-1998).

that act — I am mowing the lawn — and evaluate it with reference to themselves — because it is a sunny day and I take pleasure in being out and active in the garden. But the import of the action done in Christ goes far beyond this naming and evaluation, for the action participates in economies that suspend the local in the universal.

It is important not to fall into a nominalist error at this point. The naming and judging undertaken by the agent with respect to the Christian act is not arbitrary. It is not that this naming and judging bears no relation to how it is named and judged with respect to God. In *De Civitate Dei* Augustine observes that "ignorance is unavoidable — and yet the exigencies of human society make judgment also unavoidable."[29] It is both necessary to make judgments and also to admit one's ignorance because all judgments are contingent upon the eschatological judgment. Nevertheless, if there is a participation in the operations of God then the contingencies of the necessary acts of naming and judging will find their consummation, not their overthrow, in the eschatological judgment. Participation implies then analogical relations: our naming and judging participates analogically in God's naming and judging as the act labours in a hope for its consummation. Not that we are unable to make mistakes, to name wrongly (deceiving both ourselves and others), to misjudge. But we can recall here that analogical thinking (or imagining) is, for Gregory of Nyssa in his *Life of Moses,* inseparable from anagogical living. That is, naming and judging are part of a practice of ascent; the technologies (in the Greek sense of *teuchein*) of discipleship. We name and judge far better the more we are subject to God.

Once more, can I return then to the context in which the Christian acts today in encountering and responding to those involved in other faith-practices (or no faith practice at all)? For the finitude and contingency of all judgments mean that in the hermeneutics of any encounter there is an eschatological waiting; we wait to be revealed the true understanding of the situation, the social or cultural encounter. Ignorance, the refashioning of judgments by the judgment of God, again forestalls any Christian triumphalism or supersessionism. So, in an encounter with other practices that cannot easily be located within the system of ideas, values and practices that govern any Christian viewpoint, the avoidance of misjudgment has to predominate. Steps must be taken to understand as far as possible. There must be a listening to how the other names and evaluates his actions, for example, and a learning of the networks of association within which these names and evaluations are situated. But it is theologically necessary to de-

29. *De Civitate Dei,* XIX.6.

clare a healthy agnosticism; and to allow that agnosticism to govern our own actions with respect to the other encountered. That does not mean a judgment about the other's action cannot take place. A concrete example recently occurred with the London bombings of July 2005. An action done in the name of God that produces violence has to be judged. It was judged as morally evil by secularists, as well as people in faith communities. Furthermore, there was a validation of their judgment when the Islamic leaders themselves condemned such action as not according to the principles of Islam. But even making a judgment here should not stop us from trying to understand further what is the object of these actions.

The Object

It is the manner in which any Christian act is irreducible to its execution in the present that renders it irreducible to conscious motivations and irreducible with respect to its naming and evaluation. The same irreducibility pertains to the object of the action. The objects of an action can only be separated from the objectives of an action heuristically. The object of Judas's attention was Jesus' cheek; the object of my mowing is the lawn — grammatically. But the object of the action has been chosen in accordance with a specific objective. The object cannot be isolated from the practice governing its choice as an object. I do this rather than that — which, to forestall the emergence of the autonomous subject, we can rewrite from another direction, one attested to in a collect from the English *Book of Common Prayer:* I do this act that has been prepared for me, rather than that act which has not been prepared. This is an example of the chiasmus again. The present object/objective then is an intimation of a future and final object/objective. What is this object/objective? We return to the processes of subjectification, for I suggest the future and final object/objective is the submission of all things to Christ. The act then becomes an offering. It inhabits the logic of sacrifice. This is a positive logic, not a negative one, and it returns us again to the Greek understanding of *leitourgia*. From such a perspective, the object/objective is to facilitate all things becoming what St. Paul termed "a living sacrifice" (Romans 12:1). The particular object of any act is then situated within the schema of redemption, like a composer who submits notes, tones, intervals, and rhythms to the sovereignty of the musical score. To appreciate any single element in the composition takes time because the work occurs in and as time. Each action then (and each judgment that is also an action and will bear upon future action) is part of an ongoing politics of redemption, an economy. The object of each action either finds the place of its contribution in the divine order or it will pass as a gesture "full of sound and fury, signifying nothing" (to quote *Macbeth*). We can become more specific here, for this order is characterized traditionally by those transferable transcendentals, the so-called names of God: justice, beauty, goodness, and truth. The object/objective of the Christian act is the manifestation of what is just, good, beautiful, and true in, with, and beyond whatever is the grammatical object upon which the agent labours. In such a labouring, the agent is priestly, the act liturgical, and the object sacramental. The agent is not superior to the object, is not sovereign of it in the way some older philosophies exalted subject over object, the human over the givenness of the natural realm, and made it possible to conceive the human task as the taming and exploitation of the natural order. Here the relationship between the agent and the object is symmetrical — the lawn I mow is not my inferior. It is that which I tend, for both I and it are given to each other in this opportunity to offer, to sacrifice. To employ a distinction found in Augustine, through the act I enjoy I do not simply use and what I enjoy is the goodness, beauty, justice, and truth of God. To enjoy is to delight in, and the action ends in praise and thankfulness for what is given. To enjoy is the beginning of doxology. But to use is to manipulate for one's own satisfactions. It is an act of domination. The object of a Christian act is always a form of blessing (given and received); liturgical again.

The Effect of the Act

Only when viewed in this way can we approach the fifth of the key elements of an action in general — the effect of the act both upon the agent and the object of the action. For what takes place through the act of offering — of both oneself and the object with which one is acting — is a transfiguration. But before I detail this transfiguration, let us see what has happened to a philosophical category often examined with respect to defining an action: effect. For the language of "effect" invokes the language of causality. Aristotle, of course, distinguishes between material, efficient, final, and formal causation when discussing the economics of motion in the cosmos. The reduction of the construal of action to the autonomous subject, the emphasis on the will as animator of act, and the emphasis upon action as occurring only on an immanental plane, give priority to efficient causation. The I authors all action, and that which is executed is an effect of the will-to-cause. There are a number of difficulties with this model of causation with respect to the Christian act. First, to unhinge efficient from final cause leads to pragmatism if not (as I would suggest with Derrida) arbitrariness.[30] Secondly, the action and animation involved in a Christian act operate on a divine as well as a human level. The human action participates in a divine soteriological providence. As I argued above, this does not erase the I: the I cooperates, or the authoring of the I is authorized. Some philosophical theologians have then distinguished between primary and secondary causation with respect to divine and human action. This, to my mind, has a tendency to reify the divine and human positions such that an absolute dichotomy rules them. There is a *diastēma* between the uncreated and what is created; a *diastēma* that human sinfulness aggrandizes with respect to the human perspective — we are plunged into an ever deeper befuddlement the more we recognize the absence of the divine. But the logic of the Incarnation and the logic of living and acting as a Christian *en Christō* infer that the *diastēma* allows always for the transits of grace and adoration; the *diastēma* facilitates, it does not impede, salvation. If, then, we shift the discourse describing these transits from one of causation to one concerning chiasmic relations; that is, if we see these transits of grace and adoration in terms of a living relationship — then we are treating, in a more Augustinian manner, the way the desire of those who love each other cooperates to bring about a desired end: all things being one with Christ. It is, then, the final cause, if we wish to continue using this language, that informs Christian action at all levels and the I acts because it desires that which God also desires; it is obedient to that desire. The employment of primary and secondary causation as a means of explaining divine and human action can also tend towards conceiving God in terms of some theistic *potentia absoluta*. But, on the model I am suggesting (on the basis of my account of the Christian act to this point), God does not force but fulfills human agency.

The shift in discourse can be justified on the grounds that analysis of the relationship between cause, action and agency is undertaken on "accounts" given of agents determining something and acting. This is the third problem with respect to the language of causation. We never treat "cause" as such; we treat descriptions of cause, and the descriptions forge links so that the language of cause and effect appears "natural." Lack of attention to this representational or discursive operation leads, to my mind, to the confusions and debates concerning reason and causal explanation. Of course, rationalization is a subset of causal explanation, because explanation requires grammatical articulation and grammatical articulation requires an act of reasoning that associates subject, object and action. Both "cause" and "reason" are intrinsic to

---

30. See my "Questioning God" in *Questioning God,* ed. John Caputo, Mark Dooley, and Michael Scalon (Bloomington: Indiana University Press, 2002).

saying/writing — they cannot be attended to outside this saying/doing. Please note, this observation does not reduce all things to the level of language; it merely draws attention to the inevitable linguistic construction of events.

The fourth problem with describing action in terms of the will-to-cause is the sheer fallibility of human willing, attested to by the examples of both St. Paul and Mephistopheles. One recalls St. Paul's wrestling in his Letter to the Romans: "I do not understand my own actions. For I do not do *(prassō)* what I want, but I do *(poiō)* the very thing I hate. . . . I can will what is right, but I cannot do it. For I do not do *(poiō)* the good I want, but the evil I do not want to do I do *(prassō)*" (7:15-19). One recalls the double inversion of this when Mephistopheles first introduces himself to Faust: *"Ein Teil von jener Kraft, Die stets das Böse will und stets das Gute schafft."*[31] This does not deny the human will and its involvement in bringing about specific effects within the world. But it emphasizes both the limitations of that will — an act of love can bring about tragedy as all tragic dramatists are aware — and also the limitations of one's own consciousness. We are not transparent to ourselves. We have already observed Augustine's comments on the mystery of being human in his *Confessions:* we pose to ourselves one of the greatest of the questions we wrestle with.

On this basis no single agent can calculate the effects of his or her action. The profound interdependence of all things with respect to the providence of God implies that my act of mowing the lawn can have consequences beyond my own immediate pleasures in executing this act. It can have consequences with respect to my own spiritual development, other people who witness this act and are affected by my spiritual development, and the object (in this case the lawn itself). We can return to the word employed earlier. In the context of what Aquinas calls the effects of God's operations in the world, the object becomes a means of grace. It is transfigured; and its sacramental nature becomes apparent. Von Balthasar, speaking of the Jewish understanding of wisdom, captures this transfiguration when he describes "the realm of creation [becoming] transparent, allowing us to discern the presence of the divine Spirit within it."[32] Each created object we hold up to God bears the watermark of the *Logos* through whom all things came to be. With respect to the object of a Christian act, it is never reducible to a set of physical or visible properties. Every object, in a Christian act, is related analo-

31. Johann Wolfgang von Goethe, *Faust: Der Tragödie Erster Teil* (Munich: C. H. Beck, 1972), scene 3. Translated by George Madison Priest as "Part of that Power which would/The Evil ever do, and ever does the Good."

32. *Theo-Drama* IV, p. 220.

gously to the raising of a piece of bread at the Last Supper and its identification as "this is my body."

Dispositions and Affections

Let me clarify a point here that is important for understanding both the fifth and sixth key elements of our poetics of actions — the effect of an action and the inner intellectual and/or affective workings such that there was any action at all. What I am not saying is that because we are not totally in control of ourselves, our actions or the consequences of those actions the act itself is therefore irrational. Stuart Hampshire once remarked that the connection between reason and action is "mysterious."[33] On Augustinian lines I would agree (he would not accept such lines though). But to be mysterious, theologically understood, is not to be irrational or without reason. For Christ as *Logos* is both word and reason (as wisdom). In a Christian act, our own reasoning operates within this Christic reasoning. Or, put another way, as in Aquinas, faith perfects human reason. I can then give a rational account of my action, but the significance of my action cannot be limited by the account I give of it. The limitations are twofold: first, other accounts from friends, strangers, enemies, or colleagues also are able to rationalize my action, framing it possibly in a different way. Second, my limited reasoning participates in a higher logic such that the axiom "Abide in me, and I in you" qualifies notions of sovereignty. Both these two limitations emphasize that there is no transparency with respect to intention, but that does not mean the act is done without deliberation nor that a rational account cannot be given for it. For the agent herself these alternative frames of interpretation — that given by other people and that given by the Christian faith-tradition with respect to its unfolding meditations on the operations of the divine — are hierarchized. The latter is primary or of greater import than the former.

When we come to our sixth key element of action — disposition or pro-attitudes — we need to bear this in mind. Traditional Christian accounts of action have emphasized that the role of the passions can distort rational judgments. There must be a striving for *apatheia*. This has frequently led to a tension between affective states and reasoning; sometimes to a dualism. I am far from sure I have an adequate grasp of the issues here, and I am not an expert on Gregory of Nyssa — but I am aware of what appears to be a tension from the perspective of the twenty-first century between the fundamental

33. *Thought and Action* (London: Chatto and Windus, 1959), p. 167.

operation of a desire in his theology and the goal of *apatheia.* "[D]esire as much as you can," Nyssa advocates in his *Homilies on the Song of Songs;* "I boldly add these words: 'Be passionate about it' . . . passionate love (the Greek is *erōs*) for the divine beauty."[34] But with respect to affective states in a Christian act, as I said above a rational account can be given for them while recognizing that again we have no access to our affective states outside of such accounts. There is a long tradition that conceives sensations of the world, acts of intellection and the stirring of desire as all involving "movements of the soul."[35] The Greek word is *kinēmapsuchēs;* it is found in the work of John Damascene and it is indebted to Aristotle.[36] More recently, neurobiologists like Antonio Damasio have also drawn attention to the way acts of judgment cannot be divorced from feelings and emotional states.[37] I do not wish to enter into the difficulties and debates concerning *De Anima* Chapter Five and the Prime Mover, but on a doctrine of participation the movement of that soul is situated within the motion of divine action itself. *Anagogy* is the movement of the soul into a deeper knowledge of where it resides. As such, once more, the authority of the Christian agent is circumscribed as that agent's disposition or pro-attitudes are undergoing a discipline, a formation *en Christō.*

What, Then, Is a Christian Act?

Having hastily examined the poetics of an action in terms of six key elements, let me conclude by asking the most abstract of questions: what, then, is a Christian act? In Book Six of the *Nicomachean Ethics,* Aristotle makes a famous distinction between *praxis* (doing, acting) and *poiēsis* (making, creating): "the genus of action is different from that of production, for while production has an end other than itself, action cannot."[38] In *De Anima* the

34. *Commentary on the Song of Songs,* p. 47.

35. *De Fide Orthodoxa,* II, 11.22.46, 248 in *Schriften des Johannes von Damaskos,* ed. B. Kotter, vol. 2 (Berlin: Walter de Gruyter, 1973).

36. Aristotle distinguished between motion, *kinēsis,* and actuality or *energeia.* They were not dualistic concepts but constituted two poles of a spectrum. *Energeia* was the perfection or realization of all that was potential. *Kinēsis* was the movement that moved all things towards their formal (in the Aristotelian sense of "form") completion. The form is the "*logos* of the essence" (*Physics* II.3.194b27). See L. A. Kosman, "Aristotle's Definition of Motion" in *Phronesis* 14 (1969), pp. 40-62.

37. See *Descartes' Error: Emotion, Reason, and the Human Brain* (London: Picador, 1995) and *Looking for Spinoza: Joy, Sorrow, and the Human Brain* (London: Heinemann, 2003).

38. *Nicomachean Ethics,* tr. Terence Irwin (Indianapolis: Hackett, 1985), 1140b.

movement of the soul, *kinēmapsuchēs,* is understood as *praxis.*[39] *Poiēsis* comes from elsewhere. It has a practical aspect to it since it is related to *technē,* but it cannot be reduced to this aspect for, as Giorgio Agamben (admittedly reading Aristotle through Heidegger — which does beg a number of questions) has recently put it: *poiēsis* "does not bring itself into presence in the work, as acting *(praxis)* brings itself into presence in the act *(practon).*"[40] *Poiēsis* bears a transcendent charge, an ontological weight of bringing something into being, of genesis. It concerns bringing into being that there might be *gnōsis.* Actually, in English the sixteenth-century poet and writer Sir Philip Sydney says something very similar about the workings of "poesy" in refashioning the world.[41] After Aristotle, then, we might characterize Christian acting as a *praxis* that participates in a divine *poiēsis* that has soteriological and eschatological import.[42] It is a *technē,* a crafting, a production — of redemption.[43] As we have noted this acting is liturgical, but, returning again to Aristotle, it is also political, ethical, and aesthetic.

39. *De Anima,* tr. D. W. Hamlyn (Oxford: Clarendon Press, 1993), 433a.

40. *The Man Without Content,* tr. Georgia Albert (Stanford: Stanford University Press, 1999), p. 75.

41. *An Apology for Poetry,* ed. Geoffrey Shepherd (London: Thomas Nelson, 1965), p. 101.

42. Athanasius uses *poiēsis* in this way when, in *Orationes Contra Arianos* (I, 38), he writes of how the Logos "made men gods *(etheopoiēse)* by himself becoming man."

43. There is a very interesting use of the verbal forms of *poiēsis* and *praxis* in the Pauline passage from Romans that I quoted above, which I have not followed through. Though it may be significant that the creative doing — the doing of what is good — Paul also relates to *poiēsis.*

Morning Prayer as Redemptive Thinking

Peter Ochs

This is an essay about traditional Jewish Morning Prayer as training in how to make judgments during the day: judgments that could help or hurt and that could or could not serve us and others. For those of us who make judgments in unhelpful ways, or for those who believe that modern civilization (or some other civilization) nurtures an unhelpful way of making judgments, then this essay is about Morning Prayer as training in redemptive thinking, or thinking that redeems the ways we ordinarily misjudge the world.

Preface

This essay is offered as a heuristic exercise: not a text-historical claim about how and why the Jewish prayer book was redacted, but, within the parameters of text-historical scholarship, an exercise in imagining what the effects of praying these words may be. The exercise itself will therefore have different effects depending on what you bring to it as reader. I address the exercise optimally to those who see themselves as having inherited from modern Western civilization certain ways of seeing the world that they would rather not have (along with those they are happy to have). As complex as these ways are, I propose a simple model for identifying what lies at the heart of the troublesome way — something I call a propositional way of judging the world. I suggest that this way is not intrinsically bad — it has many necessary and good uses — but that some of us find that this way has been overdone — and the overdoing is what is problematic. For the sake of those who are socialized in this model, I suggest we may read the Jewish Morning Prayer as a way *out* of this socialization. Not a contrary way, or a way that simply negates this form of judgment (for we know that a contrary reinforces its negative), but a way to be socialized into forms of judgments that are good for us, including constructive uses of propositional judgments.

Now, if you care to include yourself in this essay's intended audience, then you might play through the exercise and only after that judge what just happened and what use or nonuse it may have. In this case, please know that I am *not* suggesting that even the bad parts of modern socialization — let alone all the other parts — can actually be reduced to this one form. I am offering the reduction only for the sake of the exercise, because I believe it is helpful for practical purposes. What, however, if you are not in the intended audience? Well, if you believe the propositional way of judging the world *is* simply the best, and if you don't agree with the brief illustrations I offer of its dangers, then I am afraid you will not enjoy this essay! There isn't space in the essay for me to try to demonstrate my many assumptions. Even so, even you might find some value in the way the essay formalizes some of the judgments framed by Morning Prayer; this may give you more reason not to like such prayer, but it may also suggest ways that prayer introduces modes of rationality you have not considered.

If, on the other hand, you feel you have not acquired these forms of modern socialization and if you were socialized, in fact, in a tradition of Jewish prayer (or some analogue), then you may indeed find that the essay fusses about things that do need to be fussed about. You may find my philosophic way of reading the prayer book a bit odd, but even so, I trust you won't find it necessarily *contradicts* what you believe abut Jewish prayer. It may in fact suggest ways that your inherited knowledge could be made to address spheres of modern life you assumed were mute to your wisdom.

If — to consider a third group — you were socialized in Jewish prayer but have strong objections to aspects of it, then you may or may not find the essay useful. If you object to the essay because you believe Judaism's failings would be corrected precisely through analyses and criticisms that draw on the clarity of propositional logic, then you and I simply have reason to enjoy extended debate.

If you object because you believe that specific parts of the prayer tradition are hurtful in some way — oppressive, muddled, overgeneralized, and so on — then I hope you will be patient with the essay, since it may in fact offer resources for you. While I look to Morning Prayer as a means of correcting one specific problem in modern Western practice, I do not presume that Morning Prayer is some panacea. I believe there are limits to the power of prayer, and I find some of our prayer texts problematic. I simply have space in this essay to focus on only one theme.

If, finally, Judaism is not your frame of reference — if, for example, you are Christian or Muslim — I trust the essay may be useful or non-useful to you in analogous ways, which means most useful if you, too, wonder how scripturally based prayer might influence the way we form judgments in the modern West.

Beginning at Night

The Jewish liturgical day begins at nightfall. While this essay's focus is Morning Prayer, how we greet any given day depends in large part on what happened, last night, to the day before. To introduce our study of Morning Prayer, I would therefore like to ask you to undertake a brief exercise of thinking about the following verse from Jewish Evening Prayer:

> Blessed are you, YHVH our God, Ruler of the universe, by whose word the evening falls. With wisdom he opens the gates of heaven, and with understanding he changes the periods of the day and varies the seasons, setting the stars in their courses in the sky according to his will. Creating day and night, rolling away light before darkness and darkness before light, he causes the day to pass and bring on the night, making a division between day and night: YHVH of hosts is his Name. May the ever-living God rule over us forever and ever. Blessed are you, YHVH, who makes the evenings fall.[1]

To enter this exercise, try this: Think of all the observations and actions you undertake during the day to be kinds of judgment: that is, think of all your perceptions, conceptions, inferences, and behavioral decisions to be either judgments of observation that take on the form "(I believe) X is y" or judgments of action that take on the form "(I will) do A to B." For now, think of all your judgments as tending to divide themselves into two distinguishable parts: subjects such as "X" or "I" and predicates such as "y" or "will do A to B." Think of these parts as corresponding to two distinguishable parts of the world: things and their qualities *or* actors and their qualities of action. And think of your judgments as actions that bring predicates into relation with subjects, thereby symbolizing how qualities are brought into relation with the things or actions they qualify. This means, as you see, that we begin the exercise by identifying our daily judgments with what we called the "modern Western" form of propositional judgments.

---

1. Throughout, translations are adapted from the range of published translations of the traditional prayer book and from the Hebrew (see note 4 for sources).

Now, consider this signal blessing of Evening Prayer as a lesson in how to align our judgments to their contexts in time as well as in space. Imagine that, according to the blessing, the universe of nightfall is distinct from the universe of daylight. Imagine nightfall as a place in time that dissolves our capacity to link subjects and predicates and, thus, our capacities to make good or bad judgments, to err or to work for the good. The fall of night marks the fall of our license, so to speak, to make claims about the relation of things to their qualities, agents to their actions, or subjects to their predicates. This is a time of relaxation and *separation*. At night, one could say, judgments go to sleep, allowing predicates to speak to themselves alone, as what we call dreams, and subjects to rest in the invisibility or darkness of the night. At night, subjects become the things of the world, mute, silent, resting; predicates become our desires of the world, but blending with other predicates rather than with the world.

Think of the dark, in other words, as a condition in which the things of the world cannot be clearly seen. They drift off, becoming the indefinite creatures they are apart from our vision of them. We may sense they are there — the way we might bump into some table or something in the dark — but they are there as only distant objects of the possibility of our sensing. They are vague things that are what they are but that could be many things. They float, and our senses of them are mere indices, pointing to something that is really out there in the dark but without any distinct identity. And we? If in the day we were agents of seeing, persons who claimed to know, now our capacity to know is also dulled. We enter a dream world where ideas are no longer conditions for discerning this versus that in the world, but a play of possibilities — wandering images — as if this were *our* way of falling as knowers into vague creature-hood. As for the third something — the subject who makes judgment — this one falls asleep, as if dead. In the realm of the night, God alone is actor, mediator, judge: in the words of nighttime prayer (blessings to be recited in bed):

> Blessed are you, YHVH, Ruler of the universe, who closes my eyes in sleep, my eyelids in slumber. May it be your will, YHVH my God and God of my ancestors, that I lie down in peace and rise up in peace. Let my thoughts not upset me, nor bad dreams or sinful fancies. . . .
>
> Those who dwell in the shelter of the Most High abide under the protection of the Almighty. I call YHVH "My refuge and my fortress, my God in whom I trust." . . . With his pinions he covers you and under his wings you find refuge. . . . Do not fear the terror of the night . . . (Ps. 91). Behold the Guardian of Israel neither sleeps nor slumbers (Ps. 121:4). . . . Into His hand I entrust my spirit when I go to sleep — and I shall awaken!

Into Morning Prayer

Blessed are you YHVH our God, Ruler of the universe, who forms light and creates darkness, makes peace, and creates all things. In mercy he gives light to the earth and all who dwell on it. In his goodness, he daily and constantly renews the order of creation. How vast are your works, YHVH! You have made all of them in wisdom, filling the earth with your creations. . . . As it is said, "Praise the one who makes great lights, for his mercy endures forever" (Ps. 136). O, cause a new light to shine upon Zion, and may we all soon be worthy to enjoy its light. Blessed are you, YHVH, who fashions the lights.

Morning Prayer offers a wake-up call. It prepares individuals to frame those judgments that, in the light of day and during waking hours, refashion dreams as predicates of desires and refashion the silent things of the world as messengers that speak to these desires and needs. The vehicle of their actual speaking is the activity through which humans make judgments: perceptual judgments, judgments of value, empirical judgments, scientific judgments. The overall theme of this essay is that Morning Prayer offers a training ground for making these judgments in the right way.

Consider the change from night to day. Daylight means a realm of experience in which creatures are perceivable. Losing the safety of their nighttime vagueness, they become what can be seen and what can, therefore, be received in some particular way as opposed to another way, in that way becoming objects of reaction and losing their freedom not to be in any particular way. And we — whose bodies also become visible — become at the same time agents of vision — actors, those who see others and in the seeing remove creatures from the ownness they enjoyed as we all slept. We become judges. Oh, that is my breath! I am alive. Oh, that is my sock — it is on the floor. It is, this is. . . . That, mine, alive. . . . Are they? Is it? The dream world in the light of day rushes away like a ghost at dawn — replaced with this-that-I-see, that-that-I-taste, this-that-I-judge. I am born, it seems, with the light. I who am I as seer, knower, discriminator, chooser-among-possibilities, remover-out of dreams, owner, *judge*. To be awake is to judge. But how?

We cannot say how all humans in all places and all times have tended to awaken in the morning. But we can guess that we modern Westerners may tend, without prayer, to awaken ready to judge the world in the way that best fits the energy, logic, and style of the institutions that have tended to dominate Western civilization since the seventeenth and eighteenth centuries. I have in mind the political institutions of the modern nation-state, the economic institutions of the modern market (now the global market), various institutions of modern scientific and technological research, various institutions of social service (with medical service as a paradigm), and various institutions of socialization — with the modern university as paradigm. While these various entities may institutionalize dozens of ways of forming judgments about the world and about how to act in it, I will ask you to imagine, for the course of this essay, that we moderns are socialized to privilege one form as if it set the agenda for all the rest. I suggest we label this one, variously, "the subject-predicate form," or "the substance-attribute form," or "the logic of propositions," or, the term I will use, "the propositional way of judging the world." I understand this to be a form of judging — that is, perceiving, conceiving, and interpreting — all phenomena in the world so that when I (someone socialized this way) awaken in the morning my first act is to see whatever is around me as an object of *my* vision and as a context for *my* action. What I see "out there" are formed things, entities, distinct one from the other, and meaningful as things that are there to be seen by me.[2] And I perceive them to "have" qualities and to enter into relations as if the qualities and relations were added on, secondary to what they are in themselves. I see them, that is, to have an essential form and then to have secondary qualities. But why?

Seeing with modern eyes, I see that these features of the world *seem* to be delivered to me though my perceptions and cognitions. I see that I can conveniently examine these by perceiving them as re-presented by way of propositions — of the form "X is y" — whose subjects name or refer to entities in the world and whose predicates indicate the qualities or relations I judge those entities to have. I see that I can think about subjects and predicates independently one from the other. On paper or in my imagination, I can perform a variety of operations on them. Perceiving them as words on a page, I can combine any subject with other subjects, predicates with other predicates; or I can re-combine different subjects and predicates with one another, forming worlds of words that seem to reflect all the elements of the world out there, except that there is no end to what I imagine into these worlds of my own art. Perceiving them as images in the mind — or in various media of visual and plastic art — I can analyze subjects and predicates into constituent elements and then vary the elements, so the subjects appear as different or new objects in the world and the predicates as new or different qualities. On paper or in imagination, I can also treat qualities as things and things as qualities: I could, for example, personify virtues so that Mercy and Cruelty become actors in a play; or I could make adjectives and adverbs of people, suggesting that you

---

2. Things, that is, whose objecthood is correlative to my own subjecthood.

"look like Cary Grant," or that he "acted the Jew." Then, with enough practice or with too much practice, I might, intentionally or unintentionally, manipulate my judgments of the world according to my experiments on paper or in the imagination. I could change my perception of someone, from "being ugly" to "being kind" or from "being a bum lying in my way" to "being someone who might be injured and need my help" or from "being a person worthy of respect" to "being a damn so-and-so worthy of mistreatment." I could potentially see clouds as pictures of people, a group of people as a pile of rocks, red as blue, dogs as people, poverty as riches, or I could even, for a second or for always, lose any sense of the difference between the world out there and the world in my imagination or on paper.

These are all ways I could go out and judge the world this morning. One purpose and effect of Morning Prayer is to prepare me to offer judgments in a different way, which means to perceive the world differently and act in it differently. The propositional way of judging the world is not bad in itself: it represents an essential part of every day's judgments and is the best way to address certain phenomena and certain calls for action. It is simply not the only way to judge; in many cases it is not the best way; in some cases it is among the worst ways; and it becomes "bad" when it replaces all other ways. Our warrant for paying special attention to this way is that, through the modern epoch (the epoch of Enlightenment and colonialism), Western civilization has tended to promote propositional logic as simply the best means of knowing the world — and, sometimes, as the only way of knowing it in a sane or rational way. The very serious danger here is not the logic itself but its being overgeneralized and absolutized: so the culprit is the logic of propositions *plus* the logic and psychology/sociology of overgeneralization. Without taking time in this essay to illustrate or argue why, I would go so far as to claim that this culprit may be a name for *the* culprit in the modern West. One illustration is the modern Western affection for "isms," which I read as a name for love of vast generalizations: making a noun, an essence, and a principle out of small collections of qualities that attend certain activities. Thus a certain set of cautions on behalf of humanity becomes humanism and individualism; a certain set of mechanisms for exchange becomes global capitalism — then there are colonialism, secularism, and even the transformation of scriptural traditions of practice into Juda*ism,* Christianity, and so on. I simply assume that the overgeneralized part of each of these isms is not good for us. Another illustration is totalitarianism as perhaps the paragon of all these isms because it is the paragon of overgeneralization. As Lévinas suggests in his critique of *"totalité,"* modern propositional logic has no defense against the tendency to totalitarian thinking, because it is based on this logic.[3] But, for those of us who inhabit the modern West, how is it possible to nurture actual, everyday habits of thinking that are not dominated by this logic?

Our theme is that Morning Prayer may serve as a means of nurturing such alternative habits in those who seek to acquire them. Within the space of this essay, we offer only a preliminary, logical argument in support of this theme: *that Morning Prayer nurtures logics of judgment that are irreducible to propositional logic and that inhibit the tendency to overgeneralization that often accompanies propositional logic.* To simplify this argument, I will make use of two overly reduced models: one of propositional logic (as the potential culprit, when overused) and one of a logic of relations — adopted as image of the culprit's redeemer. I do not, indeed, mean to reduce the force of Morning Prayer to any one logic, let alone this one. The way any redeemer needs to be dressed in the life context of the one who is to be redeemed, so too this logic of relations is simply a way of picturing how Morning Prayer might conceivably meet a propositional logic on its own terms, find room within those terms for something greater than propositional logic, and turn to that greater something as a source of better logics.

Reading the Stages of Morning Prayer

It is traditional (but not doctrinal) to speak of four sequential sections in Jewish Morning Prayer: the morning blessings *(birchot hashachar)*, the verses of praise *(pesuke d'zimra)*, the Shema and its blessings, and the Amidah (the standing prayer, or *tefillah*, "reflective prayer").[4] One thesis of this essay is

3. These days, there is much to read of and about Lévinas. On his critique of *totalité*, the classic is E. Lévinas, *Totality and Infinity*, trans. A. Lingis (Pittsburgh: Duquesne University Press, 1969).

4. I will not offer scholarly documentation for each of my claims and suggestions about the morning service. Instead, I will note here the various sources and commentaries I draw on. I offer my own translations from the traditional *nusach* of the Ashkenazi *shacharit*, aided by the following Hebrew editions with English translations:

- *Ha-Siddur Ha-shalem: Daily Prayerbook*, trans. Philip Birnbaum (New York: Hebrew Publishing Co., 1949).
- *Siddur Sim Shalom: A Prayerbook for Shabbat, Festivals, and Weekdays*, ed. and trans. Rabbi Jules Harlow (New York: The Rabbinical Assembly and The United Synagogue of America, 1985).
- *The Complete ArtScroll Siddur; Weekday/Sabbath/Festival*, trans. Rabbi Nosson Scherman (Brooklyn: Mesorah Publications, 1988).
- *My People's Prayer Book: Traditional Prayers, Modern Commentaries.* Vol. 1: *The Shema and*

that, when Morning Prayer is read as a course of nurturing redemptive thinking, then these four stages correspond to four successive stages of nurturance.
There will not be space to examine each of the stages in depth. Instead, I will
focus detailed text study on the first two stages and then simply outline where
the final two stages bring us. The Morning Blessings invite the "I think" to
greet the day as a gift from its Creator and, thus, to celebrate both the fact of
its existence ("I am") and of its serving and participating in a reality and a
subject-hood much greater than itself.

The Morning Blessings (Birchot Hashachar): A Call Both to Affirm and Displace the "I Think"

We introduce this overall theme of the morning blessings by examining several illustrative prayers in depth.

Modeh ani lefanekha: "Thankful am I"

A meditation: Let us imagine the very first moment of the morning, when the
eyes open, the body's primal waters begin to circulate, and muscles begin to
enact the morning's first desire: to move and thus to be reborn as an agent of
action. It is then that the words of Morning Prayer intervene, enjoining the
one who awakes to say this before doing anything else: "Thankful am I before
you, living and ever living leader, for you have returned my soul to me out of
your abundant graciousness and faithfulness."

Thankful am I. "I" am there; the first person is not forgotten, denied, ne-
gated. But I am secondary to you who is first person before I am: you, the living ruler (melekh), who will soon be named as YHVH (for now, the name is
missing, because, as yet unwashed after the evening's sleep, I am not yet prepared to address the one whose name *is* a form of direct address). As agent of
speech, my first act as speaker is to declare that, just as this verb (modeh) pre-

---

Its Blessings; Vol. 2: The Amidah, ed. Rabbi Lawrence A. Hoffman (Woodstock, Vermont:
Jewish Lights, 1997, 1998).

For historical background and rabbinic as well as modern commentary, I draw on:

- *My People's Prayer Book.*
- A. Z. Idelsohn, *Jewish Liturgy and Its Development* (New York: Schocken, 1932).
- Joseph Heinemann, *Prayer in the Talmud: Forms and Patterns* (New York: de Gruyter, 1977).
- Lawrence Hoffman, *The Canonization of the Synagogue Service* (South Bend, Ind.: Univer-
  sity of Notre Dame Press, 1979).
- Max Kadushin, *Worship and Ethics* (Binghamton, N.Y.: Global, 2001).

cedes me *(ani),* so do my first actions precede my agency and so does your agency precede my first actions. I have not abandoned my agency — there is no question here of non-self, since I say "I" — but I have declared that my agency is the consequence of another's agency. At this early morning's very moment of desire for movement and work and new productivity, I take a step back, bow the head through words and acknowledge the derivative character of all that I am about to do. It is you who act, I who receive, you who have brought me back to life, you who have opened my eyes, you who have hovered over my primal waters and quickened them, you who have stimulated my muscles, you who have granted me the reason for desire. At the very moment when I would have rushed headlong into the day and forgotten you, *modeh ani:* I remember you: you who are faithful to me before I even remember how to be faithful to you. What a joy to remember that that source of all energy and movement is a source of trust and personal relationship. "I am what is not mine" is how Abraham Heschel put it: "I am not even sure whether it is the voice of a definite personal unit that comes out of me. . . . I am endowed with a will, but the will is not mine; I am endowed with freedom, but it is a freedom imposed on the will. . . . The essence of what I am is not mine."[5] This discovery of limitation is also a source of relief and joy and of energy — for it means there is a place and a source on which I can fall back and refind the energy that creates me.

We may already see here a guideline for how to make judgments during the day. For, *yes,* I can make judgments, I have agency. But I have to wait to find out what will precede, accompany, and follow that agency; it is not for me alone to say.

Reshit chokhma yirat YHVH:
"Fear/Awe of YHVH is the Beginning of Wisdom"

So, yes, I will make judgments, but they do not originate with me nor do they come to clarity through my knowing alone. Judgment is grounded first in wisdom, and wisdom begins with my relationship to the Creator, not with the *cogito,* and this relationship begins with awe: a sense of amazement and of utter dependency before that which creates and sustains all this. I know that if "I see this or that," I see because of you and I see what is from you. In order to see, I therefore hope for as much help as I can get from you and from others

---

5. The title of section 8 of his phenomenology of the "Ways to His Presence," as redacted in Abraham J. Heschel, *Between God and Man,* ed. Fritz Rothschild (New York: Free Press, 1959), pp. 61-63.

who see; and what I see strengthens (all these senses).[6] Along with Immanuel Kant, I also discover who I am through both what and how I see. I discover that I see through lenses that I have received from my Creator, lenses that others have most likely received as well. I discover that my capacity to see shapes what I might call the form of what I see as well as the apparent unity that links all that I see into one world of seeing. I find reason to associate the "I" who sees to the "I" who lends form and unity to what I see. But, unlike Kant, I find no reason to assume that this "I" is self-identical, nor that it may be identified with the *cogito*, nor that I have grounds for associating it with some principle of actual self-determination that animates rational beings, human beings among them. Instead, I discover similarities among all acts of seeing — and among all acts of seeing the unity in what we see — but no strict identity. Each act, that is, appears to display both similarities and differences in both what it does (or depicts) and how it does (or depicts) it: it appears, in other words, as a non-identical repetition of whatever it repeats. Since there is no strict identity, I cannot say precisely *what* is, ultimately, repeated, but this incapacity neither surprises nor disappoints me: I take it to be a sign of the source of my amazement and awe. In this sense, unlike Kant's, in other words, my transcendental reflection leads me back to the One who gives me life again each morning, the One I know in fear and thanksgiving and without grasping.

Barchi nafshi et YHVH: *"Bless YHVH, O My Soul"*

Who am I, then, who would judge the world, but who first knows the "I" of "I see and I judge" as the "I" of "I thank you" and "I am amazed by you"? This "I" takes on a more tangible identity as, in keeping with the tradition of Morning Prayer, I next don a prayer shawl[7] and, holding it overhead and then over the shoulders, I pray "Bless YHVH, O my soul; YHVH my God, you are very great. Dressed in strength and majesty, you enwrap yourself in light as in a garment, unfolding the heavens like a curtain." Through this practice, I address this "I" as "my soul": *nefesh*, the animating soul or life's-breath. This is a soul that lives and breathes but as a consequence of others: of the One who gives it breath, of the world energies that give it energy, of the creatures that give it nutriments,

---

6. See Michael Rosenak, *Roads to the Palace: Jewish Texts and Teaching* (Providence: Berghahn Books, 1995). On his relation to Kant, see P. Ochs, "A Road to the Postmodern Palace: Michael Rosenak's Theological Response to the Postmodern Condition" in *In Search of a Jewish Paideia: Directions in the Philosophy of Jewish Education*, ed. J. Cohen, Melton Studies in Jewish Education, Vol. X (New York: Hebrew University, Magnes Press, 2004), pp. 17-31.

7. Or fringed undergarment *(tallit katan)*, depending on one's practice.

clothing, support, and shelter. And what is *its own* fundamental act? To bless the ruler, creator, and awesome one, who is named YHVH and who daily relights the world by wearing the heavenly light as a garment, wrapped as if on heaven's shoulders as I enwrap myself in a prayer garment.

A pattern is emerging that begins to indicate how this "I" of mine comes to make judgments each day. My first act is to speak (imitating, as we shall see, the "One who spoke and the world was"), and the first speech is of thanksgiving. My second act is to dress in prayer garments as if imitating the One who dresses in the heavenly lights. Although my garments dress only me (my *nefesh*), I learn that even in this modest act I can in some way imitate the very One before whom I stand in thanksgiving. We may therefore say that for me to make judgments is for me, through non-identical repetition, to imitate acts of the source of all judgment: imitating within my own creaturely context, here, what is modeled on high, "up there."

Hineni mitatef . . . k'de l'kayem mitsvat bor'i kakatuv b'torah

The next action is a physical action per se, accompanied by a voiced description of it: "I now enwrap myself in a fringed prayer shawl, fulfilling God's commands as disclosed in the Torah." In this way, I name myself an agent in the work that establishes the morning and begins the day. Note, however, the way that I allow myself to act: not immediately, following the inclinations of the muscles, but by enacting a traditional and scripturally grounded ritual of imitating visions of God's actions. In this way, movements of the major muscles of arms and shoulders follow movements of the minor muscles of lips and tongue (muscles of speech), which follow images disclosed through the imagination, which follow a focusing of attention on the words, traditions, and images of Morning Prayer.[8] The day's initial judgments, in other words, are separated from the judgments I would make were I *not* guided by a prayer tradition: what we might call more automatic movements of the muscles (responding to various stimuli of the body) along with preoccupations, wonderments, and worries of the mind. The paradigm is, apparently, *not* to act as agent only of myself, but as agent of my Creator and Guide as identified through the traditions of my people and faith. Even alone, I do not make judgments and act alone but as participant in a greater community of judgment and action.

---

8. For the general theory behind this claim, see Gavin Flood, *The Ascetic Self: Subjectivity, Memory and Tradition* (Cambridge: Cambridge University Press, 2004). For a resource within Jewish tradition, see Bahya ibn Paquda, *Duties of the Heart* (New York: Feldheim, 1996).

There appears, furthermore, to be a sequence in the way that I participate, as if my actions led through at least three worlds or domains of existence guided by three levels of prayer. The first act of the day may have been to separate myself in some way from a world of bodily and mental-emotional inclinations to act and feel, allowing the muscles of the lips, alone, to utter the day's first words: *modeh ani,* thankful am I." While muscles of the lips are a bridge to the world of language and words, my first words appear to have been separated from the language of my immediate society: in place of American English, I spoke Hebrew words of biblical origin. Uttering those words appears to have introduced me to a third world, not of inclinations or language, but of what we might call "the soul's otherworldly perceptions." Speaking of *melech chai v'kayam,* "Ever-living God," I am met by images and inclinations to action that I would not normally encounter in everyday transactions: images of divine splendor, majesty, and light and inclinations to utter blessings and bow before a sense of God's majesty. But what does it mean to call these "the soul's otherworldly perceptions"? Our answer may depend on the world through which we choose to answer. In the language of the first world, of bodily-mental-emotional inclinations, these perceptions might best be called vision or images within the "imagination." In the language of the second world, of biblical language, we might identify these perceptions with ways of "hearing" the narratives of the Bible. In its own terms, this third world appears to identify itself with "heaven" *(shamayim)* or "the world to come" *(olam haba)* and to identify the soul's perceptions with the way that the soul directly "sees" or intuits celestial beings and their actions and appearances — all of which are termed effects and consequences of the heavenly Leader, named YHVH.

We may therefore say that to engage in Morning Prayer is to move back and forth among the three realms of everyday inclinations, scriptural language, and otherworldly perceptions. While the one who prays is, by implication, a some-*one* who moves between these realms, the worshipper appears to have no single identity or form of self-reference: the pronoun "I" *(ani)* is only an indexical marker that indicates the fact that there is a "subject here who may judge, be judged, and enter into relation," but without any more discriminating details of the character of this subject. These details depend on the world of action and other contexts within it: yes, there is I, but my identity is not self-determined. I am also what is not mine, and what I am may share in what others are.[9]

---

9. The names we give ourselves as agents are not names of our being *within* any of these realms, but names or marks of specific agents of movement between the realms. If this notion

Interlude #1: *Reflections on Redeeming Judgment*

Even these initial Morning Prayers appear to have strong implications for how we frame judgments during the day. Morning Prayer already appears to challenge the propositional model of judgments in the following ways:

- Without denying individual agency, Morning Prayer renders the "I" beholden to others and conditioned by time and context in the way it frames judgments. While I have reason to assert that "I see this or that," I also have reason to assume that, on closer inspection, this "I" participates in a greater team. On the one hand, I therefore have less reason to be over-sure that, alone, I know precisely what I see, while, on the other hand, I have more reason to trust that, if I need to check on or improve my knowledge, there is somewhere to turn.
- While, at this point, I do not yet have a lot of evidence about where I should turn, I may already surmise this much: that my Creator remains

---

seems confusing to you at first, this is only because most of us are in the habit of using the same, everyday American English word, "I," to refer to the agent or place of all our experiences and understandings. But this is to reduce all the levels of our complex inner and outer lives to the terms of one limited pronoun. It is like expressing all our aesthetic insights through the medium of only one style of one art form (say, oil painting in pointillist style), or communicating all our feelings about the people we love only through a single convention of third person descriptions ("You are the person with respect to whom there have been strong feelings in my body . . ."). To defend our bad habit, we often claim that certain experiences of ours are "beyond words." But what does this mean? Do we have the experience or not? If not, we obviously have no reason to refer to it. If we *have* it, then what does it mean to say that we "lack words" to describe it? Wherever we imagine our experiences may *originate,* to experience them must mean to be aware of certain effects in our bodies: that is, certain sensations, intuitions, movements, or interruptions. On what basis can we say that certain bodily effects (the taste of salt, the feeling of being smothered) can be described in words and certain ones cannot? Certainly our bodies cannot discriminate in this way. Is it our language that discriminates? Are there only so many words in our American English? Or is it that social convention permits us to use only certain words in certain ways about certain experiences? A much simpler hypothesis is that many of us are not in fact using all the resources that are available to us in our languages. Over-using the word "I" is one example. It is most likely that we do *not* experience this "I" to be the actual source (agent or actor) of many of our experiences and actions. Sometimes, the body, or any part of it, seems to act on its own; sometimes we seem to act only as part of some group, some "we"; sometimes it seems that several "I's" are fighting for our attention and only one wins, or they agree to work in common(!); sometimes we actually sense that something else is acting for or by way of us, but we lack the words and the social convention to say what we sense, so for want of something more accurate to our own feelings, we say "I." In order to understand the Jewish prayer book, at the very least, we need to try out a new practice: recognizing that there are more actors in our own lives than "I"!

with me in whatever I do (although I do not yet know what "remaining with me" means); that I am not a simple creature but am created to inhabit several realms of experience and knowledge, all of which are united in my Creator (although I do not yet know what "united" means nor if these realms are unified in me or I in them); that I appear to participate in and derive my identity from three such realms (everyday experience, scriptural tradition, and celestial or otherworldly life); that the realm of scriptural tradition may bind me to other human beings (although I do not yet know who they may be).

• At this point, I have no reason to deny myself the capacity to judge that "I see this or that," but I also have reason to assume that such a judgment may be convertible into judgments like "We see this or that, do we not?" or "You have suggested that 'I see this or that,' have you not?" or "'this or that' have appeared here; what shall I or we do now?"

The Verses of Praise (Pesuke D'zimra): Transforming the "I Think" into the "I Praise" and "We Praise"

Baruch she amar v'haya olam:
"Blessed Be the One Who Spoke and the World Came into Being"

This signal blessing of the verses of praise tells us a great deal about the character of redemptive judgment. The one I imitate is one whose speaking creates worlds, ours and all other ones. Divine speech appears to be something I am, indeed, able to imitate, for I too speak, and speech was the first act I was enjoined to perform in the morning. The question will be, what can my speaking imitate in the Creator's speech and what can it not imitate?

Baruch she amar is a praise of the God of Genesis 1: "In the beginning of God's creating heaven and earth, the earth being unformed and void and a spirit of God hovering over the face of the deep. . . . God said 'Let there be Light,' and there was Light!" *(amar elohim yehi or vayehi or).* It is as if Morning Prayer were itself a repetition of the first act of creation: just as this world begins with God's proclaiming "Light!" so too do I begin each day by proclaiming my gratitude to the one who restores life; just as each day begins with God's enwrapping himself in the heavenly lights, so too do I begin each by enwrapping myself in the *tallit.* As one proclaims later in the Morning Prayer, "(God) everyday and continually renews the order of creation" *(hu mechadesh b'khol yom tamid maaseh b'reshit):* each day is truly a renewal of creation, the world's creation and my creation. God's speaking is thus an activity of bringing into being. And my speaking? To understand how to answer that question, let us first reflect further on what it means for God to bring it into being.

While, in both Genesis 1 and in our verse of praise, the verb used for "speaking" is *amar*, the biblical synonym is *diber*, as in "God spoke to Moses, saying . . ." (*vayidbar YHVH el moshe l'emor*: Deuteronomy, passim). The synonym is significant, since in this form, the verb "to speak" is the root of the word "thing," *davar*, referring to any created thing in the world or any everyday thing. Just as a "creature," *b'riah*, is that which God "created," *barah*, so too is any thing, *davar*, that which God spoke, *diber*. Looking from the side of the Creator, one might regard any thing in the world as God's reified speaking: a living dog is God's having spoken "dog." Looking from the side of the creature, one might regard any thing in the world as a hidden face of its Creator: this dog is not just this dog, but God's voice still speaking "dog." If so, we might consider how the entire world one enters in the morning may be transformed by the words of Morning Prayer and, in this case, of *baruch she amar* in particular:

Judging the World without Morning Prayer   If I rush into the day without Morning Prayer, then (speaking at least for myself as one person nurtured in modernity) I believe that I perceive the leaves on that tree outside my room as something like "those green, oaken leaves hanging over the dogwood by the car" that might soon lead me to consider, "But I need to drive to school, what time is it? Oh dear, what shall I say to E— at our meeting? I am hungry." Later, something might possibly draw me outside to look again at the leaves — perhaps some color or shape I am not accustomed to seeing, or perhaps remembering that I had planned to prune the tree. In one case, I may think, "This leaf has an odd splotch. . . . It may be a fungal growth"; in the other case, "I need a ladder to get to that old branch and cut it down." These various thoughts and perceptions illustrate what I mean by seeing a thing, *davar*, as a thing: a reflection that bears some relation to Martin Buber's words on "I-It" relations.

Judging the World with Morning Prayer   At least for a few moments after Morning Prayer (before resuming my old habits), I might perceive those leaves, instead, as not just things but something like words-still-being-spoken. But how I talk about this perception depends on which of three worlds I choose as context for my speech. If I were to speak in the terms of the third or celestial world we considered earlier, I might say something like this: the leaves appear to me not just as "leaves" — green, yellow-veined things

there in that tree — but as words spoken by God to me and to anyone else listening: as if to say, "Here I who created the world have taken time off just to
bring you these leaves as palettes of color to paint your imaginations these
hues of ochre, garden green, with spidery lines and hints of spider webs," or
". . . to bring you these messengers of calm, complexity, wonder," or ". . . these
warnings about the state of the environment," or ". . . these reminders that I
am here and with me is all that is past and future." If I were to speak in the
terms of the second world, of scriptural language, I might, if the leaves were
very beautiful, recite a blessing such as "Blessed are you, YHVH, Ruler of the
Universe, who has such beauty in his world." Or I might recite words of a
psalm: "How manifold are the things you have fashioned, YHVH, you have
made them all with wisdom; the earth is full of your creations" (Ps. 104:24).
Or I might speak of the laws of trees, "When you in your war against a city
have to besiege it a long time in order to capture it, you must not destroy its
trees, wielding the axe against them. You may eat of them, but you must not
cut them down" (Deut. 20:19). Or, if I were to speak in the terms of the first
world of everyday inclinations, then I might speak more as I already have spoken in the beginning of this paragraph: about the leaves I have seen that appear to me now in new ways, not as things closed off and finished and sitting
out there for anyone to see, but as brief glimpses that I have been afforded
into ongoing processes: of fluids flowing up and flowing down; of photosyn-
thesis; of cell division; of inchworms chewing; of rain falling, acid rain and
sweet; of bulldozers and land use; of ancient trilobites; of stars formed; of the
Civil War in old Virginia; of new roads cut today; of local churches; of Bible
stories; of nightfall.

Reflecting now on the judgments I might articulate in any of these worlds,
in what grammatical and logical forms would those judgments be displayed?
This is the defining question for our study, and, to respond to it, it is best to
interrupt our reflections on specific prayers of the morning and engage in an
extended exercise in the logic of making judgments:

Interlude #2: An Exercise in the Logic of Making Judgments

The judgments I offered without Morning Prayer fit rather well into the
propositional model of judgments: "A is y," and "I do Z," yielding such judgments as, "The leaves are green and yellow," or "I must go to school." But what
of judgments offered with Morning Prayer? Let us first see if I could make use
of the propositional model. With respect to the first world, I might say, for example, "I see in these leaves a metaphor for ongoing processes, such as pro-

cesses of cell division or inch worms chewing." This judgment would indeed deliver something about what I wanted to say. The use of the term "metaphor" would signal my effort to link together two different elements of my consciousness: one part referring directly (or indexically) to the leaves, another part to other occasions on which I have observed temporally extended activities of one sort or another. But this form of judgment would also occlude major aspects of what I saw, and in that way misrepresent what I want to say about "ongoing processes." The most egregious misrepresentation would come from the presence of an implicit "I think" behind each side of the metaphor: linking only *my* vision of the leaves to *my* memory of occasions in which I have observed complex processes. According to this linkage, my judgment is about two aspects of *my* own experience. But my perception of the leaves as "words-still-being-spoken" was *not* reflexive in this way: it was of a process of which I had some sense but which also extended beyond the limits of my comprehension. Metaphor cannot carry this latter sense, because to speak of the leaves as metaphors is to speak of my perception as limited by what Emmanuel Lévinas called "the logic of the same": the sign and object of metaphor are linked by what they *share* in the "I think." The force of judgment after Morning Prayer, however, is to discover something in the leaves that is *not the same:* that, right here in my everyday perceptions of green and yellow ribbed, is a perception of something extending into an unknown space and time that is of the leaves but more than the leaves and that therefore links what I already know (the same) to something I do not know. Judgments after Morning Prayer bring me into intimate relation to what I do not know and, therefore, to "what is not mine," and that is what is truly amazing.

The propositional form of judgment is all the more limited when applied to the two other worlds of expression, since they are explicitly addressed from and to what exceeds the grasp of the "I think." In the case of scriptural language, the worshipper simply receives, in which case the "I think" displays itself only as the source of choice and redaction. "I chose" to cite Deuteronomy. In this case, however, the "I chose" is not explicit, but displayed only in the consequences of choice. Adopting a propositional form would require restating such citations in this form: "I chose to cite 'When you eat of them you must not cut them down.'" In this case, the predicate remains opaque, so that the consequence of adopting a propositional form is to over-clarify what we really do not need to hear more than once — "I chose to cite x," "I chose to cite y," "I chose to cite . . . n," — and import the citation as basically a black box, that is, a text that is simply imported but as yet unarticulated.

The case of celestial language is more complex. Because each vision is specific, we may assume, to the imagination, and because the imagination expresses itself by way of perceptions, we might adopt the propositional form in either of two ways. On the model of importing scriptural language, we might simply adopt "I imagined that" (or "It entered into my imagination that") as subjects of each judgment, followed by another black box, such as "the leaf is a sign of God's creativity" or "we are showered by divine wisdom." Or, on the model of the first world, we might bracket the "I imagined" and articulate the celestial perception as we would any natural perception: "The leaf is a sign of God's creativity." Here we have a paradigmatic illustration of how using the modern form of propositional judgment leads us to reduce otherworldly claims to unmediated pairs of contrasting claims, both of which elide at least one elemental feature of the original claim. In this case, the original judgment had to do with the *movement* from perceiving a leaf to perceiving God's creativity. When the claim is translated into propositional form, we are offered two mutually exclusive options that identify either side of what is moved, but that fail to identify the movement itself. On the one hand, we have the claim — "I imagine that x . . ." — that tells us only about the "I think," reminding us that what follows belongs to the realm of imagination. Beyond its incompleteness, this option is also misleading, because it implicitly assigns the "I think" to each side of the movement I had perceived, as if we already *knew* that not only "the leaf" but also "God's creativity" was exclusively a part of *my* imagination. As with the case of metaphor, the translation of my perception into propositional form has transformed a perception of my moving into the other (beyond the limits of "I think") into a perception of self-movement (from one part of my consciousness to another).

If you object — "Do you really mean to suggest that 'God's creativity' belongs to someone else's imagination?" — we must reply that the only evidence we have to go on is this otherworldly perception, so that if *you* claim to know beforehand what limits the perception must respect, then you have acknowledged that your goal is not translation but reinterpretation. In this case, the most likely source of your confusion is that you have imported a specific ontology along with your propositional logic, presuming that imagination must be either "mine or not-mine," thereby excluding the possibility that imagination, like everyday perception, can be a conduit from one subject to another — that, just as I can see a flower that, even on Kantian terms, is not-mine nor merely part of me, so too I can encounter objects of the imagination that are not merely part of me. You may admit that I can imagine the form of triangle that belongs to the universe of mathematicals and not just to me; if so, you should also admit *the logical possibility* that, by way of the imagination, I may perceive celestial things that are comparably not merely of the "I think." I am not suggesting you have to believe or accept what I perceive, only that your logic is inadequate if it does not allow you even to consider or hear my claims. To return to the translation: the second option goes to the other extreme, delivering my claim as if it were indistinguishable from a this-worldly perception: "The leaf is a sign of God's creativity." If this translation, for example, expressed your effort, this time, really to hear what I have to say, then I am afraid you would have failed again, but for the opposite reason. By removing any signs of the *difference* between the everyday and the otherworldly realm, you have translated my perception into a weird portrait of the two worlds as identical — producing the kind of judgment that either makes my perception look silly (for then you might also hear me suggest things like "the burning bush is down the road to the left") or else absorbs this world into the other one in a fashion pleasing only to millenarians and religious fanatics.

In sum, to speak in the form "A is Y" and "I do Z" is to be limited to speaking only of aspects of ourselves and of the same. The lesson of Morning Prayer is, however, that we can see beyond ourselves and beyond what is the same. Through what other logic, then, shall we articulate this seeing? While many other logical forms may be available to us, we need, for our present purposes, to identify only one. If we could identify one non-propositional logic that successfully modeled the way judgments are formed after Morning Prayer, then we would have demonstrated that there is no need to accept the limits imposed on our judgments by the logic of propositions. We would have shown that we *can* judge the world in reasonable and reiterable ways without limiting our judgments to the "I think" and, thus, that there *are* ways to reason about "what we are not." For the sake of this demonstration, I will adapt a version of Charles Peirce's logic of relations as a means of shaping judgments in conformity with Morning Prayer. I do not mean to suggest that the logic of relations is *the* logic of Morning Prayer or the best way of shaping judgments. I mean to suggest only that this logic succeeds in mapping the judgments of Morning Prayer that propositional logic fails to map and that, if so, we moderns can find ways of reasoning that are not limited by the conditions of propositional logic.

Before introducing the logic, I suggest we engage first in an exercise of imagination that might help make a place for the logic within our reading of Morning Prayer. Here are instructions for the exercise. Recall for a moment our account of the way Night Prayer allowed the judgments of the day to fall apart: allowing subjects to fold into those unknown and vague things of the dark and allowing predicates to fall into our dreams. Now, consider what held the world together when we slept in the dark. According to Night Prayer, the Creator's never-ending activity held the world together, suggesting that it is not we, after all, who hold the world together, nor is the unity of the world a product of our own efforts to bring ideas and things together. When the day-light rouses us to judgment once again, we might consider that, while *we* may make sense of the daylight world by actively linking predicates to subjects, we have no reason to presume that is the Creator's way nor, in that sense, a source of great insight into the way of the world as it is spoken. Should you object, "But this is how we humans know the world and how else can we imagine the work of the Creator other than by way of analogy to the way we know?" — then we may respond, "Yes, we should reason by analogy. But why assume that the prototypically 'human' is represented by the way individual judg-ments link subjects to predicates? There are richer, more helpful and more ac-curate ways of articulating how we know the world; and these may be ob-served through Morning Prayer." *Now then,* the purpose of our trying out a logic of relations is to demonstrate this fact by showing these four things: how Morning Prayer displays patterns of judgment that cannot be fully artic-ulated in the terms of propositional logic; how those patterns *can* be articu-lated through other models of judgment, illustrated here through the one al-ternative of a logic of relations; how discrete claims (the kinds mapped by propositional logics) can also be mapped through this alternative; and how Morning Prayer may therefore nurture ways of judging the world that move past the limits of modern propositional logic and the "I think" that accompa-nies it.

Here is the simplest way I can think of to construct and illustrate the use of Peirce's logic of relatives. Begin with a letter, say, R. Let us suppose that R stands for this whole process of which we have an immediate intuition, direct but vague and undifferentiated, as if to say: there it is, this whole blooming confused reality, confusing but really there and we are as sure of it as anything else we can be sure of: R. Then, imagine that, little by little, depending on the specific context, space, time, realm of experience, and presuppositions we bring to it, we come to perceive more and more different dimensions of R. Consider, therefore, that each dimension that we come to know is not per-ceived by itself, but as one part of a minimally two-part relation. The simplest example might be the way that, when addressing some complex process, I sense "blueness" when I "stand here." Let us call the blueness "b," and the con-text of standing here "s." Let us then use the symbol "sRb" to express the way that, when I stand here, I perceive blueness in this process. Now, to get a clear sense of the difference between this emerging logic of relatives and our more habitual propositional logic, compare these two sets of representations. First, illustrations from propositional logic: "The sky is blue," or "I see a blue sky." Now an illustration from the logic of relatives: "There is blue here."

For starters, we should expect the second judgment to elicit from an interlocutor the question, "Where? What are you talking about?" and this should elicit a second judgment, perhaps something like "I mean up there, in the sky." The second judgment begins to take on some of the propositional logic, but only for a moment. We must imagine that the speaker is trying to communicate a sense that no single word like "the sky" would suffice to identify the subject of experience, since that word might bring with it a very limited set of expectations about what was seen: for example that it had to be something "up there," with certain kinds of blues and white and so forth; but the speaker wasn't referring to that, but to some much less demarcated splash of experience, of which he or she only meant to indicate one small clarity — that, whatever else it has, this experience or process has blueness in it. Here, the whole point of voicing a judgment is to draw the interlocutor into discussion and comparison and more observation, call it participation in an as yet unidentified, ongoing process and experience. In this approach, *it takes a lot of time to offer and share judgments*. In fact, there is an analogy between the vagueness and open-endedness of the experience and the vagueness and open-endedness of the process of communicating it. Both processes involve relationship, participation, and exploratory efforts to see more clearly some aspect of what is going on. This analogy, in fact, may provide us with what our imagined reader requested of us earlier: a way of drawing analogies between our human experience and activities we may attribute to the Creator. If, according to night prayer, linking predicate-like qualities to subject-like things does not put the world together, then we may suggest that it is put together somewhat like our complex process of experiencing the world and of communicating what we experience. It may be put together all at once, as in a big bang, with all things present but vague and complex, amazing but largely indiscernible, until probatively, moment by moment or place by place, clarifications happen or context-specific events of relation, like red appearing here, or cold there, or this-here communicated to you-there.[10]

Within the world of everyday inclinations, judgments of the form "sRb" might therefore sound like this: "There is ochre here, when this leaf is bent toward this side," or "I am drawn to that violet-blueness in this part of the sky as I walk home remembering Mom, hoping for a better time, and. . . ." In the first case there is "oRb": some experience in which the "ochre" quality accom-

---

10. Readers may note that there are parallels here to A. N. Whitehead's understanding of events and how we identify them. See, for example, the section "From Substances with Attributes to Events with Relations" in John B. Cobb, Jr., "Alfred North Whitehead," in *Founders of Constructive Postmodern Philosophy,* ed. David Ray Griffin et al. (New York: SUNY Press, 1993), pp. 170ff. Also A.N. Whitehead, *The Principle of Relativity* (Cambridge: Cambridge University Press, 1922) and *Process and Reality* (New York: Free Press, 1929).

panies this activity of my bending the leaf this way. In the second case we have "vRm": some experience in which the "violet-blueness" accompanies the whole series of associations I have with Mother, the projects of today, and so forth. In either case, "R" stands for what William James dubbed an aspect of "absolute experience," that is, a fairly undifferentiated wholeness of the world that comes to us in perception before we attend for specific reasons to particular parts of it. The letter "R" may be used to suggest that this absolute experience is known only as an indefinite set of *relations*, each one of which will relate some aspect of the experience to some context of having and communicating it. It is as if one consequence of Morning Prayer is to remind us that our immediate experiences of the world may be very vast and amazing before we whittle them down to the specific contexts of our momentary and passing concerns.

If this is, in fact, to *recover* the world in its wholeness, amazingness, and blessedness, then this recovery need in no way preclude the possibility nor the usefulness of more discriminating judgment. It simply reminds us that, in each moment, we have available to us something much vaster and richer than what we are in the habit of discriminating within it. But the bigger picture also allows the smaller one. While aRb might guide our judgments about the whole, it could also guide judgments about particulars: it may indeed be appropriate to say that "the leaf is ochre" (A is y) when I take it and bend it this way in this light (and when "the leaf" refers to this thing I am holding here). In symbolic form: $(A = y)R(b = 1)$, which is to suggest that the propositionally formed judgment is *inside* the relative judgment.[11]

Applied to the second world of scriptural language, "sRb" would, for example, model the way that the broad experience of a leaf (R) may, at a given moment, link my sense of the leaf's beauty (s) to an occasion for uttering the traditional blessing for "He who has such beauty in his world" (b). We might also write R $(s_1b_1, s_2b_2, s_3b_3 \ldots s_nb_n)$ as a map or convenient sign of the way that R may link together a potentially indefinite series of perceptions and actions. We cannot, however, identify this with the propositional function $f(x) = R(s_1b_1, s_2b_2, s_3b_3 \ldots s_nb_n)$, because R cannot be reduced to any predictable function or rule for the *cogito* or "I think." The character of R is displayed

---

11. I am providing this cumbersome formula just to suggest that the patterns of identity displayed in something like "the leaf is ochre" (A = y) are meaningful as discrete elements *inside of* an overall experience, so that each pattern of identity is displayed in relation to some other one: in this case, the character of the leaf in relation to some way of manipulating the leaf. The reason for displaying a formula like this one is to show that the kinds of discriminations that modern logicians make can still be made in a logic of relatives, but only when they are situated within a vaster *process* of logical reasoning.

only through narratives or series of thick descriptions that I or we offer of R. Those who privilege the propositional model of judgment will most likely object that "if so, accounts of R are nonrational and you have only verified our assumption that either R = f(x), or R, and Morning Prayer along with it, lies beyond the ken of reason." Our reply is then: Indeed, accounts of R are nonrational if rationality is identified only with the rules I set myself through my individual judgments; but, in this case, rationality is only the rationality of what "I think," displayed in a logic of the Same. Morning Prayer introduces us to other rationalities, however, in which the "I think" is brought into relation to what exceeds its grasp and its limits. If you misrepresent our argument, perhaps it is because you conceive of rationality as something internal to the individual act of judgment or perhaps, after John Locke, you identify the process of reasoning as steps through which what was internal to judgment is displayed externally or to the public eye. We approach rationality differently: assuming that individual judgments of any kind — of sense, of perception, of cognition — are *per se* neither rational nor non-rational, but elemental components of a *process* that may be rational or non-rational, the way that a single letter is a component of some word or other and usually lacks semantic meaning except as it contributes to the meaning of that word. An *argument* is one example of a process of reasoning. But when is a process — including an argument — to be judged as rational or non-rational? By your standards, there is perhaps some single model of rationality and you will judge a process rational whenever it matches this model — perhaps when it is compatible with clear judgments + some rules of propositional logic. Since we recognize multiple models of rationality, we are not wont to use the term "rational" as a single standard or perhaps as a weapon. Perhaps the term is best defined as "some publicly agreed-upon standard of reasoning," where each standard serves some specific public or community and for the sake of some specific activity or goal.

To return to our example, "R" refers to a field of experience and should not itself be considered rational or nonrational. Some pair a/b refers only to the context and content of some aspect or discrimination of and within that experience, so that, again, it should not be considered rational or non-rational. "Rationality" may properly appear as the character of *some activity that we perform with respect to R or to any aRb* (or set of them): for example, activities of measuring, or building buildings out of, or talking about, or praying with regard to. Standards of rationality — just another name for standards for successful practice — should emerge from out of each activity as it is understood by the community or society that sponsors it. And this brings us to the next signal characteristic of a logic of relation: logics of relation are also logics *in relation,* that is, they display their rules of practice with respect to some community of practice, rather than presuming their rationality to be "of the world of nature as it is." Judgments articulated in scriptural language are articulated *for* particular communities of scriptural practitioners. This fact is displayed most clearly in the way Jewish Morning Prayer addresses the community of worshippers and not just the individual. To complete our reflections on the second world of judgment, let us therefore return to our textual study of prayers but in a somewhat different way: reflecting, this time, on how a broad movement of prayer, from "Verses of Praise" to "The Shema," implicates the worshipper, first, in the community of all creatures and then in the community of Israel.

From Baruch She Amar *to the Shema:* How the "I" Comes to Share in "We"

As we read it earlier, the prayer *baruch she amar* opens the Verses of Praise by introducing the double wonder of Jewish worship: that the worshipper is both creature and potential imitator of the God "who spoke and the world was." As we reread the prayer now, our attention is drawn to the "I think" of the worshipper and how it may evolve from one to the other through the process of praying the Verses. More precisely, our attention is drawn to a series of relations in which the "I think" is implicated, until we reach the *telos* of the verses of praise: the Shema, and its identification of the worshipper with the covenantal and corporate community of Israel.

Our *starting place* is with the "I" as "only an indexical marker that indicates the fact that there is a subject here who may judge, be judged, and enter into relation," with any further details depending on specific contexts of action. The "I" is thus a mark of both agency *and* a dependence on others. These two are not mutually exclusive, but complementary yet different characteristics — the reason why Morning Prayer may be redemptive for those of us nurtured in modern binarism: for us, the force of Morning Prayer is not to uproot our two warring tendencies but only to sweeten their conflictual difference into a complementary difference. The movement from this kind of war to this kind of peace begins with *praise.* Like the very first words of the morning — *modeh ani,* "Thankful am I" — the Verses of Praise all resituate the "I" from the place of master of a small universe to the place of a smaller someone in a vast universe. The work of prayer will be to identify the company of other I's with whom this one acts in the world and how they relate, one to the other and to the world.

Since the "I think" becomes the "I speak," it is helpful to re-describe this "I in the company of others" as an "I in a chain of spoken-words," where each I both hears words and speaks them, one I to another and another. If, again with Charles Peirce, we characterize a spoken word, more formally, as a spoken unit of communication or sign, then we may re-characterize the "company I keep" as a chain of signs — or what, more technically, Peirce calls a semiotic chain. In these terms, all creatures participate in the "semiotic chain" of being created or receiving the gift of God's creating word, then speaking that word in praise, then hearing others' words. This chain implies, for one, that, while God creates distinct and identifiable creatures, these creatures are not wholly distinct in the sense of being wholly autonomous, self-referential and self-identical: their identities implicate them in the existence of others. In this sense like a Leibnizian monad, each creature is also an observer of others (potentially all the others). This means that, whatever we mean by "the being of each creature," that very being includes a manner of relating to the other creatures and thus to the Creator as known through what he has created. This is why such being is best stated in terms of the spoken word *(dibbur):* what is created is spoken and what is spoken is a spoken-word that is an actual entity in the world *(davar)*, so that each creature is a spoken word, so that to be is to be spoken. As Lévinas points out, however, only to be spoken would be to be wholly determined or finished, like the past: *le dit,* "the said," rather than *le dire,* "the saying" that is still being said. As depicted in both Genesis and Morning Prayer, creation is an ongoing affair, rather than one of the past: as noted earlier, the blessing before the Shema is to "he who daily renews the order of creation." Creation is a continual creating, as Buber writes; "In the beginning was the Word," not in the past, but in the beginning of each moment is a speaking which, or out of which, all being is. So the creature is not merely a spoken-word but also a word-being-spoken, a speaking. This is why semiotics works so well as a logic for scriptural language: if "sign" is taken as synonym for "word" (or as the type of which "word" is a token), then the act of creating is a signifying or semiosis, what is created is a signification or word-being-spoken, *and "to be" such a creature is at once to be signified* (to display the meaning of some speech or some signifier) *and to signify afresh* (to offer oneself to another as signifier and source of meaning).

As Buber suggested, the tree that I encounter is therefore not identical to some list of characteristics I may ascribe to it: in Buber's terms, it is not identical to some "it" or object of my consciousness; in Lévinas' terms, it is not only a "said." The tree is, rather, a speaking of tree, so that my access to it is not so much to observe it "out there," but to listen to it, read it, or, ultimately, engage it in conversation. With Buber, we may speak here of "conversation" (at least as a metaphor for "relation"), since what I am as creature is also a speaking, so that when "I observe," my speaking has in fact entered into relation with its speaking, and "observation" is a reduced way of referring to some encounter or *relation* between these two speakings. In different terms, if Morning Prayer renames the "I think" according to any of a series of encounters, of which one is "I observe," then "I observe" may also be renamed "we encounter one another." I may still refer to my observations in propositional terms, "I see the tree," but, when I do that, I now regard this judgment as only a momentary specification of something within the broader reality of an encounter or relation between streams of signification. If I stop, as in Morning Prayer, to reflect further on those streams, then I may begin to rename each of them a "creature" — or a consequence of God's creativity — and I may begin to rename the relation between them as itself a creature, albeit of a different kind: *a sign of the only One who creates both streams and in whom, or in whose creativity, alone, the two are actually and literally in relation.* This is, in sum, to rename "my observation of the tree" "our relation . . . ," to rename "our relation . . ." "this sign of our one Creator," and thus *to locate what we might now call the "truth" and the "reality" of my observation in a three-way relation among this creature that I am, that creature there, and our Creator.*

Locating this truth and reality is also another way of comprehending what it may mean, in Morning Prayer, to say both that "I praise God" and that "all creatures praise God." It may mean, in part, that all of us creatures encounter one another as co-creatures of the one God and as brought into relation through the one God. Revisiting our exercise of reflection, we could indefinitely expand the semiotics of each member of this relation, since, on further inspection, I would find that this tree and I are also each implicated in these indefinite sets of other relations, as is this particular three-way sign of our relation to the Creator. This kind of inspection would generate what we might call "thick descriptions" and "narratives" of my life, the life of this tree, and the new life of our encounter. The work of inspection would add two dimensions to the sense I now have of how the "I observe" becomes the "we encounter" and "we are with God." One is the dimension of what we might call *expansion:* a sense of how our being and our relations implicate us in the whole of creation. The other is the dimension of what we might call *contraction:* an awareness of the process of selection and attention that led away from all these narratives and sets of relations to the one triadic relation that is named by my observation. In this way, Morning Prayer both ennobles and humbles our personal agency: ennobling my sense of the "I observe" as an element of divine activity itself while also humbling it as but one act of attention within this vast universe of relations.

We may associate the *ennobling* dimension with the "reality" of the judgment, for Morning Prayer teaches that indeed we directly encounter not only the created world but also the Creator.[12] We may associate the *humbling* dimension with the "truth" of our judgments, for Morning Prayer teaches that our knowledge of the world, while real, is nonetheless hypothetical. Our judgment *selects* from what is available to us and, while each selection has its own reality, it may not necessarily accord with what we think it is. Truth is a measure of our success in achieving what we have intended, rather than a measure of reality as our being present to what God intends for us. This leads us to the question of testing or verification. How do we move from hypothesis making (abduction) to true judgment? Morning Prayer suggests that it is a matter of testing, understood as a way of examining the consequences of our choice, and this is where the expansive character of our judgments comes into play. Criteria for testing our judgments are drawn from out of the broader set of relations that are also implicit in our judgment. This is a rough version of Peirce's "pragmatic maxim," which he believed was also signaled in Jesus' recommendation, that "you shall know them by their fruits" (Matthew 7:20) — "fruits" referring, in this case, to the way the contents of your judgment would relate to the rest of the observable world. Here we glimpse a mark of our humility: God's glory is shown in the consequences of his actions, all of whose consequences are trustworthy. As we read in the prayer that follows the Shema, *emet v'emunah,* "true and trustworthy are all these things that God had told us and done for us." In our case, however, the consequences of what we say and do disclose our errors and our failings as well as our moments of truth telling and successful action.

The hypothetical character of all of our judgments is a mark of the relational and social fabric of our being. Because our being is enmeshed in an indefinite series of relations, our individual judgments are always selective, partial, and therefore no more than hypothetical. At the same time, the relational character of our being is also the source of our ability to test and confirm our judgments, learning, over time, which kinds of judgments tend to be more trustworthy than others and learning, thereby, how it is possible, after all, often to act in the world as if we saw things just as they were, self-evidently. We can think of this relationality in several ways. On one level, we live in such intimacy with a myriad range of creatures that there are always more things to observe as evidence to support or counter what we think we just observed. On another level, we share such a unique relation with creatures that are most

---

12. The term "reality" is used here to refer to "that which is what it is independently of what I may think of it."

identical to us that we can speak to them, share personal memories with them, and call on them directly to *help* us verify what we believe we observed. These are members of our species, called "our people" (*'am*), with whom we share a unique, three-part relation among the "I observe," what I observe, and the Creator. In Morning Prayer, my place in "the people Israel" serves as prototype of how any creature shares in a collective community of creatures — of how the "I think" that is "I speak" becomes part of a "We speak."

In Morning Prayer, we may read "Israel" not only as that people in the Bible story whose language becomes the language of this prayer book, *but also as a name for what a community of creatures would look like*. When creatures become an agental we, they look like Israel.[13] While there are other grounds, within the scriptural and rabbinic sources, for talking about differences between this Israel and other peoples and between human and non-human communities, these differences are not germane to our focus in this essay. To understand how Morning Prayer may redeem modern habits of judgment, we need consider only how this prayer transforms "I" into a participant in "we": whether I am Jew or ant, the paradigm is "Israel." It should suffice for our needs to consider three stages of transformation, each as illustrated by one or two specific prayers from the verses of praise and the Shema.

(a) *To move from "I" to a distributive "we" is to observe the world as a collection of creatures who are spoken and who speak and to recognize that I am one of them.*

This does not mean that I share in the collective action of any "we," but only that I appreciate the analogy of creaturehood that is distributed among everything that I observe. This stage may therefore correspond to "inter-

---

13. In the case at least of human creatures — and as typified here by the case of Israel — praise of the Creator entails the step of proclaiming, announcing, and teaching others the glory of the Creator, or the good consequences of what God does. To *be* a human creature is thus, ideally, to celebrate and transmit news of God's acts to other humans. This suggests that to receive being from YHVH is to receive that which in the receiving is also to be given. This last phrase may bring to mind the theories of "gift" that are given considerable attention in contemporary literature, for example in John Milbank, *Being Reconciled: Ontology and Pardon* (London: Routledge, 2003) — characterized on its jacket-cover as "a fresh theological treatment of the classic theory of the Gift in the context of divine reconciliation." There are overlaps between claims like Milbank's and like ours, but there is also at least this difference: we do not intend our claim to be a normative claim, per se, nor an argument about what alone being must be if it is to be being. I hope at least that there is no triumphant discovery here that our God is a gift-giver per se. Our effort is instead to unpack implications of traditional texts of prayer and of Scripture, so that the claim is not that "Being is this!" but only that "these traditional texts recommend this account of being." Our account of gift, moreover, derives from an account of the word.

subjectivity" as portrayed by Kant and Husserl (until very late in his work): that I know of your subjectivity only by analogy with mine, not by participation.[14] This stage is illustrated by Psalm 105 (= 1 Chron. 16): *hodu l'yhvh, kiru 'shmo:* "Give thanks to YHVH, call upon his name." Placed immediately following *baruch she amar,* this psalm anticipates much of what is to occur through all the verses of praise. As a singer of praise, the "I speak" sings and speaks God's *name,* before all else. But how can the unspeakable name be sung? *hodiu va'amim alilotov:* "teach (make known to) the peoples about His deeds" (16:8). The immediate focus of attention will be the actions of YHVH, as observed in their *consequences* in this world: first in our world of social and political history, then in the wonders of natural creation itself. The immediate purpose of observing these consequences will be *to teach or announce them to all the nations:* to know YHVH, in other words, is to observe his actions and proclaim them to the world. The "I speak" is one who praises, observes, and proclaims a series of specific things: the "marvelous works [*nifl'ot*] YHVH has done," from the specific acts of his making a covenant with Abraham and bringing Israel to the Land of Canaan to the "honor and majesty" (*hod v'hadar*) of his making the heavens. Reference to the heavens turns the worshipper's (and the psalmist's!) attention to all God's creatures, who are now addressed as fellow singers of praise: "let the ocean roar . . . the field rejoice . . . the trees of the forest." All creatures share in the worshipper's activity of praising the Creator, and this implies that, regardless of whether they all "speak" and regardless of whether we share in any collective action, all creatures share with me the capacity and obligation to sing praises to YHVH. Since observing the Creator's actions is a condition of praise, I see that neither the "I sing" nor the "I praise" nor the "I observe" (and at least that dimension of the "I think") is unique to me. I have reason to infer, therefore, that being a creature of YHVH *means* to be something that observes and praises its Creator. I am but one of many such "somethings," so I share, distributively, in this call to all of "us" creatures: praise God!

(b) *To move from member of a distributive "we" to member of a collective "we" is to see the "I speak" both as consequence and as agent of creaturely events of speaking. In Morning Prayer, this movement comes from seeing that I share in a history of God's actions that implicate me only as participant in the "we" of Israel.*

This stage may correspond to "intersubjectivity" as portrayed by such dialectical philosophers as Hegel and Buber, to the extent that they attribute

---

14. It also implies that the intersubjectivity I recognize may be only inter-human and perhaps visible only among those whose mode of speaking I can recognize.

to me the characteristics of being both "I" as cause or agent and "me" as effect or object. As in this stage of prayer, however, dialectical philosophy keeps the "I think" in play as autonomous agent, sometimes in power as "I," sometimes out of it as "me," so that tendencies to binarism may be heightened as much as they are lessened through this stage. The Psalmist's voice is paradigmatic of this drama: *Halleluyah, shiru l'yhvh shir chadash:* "Sing to YHVH a new song, sing praise to him in the assembly of the faithful *(kehal chasidim).* Let Israel rejoice in his maker, the children of Zion exalt in their ruler" (Ps. 149).

Through psalms of Halleluyah like this one, the worshipper's attention is drawn to Israel as the focal point both of agency and of petition. Praise for the way that "he takes pleasure in this people" *(ki rotseh yhvh v'amo)* is epitomized in the way he protects them from the other nations who are their enemies. The truthfulness of Israel's understanding of its covenant with God is therefore measured by Israel's capacity to have lived, and not died, when confronting nations "who did not respect Israel's covenant" or its consequences for Israel's earthly life. And where am "I" when I speak this praise? "I speak" only by praising Israel as well as God, but I cannot yet locate *how* I am part of this assembly, except by way of the following inference: God is praised by way of the visible consequences of his acts; God's protecting Israel from the nations is among those consequences; I am part of Israel; therefore, by way of my place in Israel, I share in the praiseworthy consequences of God's acts and, thereby, share in what is praiseworthy. But where am I as agent of action rather than effect? I see now that "I praise Israel" as well as "I praise God," but I do not yet see what else "I do" in Israel other than receive God's protection: beyond offering praise, "I" appear only as "me."[15] As for who the active "I" is in Israel: this "I" remains either autonomous or undefined.

(c) *There is a dualism here that is not binarism: I am creature in this world of consequences and I am image of God in a world of agency. But where is the unity that joins my two aspects?*

This stage challenges efforts to account for my participation in Israel strictly within the this-worldly terms of my natural inclinations. This is to challenge the dualism played out in philosophic debates between modern liberalism and a later-modern communitarianism: in different terms, between claims that I am a self-begotten agent and that I am a member of an interper-

---

15. Perhaps "I praise" is a name for the relation to the Creator that is implicit in all that I (along with Israel) do in the world. If so, however, I still do not *understand how* the specific things that I say and do share in this "I praise."

sonal agency. The verses of praise approach their climax with an excerpt from Chronicles that dramatizes a third alternative:

(ci) *Within Israel it is the "I praise" who addresses God actively:*

vayevorech david et yhvh l'eyne kol hakahal:

"Then David blessed YHVH in the sight of all the entire congregation . . . saying, 'Blessed are you, YHVH God of our father Israel, for ever and ever'" (1 Chron. 29:10-13)

The creaturely "I" of the passage is the "I" of King David, which now embodies the corporate character of Israel. On behalf of the entire people, this "I" sanctifies their covenantal unity by intoning a blessing that anticipates the classic form of all blessings in the prayer book: "Blessed are you, YHVH our God." Here, the focus of blessing appears to be the power of God himself, for, "yours, YHVH, are greatness and power and glory and victory and majesty, yes, all that is in the heavens and on earth. Yours, O YHVH, is the dominion and you are exalted, supreme over all. . . . In your hand are power and might . . . to make great and to give strength to all. Therefore, we thank you our God and we praise your glorious name." In the texts that follow, gathered from the books of Nehemiah and Exodus, God's power is proven by the events that mark Israel's salvation history: God redeemed Israel from slavery in Egypt, from the oppression of task masters, and from the hot pursuit of angry kings. All these proofs constitute the "glory," *kavod*, of God: that is, his reputation, or what we are able to know of his power, as displayed in his saving acts and as narrated in this history. By proclaiming this glory and identifying it as the engine of Israel's covenant, David's "I praise" becomes a witness to Israel's more than this-worldly identity: beyond creaturely inclination, Israel is gathered-together only by the name of YHVH, her redeemer who is also the Creator.

What does this tell us about the agency of David's "I praise"? Against neoliberal efforts to defend the primacy of the "I think," here the paradigmatic "I" within Israel — the "I" of King David — proclaims its utter humility before the one "I" in whom all power rests. But against communitarian alternatives to the liberal "I think," this creaturely "I" asserts itself in relation to the corporate "we" of Israel: it is David who calls Israel to blessing. We therefore find ourselves with no easy resolution to what appears to be an elemental three-ness in Morning Prayer: we, I, and the I of God.

(cii) *The "I praise" within Israel is also the I who sees the glory of the Creator God by way of the imagination:*

baruch ata yhvh . . . yotser or uvore choshekh:

Blessed are you . . . who forms light and creates darkness; . . . who mercifully gives light to the earth and to those who dwell on it. And who, in his goodness, daily renews *(m'chadesh)* the order of creation *(maaseh b'reshit).*

This first blessing of the next section of prayer, "the Shema and Its Blessings," offers the worshipper not only words for praising the Creator, but also a remarkable series of images for understanding something of how creation works.

Blessed God, great in knowledge, designed and activated the sun's rays. . . . he placed lights around his throne. . . . he fashions ministering angels who . . . reverently proclaim in one voice words of the living God, eternal Ruler.

To praise and then behold creation is to examine details of the object of praise through the imagination rather than through language. Previously, I observed the world, learned its name and, then, by way of language, beheld the word that is also world. This time, however, I am offered an image, or vision of the imagination, and I perceive it, but through the mind's eye. I have been led, that is, from objects in the world of my senses, to words in the world of Israel's language, to celestial visions received by way of the imagination. In this case, the vision is of the glory of God, but a glory that differs from what I encountered previously. Previously, this glory was displayed through narratives about the consequences of God's redeeming actions in the world and in Israel's salvation history. Now, it is displayed through images of the process of creation. In either case, we may now suggest that perceptions of glory emerge through a transcendental regress: in one case from sense object to word to realm of words or Israel's language; in another case, from word to image to realm of images or imagination, which is known in Morning Prayer as our means of observing the heavens. The first regress brings me from worldly objects to Israel's language as the transcendental condition for my knowing the world as creation: here I know myself only as recipient of Israel's language and, by way of Israel, of God's saving help. The second regress brings me from worldly objects to images of divine creativity as the transcendental condition for my knowing the world's Creator: here, I know myself as "I who have been given an eye to see the celestial realm," but I do not yet know more about who this "I" is in relation to Israel or to God. The active I remains that of King David, with all the tension and danger that that implies.

(ciii) *God's love appears as the place of unity that joins together the "I who sees the heavenly realm" and the "we praise" of Israel.*

Ahavah rabah ahavtanu, yhvh elohenu, chemlah g'dolah viytera chamalta alenu:

"With a great love have you loved us, YHVH our God; great and abundant mercy have you bestowed on us. Our father, our sovereign, for the sake of our ancestors who trusted in you and you taught them the rules of life, have compassion on us and enable us to understand and discern, to hear, study, and teach, to observe, enact and lovingly fulfill all the teachings of your Torah. . . ."

The God who creates and redeems is also the God who loves. God's "great love" appears in this blessing as the abundant gift of understanding and discernment that will open Israel's heart and mind to receive and embody God's word. Since, however, the "I who sees the heavenly realm" is the one who voices this blessing, we have reason to infer that Israel's scriptural language is brought to the light of daily life only by way of the "I see" of Israel's individual members. This would imply that there is no embodied knowledge of God's word without the cooperative work of both the "I see" and the "we praise" and that it is therefore in David (as prototype of the "I see") that Israel is given eyes to see the Creator's light, and in Israel that the dangerous impulses of David are given an ear to hear the redeemer's instruction. Love and knowledge appear, therefore, as agents of the unity of we, I, and God. We need now only to see and hear how the unity is enacted in fact.

(civ) *A surprising proclamation: the "I" is itself an instrument of unification. Redeeming the "I think" without losing the I: modern logic resituated in scriptural logic.*

shema yisrael yhvh elohenu yhvh echad:

"Hear, O Israel, YHVH is our God, YHVH alone" (Deut. 6:4). "Blessed is the glorious name of his sovereignty for ever and ever."

This defining proclamation of the people Israel is a call to Israel by its leader: not David, in this case, but Moses. In Moses, the "I speak and I praise" become the "I call": the first event in Morning Prayer where the "I" addresses and leads the "we" of Israel. Here is a surprising introduction to the movement that may unify the I, the we, and God: for the movement is introduced by a creature, taking on the active I that one might otherwise associate only with God. This may be the most dramatic moment of prayer for anyone seeking to redeem the binary "I think" of modernity. The "I call" of Moses suggests that the "I think" may be engendered by Israel's scripture before it is redeemed by it.[16] The one "I" on which we ground our faith and knowledge is the *ehyeh imach,* the "I am with you" of the God of Israel (Exod. 3), but the purpose of God's gift of Torah is not to replace any human agency with this "I am." It is, to the contrary, to offer Torah as the means through which the "I am" comes alongside the "I see" of Israel to recommend ways of learning more and knowing more so that our judgments will more likely be true and not false, serving life and not death. It is as if we heard this: that "I am with you," not in place of you; it remains your choice to hear and see and make judgments; I will simply tell you all I can about how you would judge best; then it is for you to act; I suggest, in other words, that you learn to adopt the "I act" as *I* do; this should indeed help you live in this creation: if you misuse this "I," it will, I fear, hurt you all the more, but that is the chance I have taken with you. . . .

There is much more to learn from Morning Prayer about what comes next for this reaffirmed yet chastened "I" of the "I think" that is also the "I see, I praise, I participate-in, I become. . . ." Perhaps the most powerful movement of all comes in the Amidah, or "eighteen blessings," that follows the Shema, for here the creaturely "I think" is offered actual entry into a cloud of holiness and, with it, an opportunity to place the "I think" as fully as possible into service of the redeemer's "I." For now, however, the Shema completes a minimal account of how Morning Prayer can redeem the modern "I think" without undoing it. Let us therefore conclude with this accounting of five lessons of the proclamation that the Creator and redeemer is YHVH alone, so that all creatures and all acts of God are unified in the one name of YHVH:

---

16. This, in fact, is the claim of Peirce's pragmatism, albeit in the name of Jesus' Scripture. Let me summarize the claim as a series of statements, each one prompting a challenge that is answered by the next one:

  (a) The logic of modernity can be repaired only from within.

  (b) The "I think" of modernity is typically posed as *causa sui,* but this claim lacks logical or epistemological warrant. The only *causa sui* is the divine "I am I" of Exodus 3, incarnate in the I of Jesus. If I say "I think," it is only to introduce a hypothesis, that "this may be the case," verifiable only by the "I am I," which means by the creator of the universe, about whose judgment we have verified knowledge only in the end of days, or the "long run of experience."

  (c) In this reading of Morning Prayer, the Jewish analogue to Peirce's argument is that God's will is disclosed now in the words of Torah but verified in its embodied enactments only in the end of days. In the meantime, our judgments are tested by the disciplined opinion of the community of scriptural readers and reasoners.

1. Against neo-liberal efforts to defend the primacy of the "I think," here the greatest "I" of Israel, the "I" of Moses, becomes agent of the unification of Israel as servant of God, enmeshing each individual "I" of Israel in an indefinitely expanding network of relations. Responding antiphonically to Moses' call — in imitation of the angelic chorus of Isaiah 6 — the collectivity of Israel freely donate their active wills and intellects to the angelic ideal of imitating, each and all, the subjecthood of their Creator and redeemer.[17]

2. Against communitarian alternatives to the liberal "I think," the creaturely "I" of Moses still asserts itself in relation to the corporate "we" of Israel: it is Moses who calls Israel to serve God and one another. The I who comes to serve Israel *freely enters* that service.

3. Furthermore, against neo-orthodox efforts to reject the modern "I think" altogether, the creaturely "I" of Moses retains a degree of autonomy in relation to the Creator God as well as the people Israel. The I who comes to serve God freely enters that service.

4. But how then has Morning Prayer offered a means of redeeming the binary character of the modern "I think"? Because, while affirmed as a legitimate part of this created world, the "I think" discovers through Morning Prayer that it is only one miniscule integer in an infinite array of infinite series of integers. The "I think" is therefore both indefinitely humbled and also preserved in its nobility, since God says even to that miniscule integer, "I am with you": that is to say, not just that he is with you, but also that the I itself is with you.

5. What then are the implications for how we judge "I see the tree"? First of

---

17. The resulting, covenantal collectivity appears to display features of what Peirce calls "material continuity." Adapting his logic of continuity as a model of how each member of Israel relates to each other and to the whole, we might portray covenantal Israel as follows: Israel is a "people" *('am)*, defined as a collection of individual "children of Israel," each and every one of which also shares in a single collection-identity "Israel" (comparable, in set-theory, to a "class character") *so that:* (1) all relations among every member of the people *also* share in the identity "Israel" and (2) each member of "Israel" may be redescribed as a human being *(adam)*, defined as a collection of its own attributes, each and every attribute of which *also* shares in the individual-identity "Israel"; *furthermore,* (3) "Israel" as a people may also be redescribed as a collection of its own attributes, with the features characterized in (2), *so that:* (4) these attributes are also collected into sub-groups, defined by such dimensions as "historical identity" (relation to itself in different periods of time), "political identity" (relation to other such peoples), and "covenantal identity" (relation to God). See P. Ochs, "Continuity as Vagueness: The Mathematical Antecedents of Peirce's Semiotics," in *Semiotica* 96-3/4 (1993): 244; and Charles Sanders Peirce, *Collected Papers,* vol. 6.174ff; 4.561n; 4.642; 7.535n (Cambridge, Mass.: Harvard University Press, 1931, 1932, 1958).

all, we need *not* remove either the "I" or the "I see" or "I think" in order to redeem the binary character of this judgment. There really are "I" and "I see," but, verbally and ontologically, each element of the judgment extends in every way to infinity — drawing not only the "I think" but each element of each element into indefinite possibilities of relationship and thus indefinite calls to relationship: I in relation to me, I in relation to each creature I see, I in relation to the we of my language community, I in relation to each other I in that we, I within each we in *its* relation to each other of we, I in relation to the angelic I's, I in relation to the I who is with you. And that "_____ see _____" also belongs to indefinite series of series: the narratives and histories of all that "I do" as well as see, and of who else "sees," and of what else I see, and the whole life and series of relations of what I see, the tree in its own series of relations. And the form "I see the tree" also belongs to a language in which there are many other forms of judgment — of which the relational judgments "there is tree here," " — is tree," and (I)SEE(tree) are only one set of examples. And many other languages and modes of perception and realms of being and non-being. Yes, I judge. But there is so much more to do.

What lesson is there, then, for those of us who seek a way out of the binarism we believe we received from being nurtured in the modern West? I learn that a "way out" needs to come as an alternative source of nurturance, rather than as some more abstract claim or critique. Here, nurturance means a reiterable practice that engenders integrated habits of thinking, feeling, imagining; and it means a practice that is suitable for reforming the ways of older folks, as well as bringing up the young. I don't assume that Jewish Morning Prayer is the only way! But I believe it illustrates some more broadly instructive features of "the way." For me, the central feature is that "very big problems" may have "very small solutions": in this case, that the colonialism that is "writ large" into the dominant political and economic institutions of the West displays the binary logic that is "writ small" into the way modern folks learn to make judgments about the world and one another. Morning Prayer shows how other logics can be "writ small" into the ways we learn to make judgments and how prayer can serve as a daily exercise in these ways. In this essay, we have examined only the logic of the thing. The next step would be to test the logic ethnographically: to see if there are observable differences between the practices of judgment-making among those who are habituated to Morning Prayer, for example, and those who are not.

In the meanwhile, we may conclude only with a recommendation for your "self-testing": Consider the politics of binarism. See if your criticisms of large-scale modern institutions may be translated into criticisms of "colonial-ism writ large" and if these, in turn, may be translated into criticisms of "co-lonialism writ small," or the logic of binarism. Consider next what alterna-tives you tend to offer: are these practicable alternatives or abstract pronouncements? If practicable, do they display alternatives to the logic of binarism? If not, back to the drawing board! If so, what practices of nurturance or habit-formation tend to engender these alternatives? Are these practices readily available — the way, for example, that Jewish Morning Prayer is available to folks who inherit traditions of Jewish practice? If not, is your critique utopian or practicable? If they are available, then what is the next step of your critique? How, in other words, does your critique connect what is to be writ large, politically and economically, to what is to be writ small, in our daily practices of judgment?

PART II

LITURGICAL TIME

Figuring Time: Providence and Politics

Scott Bader-Saye

All things proceed to a joyful consummation.[1]

Thomas Becket in *Murder in the Cathedral*

My five-year-old son is learning to tell time. He is learning to match digital clocks to analog clocks, to count in base sixty, and to name thirty minutes as "half an hour." His favorite question is "How many seconds have I been alive?" He is also learning that not all time is the same, that time has quality and not just quantity. For instance, the stay-in-your-pajamas-and-watch-TV time of Saturday morning is not interchangeable with get-up-get-dressed-and-go-to-church time of Sunday morning. He is learning that we live differently during Lent than we do during Easter. In many ways he is learning how to mark time so that one day is not the same as another. The harder task is to teach him not just the cyclical patterns of weeks, months, seasons, years, but that God's work in history indelibly marks time so that the time framed by incarnation and consummation needs to be lived in a way that recognizes God's intervention in history. We have to work hard to remind ourselves of this characteristic of time, since modern Western culture teaches us to tell time in a very different way.

Recently, while reading a book entitled *The Becoming of Time*, I noticed the word "time" printed on my paper coffee cup. I lowered the cup and saw the message: "Time. It's a valuable commodity." I was thankful that my coffee cup was ready to teach me such an important life lesson. So then I asked myself, was I "wasting" this precious commodity, time, by sitting in Borders

1. T. S. Eliot, *Murder in the Cathedral* (New York: Harcourt Brace Jovanovich, 1963), p. 70.

91

reading and sipping coffee? (Note to Borders: your coffee cups may be bad for business.) Was I "spending" my time well or did I need to "manage" my time better? If time is a commodity, then it can, presumably, be bought, sold, and exchanged. Does it then follow that, as Benjamin Franklin taught us, "time is money"? But if time and money are interchangeable, how does that shape the way I think about time?

Economists speak of "opportunity cost" as the recognition that "the cost of using a resource arises from the value of what it could be used for instead."[2] Opportunity cost includes, for instance, the difference between spending money and saving it, so that over a ten-year period the $1.50 I spent on that cup of coffee could have been invested at, say, a modest 5% interest yielding $2.44. But we shouldn't stop there, since *time* is also a "resource." The hour I spent sipping coffee and reading could have been spent earning money, so that, even at minimum wage, I've now turned that cup of coffee (which cost me the resources of $1.50 plus one hour) into roughly an $8 expenditure. The logic of "opportunity cost" assumes that all time could be financially productive; thus, every hour spent taking a walk, cooking dinner, or playing ball with the kids could be thought of as money lost or spent. By this logic we are encouraged to become consumers of time, to think of every moment as having a monetary exchange value (and all of this from a cup of coffee!).

David Foster Wallace lampoons such commodification of time in his novel *Infinite Jest*. He imagines a day, not too far in the future, in which there will be corporate sponsorship of time. So, he suggests, we might look forward to the "Year of Glad," "Year of the Depend Adult Undergarment," "Year of the Tuck's Medicated Pad," "Year of the Trial-Size Dove Bar" and "Year of Dairy Products from the American Heartland."[3] It is not too difficult to imagine standing in Times Square watching the giant ball drop from the hand of one corporate sponsor into the clutches of another: "Welcome to 2025, the Year of the McDonald's Big N' Tasty®."

Time in the Modern World

We do not know very much of the future
Except that from generation to generation

---

2. David R. Henderson, "Opportunity Cost," in *The Concise Encyclopedia of Economics*, available online at http://www.econlib.org/library/Enc/OpportunityCost.html, accessed April 25, 2005.

3. David Foster Wallace, *Infinite Jest* (Boston: Little, Brown & Co., 1996).

The same things happen again and again.
Men learn little from others' experience.
But in the life of one man, never
The same time returns. Sever
The cord, shed the scale. Only
The fool, fixed in his folly, may think
He can turn the wheel on which he turns.

Thomas Becket in *Murder in the Cathedral*

The modern conceptions of time that have led to its commodification arose during the period of transition between the Middle Ages and modernity. What emerged was, to borrow Walter Benjamin's phrase, "homogeneous, empty time," in which time was no longer thought of as qualitatively determined by a divine plan but as quantitatively constructed in an unvarying linear progression.[4] In this modern view, history is "additive"; the whole is no more than the sum of its parts. History writing merely arranges events "like the beads on a rosary" and "contents itself with establishing a causal connection between various moments in history."[5] What this modern historicism does not do, says Benjamin, is leave room for the "Messianic cessation of happening,"[6] that is, the moment of decisive transformation, the now *(jetztzeit)* that is not just one event among many, but the turning of time that defines the quality of time itself.

Benjamin suggests that the medieval chronicler (the "historian" of his day) shares more in common with the contemporary storyteller than with the modern historian. Neither storyteller nor chronicler is content "with an accurate concatenation of definite events";[7] rather, they seek to show "the way these [events] are embedded in the great inscrutable course of the world," which, in the medieval chronicler's case, meant embedding them in "a divine plan of salvation."[8]

In 1898 Ernst Troeltsch described the methodology of critical historical scholarship in a way that underlines the triumph of "homogeneous, empty time": "The observation of analogies between similar events in the past provides the possibility of imputing probability to them and of interpreting what is unknown about the one by reference to what is known about the other. . . . This omnipotence of analogy implies the similarity (in principle) of all his-

---

4. Walter Benjamin, *Illuminations* (New York: Schocken Books, 1968), pp. 263-64.
5. Benjamin, *Illuminations*, pp. 262-63.
6. Benjamin, *Illuminations*, p. 263.
7. Benjamin, *Illuminations*, p. 96.
8. Benjamin, *Illuminations*, p. 96.

torical events."[9] One of the results of this democratizing of history is that "Jewish and Christian history are thus made analogous to all other history."[10] The possibility that a certain history could become determinative of all other time holds no purchase on a modern mind that sees time and space as analogically interchangeable.

While modernity eschewed any theological framework for understanding time and history, it still presupposed that we inhabit a "narratable world."[11] Indeed, the Enlightenment fed us optimistic visions of human progress. But in the wake of the twentieth century, the deadliest yet known, this story of inevitable progress strikes us as untenable and perverse. Indeed, for many "postmoderns" the very idea that world events hold together as a coherent narrative seems overly optimistic, if not naïve. Thus, while modernity gave us a story without an author, postmodernity has given us a world without a story.[12] Jean-François Lyotard famously declared, "The grand narrative has lost its credibility."[13] Others have joined in sounding the death knell of the "metanarrative," seeing it as an obfuscation by which the powerful legitimate their domination. The beads have come off the rosary, their linkage now appearing arbitrary, not necessary. Yet once each event, each moment, constitutes a singularity, there is no past and no future. And in a sense, then, there is no present either. Life is "just one damn thing after another."

Without an overarching narrative in which the self might locate an enduring identity, the smaller narratives of human lives easily become fragmented into dislocated moments. Alasdair MacIntyre has argued that this turns us into "unscripted, anxious stutterers in [our] actions as in [our] words."[14] It should be noted that this dissolution of the narrative unity of the self and the world is not merely a postmodern apocalypticism foisted on us by French intellectuals; it is the everyday experience of compartmentalized

9. Ernst Troeltsch, "Historical and Dogmatic Method in Theology" (1898), in *Religion in History,* trans. James Luther Adams and Walter F. Bense (Minneapolis: Fortress Press, 1991), pp. 13-14.

10. Troeltsch, "Historical and Dogmatic Method," p. 14.

11. Robert Jenson, "How the World Lost Its Story," *First Things* 36 (October 1993), pp. 19-24, available online at http://www.firstthings.com/ftissues/ft9310/articles/jenson.html, accessed May 18, 2005.

12. As Jenson has put it, "Modernity has supposed we inhabit what I will call a 'narratable world.' . . . Postmodernism is characterized by the loss of this supposition in all of its aspects" ("How the World Lost Its Story").

13. Jean-François Lyotard, *The Postmodern Condition: A Report on Knowledge,* trans. Geoff Bennington and Brian Massumi (Minneapolis: University of Minnesota Press, 1993), p. 37.

14. Alasdair MacIntyre, *After Virtue: A Study in Moral Theory* (Notre Dame, Ind.: University of Notre Dame Press, 1981), p. 216.

people, whose work lives are disconnected from their home and church lives, whose public speech does not coincide with their private convictions, whose youth and old age sit uncomfortably as disjointed bookends to an autonomous adulthood.

It is not the case that in postmodernity chaos replaces order but that the two become indistinguishable. The homogenous, empty time ushered in by the modern era continues to reign supreme, but now without the optimistic assumption that human beings could imprint order on its pristine sands. All moments become interchangeable. In contrast to the Enlightenment faith in progress, postmodern "history" becomes "a book you read in reverse, so you understand less as the pages turn"[15] (to borrow a phrase from the indie-rock group The Shins, who exude postmodern cynicism despite their valiant attempts not to).

Time, Community, and Politics

Destiny waits in the hand of God, shaping the still unshapen:
I have seen these things in a shaft of sunlight.
Destiny waits in the hand of God, not in the hands of statesmen
Who do, some well, some ill, planning and guessing,
Having their aims which turn in their hands in the pattern of time.[16]

Chorus of Women in *Murder in the Cathedral*

The breakdown of our assumptions about ordered time has implications beyond theory, since time, community, and politics interweave in significant ways. Benedict Anderson has linked the shifting perceptions of time in modernity to the rise of the nation-state. "Beneath the decline of sacred communities, languages, and lineages, a fundamental change was taking place in modes of apprehending the world, which, more than anything else, made it possible to 'think' the nation."[17] The nation has to be "thought" or "imagined" because like any community it rests on a construal of one's unity with others whom one has never met and likely will never meet. By "imagined" Anderson does not mean fictional or unreal, but rather something that is not apprehended directly. The imagining of community re-

---

15. The Shins, "Pink Bullets," *Chutes Too Narrow* (Sub Pop, 2003).
16. Eliot, *Murder in the Cathedral*, p. 13.
17. Benedict Anderson, *Imagined Communities: Reflections on the Origin and Spread of Nationalism*, revised ed. (London and New York: Verso, 1991), p. 22.

quires that we perceive a simultaneity between ourselves and others; that is, our conception of political unity has to do without our conception of temporal correspondence.

Changing perceptions of history and simultaneity helped make possible the rise of the nation-state just to the extent that they disrupted the synchronic community of the church created through the figuration of divine providence. The reading of Scripture, the celebration of Eucharist, and the marking of saints' days serve to create an imagined contemporaneity among God's people stretching from the biblical world to the present, from the living to the dead. Isaiah, Mary, Jesus, and St. Augustine are as much a part of one's community as are one's chronological contemporaries (perhaps more so). The "communion of saints" constitutes one's true community. But in order to make European Christians see themselves primarily as Italian, French, German, or English it was necessary to reimagine contemporaneity and thus to imagine a new communal identity. Rather than leaping across time to envisage a vast Christian community extending back to biblical days, the new view of history created an ever-widening gulf between the present and the past. It no longer made sense to view oneself as a contemporary of Abraham, Moses, St. Paul, or St. Benedict for chronological time made us contemporaries only of those with whom we shared temporal coincidence. The link to past and future was not figural or providential, but rather calendrical. In modernity "simultaneity is, as it were, transverse, cross-time, marked not by prefiguring and fulfilment, but by temporal coincidence, and measured by clock and calendar."[18] Time turns out to have significant political consequences.

One striking instance of this linkage between time and politics can be found in the story of the French Revolution, which ushered in not just a new regime but a new calendar. The "French Revolutionary Calendar" was adopted in 1793, proclaiming September 22, 1792 as day 1 of year 1. Despite the rise of modern conceptions of time as uniform, the revolutionaries understood that calendar functioned to name a politics and define a people; thus the old calendar had to be overthrown and reinvented with the rise of the first French Republic. Though this new calendar did not last (it was abolished by Napoleon I in 1806), its very existence bears witness to the political significance of how we name time.

Israel's Scripture narrates a similar moment of reinvention so profound that time itself had to bear the mark of this event. The Book of Exodus tells the story of Israel's liberation from Egyptian slavery. The story begins in

18. Anderson, *Imagined Communities*, p. 24.

chapter one with accounts of oppression and forced labor. Quickly the narrative progresses through the call of Moses, the confrontation with Pharaoh, and the first nine of ten plagues. Chapter 11 of Exodus ends with the warning of a final, devastating plague: the death of all the firstborn throughout Egypt. At this moment of great suspense, as we finally move to the critical showdown that will make or break this great escape, as we sit on the edge of our seats wondering what will happen next, the biblical story screeches to a halt. Chapter 12 begins with the words, "The Lord said to Moses and Aaron in the land of Egypt: This month shall mark for you the beginning of months; it shall be the first month of the year for you." One can only marvel at this interruption of the story to command Israel to recalibrate their calendars. Surely John Grisham would never make the mistake of wrenching his readers out of the narrative flow of a novel in order to treat something as mundane as negotiating the date of a religious holiday! Nonetheless, at the pivotal moment of Israel's exodus tradition, we are told how the calendar is to be set up and on which date the Passover is to be celebrated. Once the text returns from legislation to narration in Exodus 12:21, the pivotal events quickly follow: the slaughter of the passover lambs, the marking of the doorposts, the destruction of the Egyptian firstborns, the parting of the Red Sea, and the drowning of Pharaoh's army. Just as the events end, the text turns again from narration to ritual, giving, for a second time, instructions on how to celebrate Passover (12:43-49).

One might conclude that this is a poor job of editing, but I would contend that the point lies precisely in the disruptive seams. The actual escape from Egypt is effectively bracketed by instruction in calendar and ritual; thus the foundational story of the people of Israel cannot be reached, textually or experientially, except by means of a set of calendrical and ritual practices that make the story more than one story among others, more than one event among others. Time itself has been transformed by this event. Through the practice of Passover, Jews from antiquity to the present participate in a ritualized simultaneity, creating a community, even a polity, that spans time and creates identities that cannot simply be circumscribed by nation.

Providence and Time

What is the day that we know that we hope for or fear for?
Every day is the day we should fear from or hope from. One moment
Weighs like another. Only in retrospection, selection,
We say, that was the day. The critical moment

That is always now, and here. Even now, in sordid particulars
The eternal design may appear.[19]

Third Priest in *Murder in the Cathedral*

The ways we experience, name, and interpret time contribute to the kinds of communities we imagine and inhabit. Traditionally, Christians have used the language of providence to speak of God's time as determinative of our own. Here "God's time" does not mean a time above or alongside human time, but a quality of time that is the internal basis of human time. To put it another way, the central events of Israel, Christ, and church occur within history while also enacting the goal of history. In this way, they give history its coherence and trajectory. As Karl Barth puts it, "The history of salvation attested in the Bible cannot be considered or understood simply in and for itself. It is related to world history as a whole. It is the center and key to all events. But again, world history cannot be considered or understood simply in and for itself. It is related to the history of salvation. It is the circumference around that center, the lock to which that key belongs and is necessary."[20]

The witness of the church in the postmodern world must include a way of construing time, and thus politics, that is driven neither by the presumption of homogeneity nor the incoherence of singularity. The church's conception of time must show itself able to produce communities that bear witness to a redemptive politics, a way of being in the world that trusts the future precisely because of the way it narrates the past. Part of what is required, then, is to give an account of providence that can sustain this community-forming work. To do so, we need to rethink providence in ways that are more literary and less philosophical; that is to say, when engaging the mystery of the divine drama, we would do well to attend to narrative, figuration, and practice rather than seeking to resolve abstract problems concerning sovereignty, determinism, free will, and causation. These philosophical problems are not unimportant, but they have so dominated the conversation about providence in the modern era that we have lost sight of the practical (and political) force of confessing time as the arena of divine provision.

The central affirmation of the doctrine of providence, that God is Lord of history, is not neutral news and certainly not bad news but in fact good news. This good news of providence is threefold: first, that the world's story (and one's own) will finally hold together as a coherent narrative (it's not all chaos

---

19. Eliot, *Murder in the Cathedral*, p. 57.

20. Karl Barth, *Church Dogmatics*, III.3, ed. G. W. Bromiley and T. F. Torrance, trans. G. W. Bromiley and R. J. Ehrlich (Edinburgh: T&T Clark, 1960), p. 186.

after all); second, that in the course of this life's difficult journey God will provide; and third, that the world's story (and one's own) is not ultimately tragic but comic, that is, redemptive. Trusting this good news enables the Christian community to live a risky kind of discipleship precisely because we can relinquish control of the future to God's hands. We can risk being faithful even if we don't appear effective. We can trust that what we risk for Christ's sake, and even what we lose, will be returned to us in the "joyful consummation" of all things. Providence, as the narrative of divine provision and redemption, thus sustains practices of generosity, peacefulness, and hospitality.

The first shift we must make in our discourse about providence, then, is to think of the doctrine less as explanation and more as narration. Or, to put it another way, narration is a certain kind of explanation that allows us to "give an account" of something that remains in large part mysterious. As Hans Frei affirmed, "The providential action of God over and in his creation is not that of a mechanical fate to be read off of one occasion. God's work is mysteriously, abidingly mysteriously, coexistent with the contingency of events. The history of his providence is one that must be narrated. There is no scientific rule to describe it and eliminate the need for narration."[21] The doctrine of providence makes the dual affirmation that our particular lives will prove to be intelligible as unified stories and that God's action in the world will be revealed eschatologically as an intelligible narrative of provision and redemption. We do a disservice to Scripture, tradition, and experience when we try to reduce providence to formulas such as "when good things happen you are being rewarded," or "when bad things happen you are being punished," or "this suffering is meant to teach you something." Such explanatory formulas provide simplistic accounts of God's engagement with the world. They may be attractive to some precisely because of their clarity, but ultimately they stifle our imaginations and belie both the mystery and variety of divine action. This is why, I think, there is a backlash within Israel's wisdom tradition when the neat formulas no longer seem adequate to account for life as we know it. The books of Job and Ecclesiastes challenge the sometimes naïve assurances in Proverbs and Psalms that goodness will bring blessing. They suggest instead that evil and suffering are more complicated, that they assail both the good and the bad, so that the real issue becomes the practical one of sustaining life, faith, and hope when the arc of the universe does not seem to bend toward justice.

In order to affirm divine providence, we need to learn again the skills of figuration by which we read one person, thing, or event in light of another,

---

21. Hans Frei, *The Identity of Jesus Christ* (Philadelphia: Fortress Press, 1975), p. 163.

thus enriching the meaning of both. This "mutual enriching" is one way in which figuration can be distinguished from allegory, in which one "figure" points so completely to another that the first is no longer needed once the second has arrived. Christian allegorical readings of the Old Testament, for instance, long served to make Israel's existence superfluous after the coming of Christ. With figuration, by contrast, both of the figured elements maintain their integrity and significance. We find examples of figuration already in the New Testament; for instance, in the Book of Acts, Luke interprets the story of Jesus in figurative relation to the Suffering Servant of Isaiah (8:30-35), and in Matthew Jesus himself uses Jonah's three days in the whale as a prefiguring of his own upcoming death and resurrection (12:39-41; 16:4). We also find examples of figuration beyond the biblical text itself. St. Augustine used the biblical figure of Babylon to interpret the Roman Empire, and Ronald Reagan used Jesus' reference to "a city on a hill" to describe the United States. Of course, figurations can be contested. Far from seeing Rome as a kind of depraved Babylon, Eusebius interpreted the Roman emperor Constantine positively as a type, or figure, of Moses.[22] And some would argue that Reagan's use of "city on a hill" in reference to the United States is more a rhetorical justification of national interest than a true assessment of America as the embodiment of Jesus' Sermon on the Mount (Matt. 5:14). What these contested figurations reveal is that God's action in history is not something we read clearly off the surface of events, but which we discern through prayer and often have to reinterpret when time and patience give us the wisdom of hindsight.

Figuration is a way of bringing the whole of our world into the descriptive penumbra of the biblical world. In this way it is the primary means by which we answer the question, "How is God at work in world events and in our own lives?" John David Dawson explains the relation of figuration, providence, and politics this way: "Figural readers turn to the text of the Bible for clues and models useful for unraveling as much as they can of what they think they discern as the mysterious working of God in the lives of people over time. What is always ultimately at stake is the reality and the proper characterization of a divine performance in the material world of space and time, a performance that defines the personal, social, ethical, and political obligations of Christians in the present, as well as their stance toward past and future."[23]

---

22. See Peter Hodgson, *God in History: Shapes of Freedom* (Nashville: Abingdon Press, 1989), p. 16. George Lindbeck's suggestion that the Constantinian shift be figured in relation to the rise of the monarchy in Israel (with all the same ambiguities reflected in 1 Samuel 8–12) may turn out to be closer to the mark.

23. John David Dawson, *Christian Figural Reading and the Fashioning of Identity* (Berkeley: University of California Press, 2002), p. 216.

Dawson rightly points out that there are material, political implications for how we interpret the times in light of the "divine performance," that is, divine providence.

The second important shift we need to make in our discourse about providence is from language of control to affirmations of redemption and provision. The theological point of providence is not to confess an abstract sovereignty, as if God were simply and purely a controlling power, but rather to confess that God's sovereignty takes a very particular form, most clearly seen in the life, death, and resurrection of Jesus Christ. We thereby affirm not so much that God is in control (by some analogy to the ways in which we "control," i.e., coercion and violence) but rather that God's lordship takes the particular form of provision and redemption. Karl Barth has noted that the Protestant Orthodoxy of the seventeenth and eighteenth centuries was infected by a loss of *telos* which corresponded to a generalized, that is, insufficiently trinitarian, doctrine of providence. This produced strong affirmations of divine lordship without a clear sense of the purpose for this lordship, becoming, then, a kind of counterdeterminism to the materialist determinisms of modernity.

> The orthodox Lutheran and Reformed teachers are rather at one in teaching the divine lordship over all occurrence both as a whole and in detail without attempting to say what is the meaning and purpose of this lordship. . . . It does not seem to have occurred to whole generations of Protestant theologians to ask what this lordship has to do with Jesus Christ. . . . What does this imply but the absolute exercise of the absolute will of an absolute power in an absolutely subjected sphere of power? The meaning, goal and purpose of this action are one with the action itself. In other words, it is its own end. The *gloria* of God consists in the fact that He is so powerful in relation to the creature; that He asserts Himself so thoroughly. And the question what this controlling God actually wills of His creature can be left open.[24]

Such "openness" without reference to the goal of divine providence tended to magnify God's power precisely as it diminished the importance of the particular biblical and trinitarian patterns of divine activity. Perhaps one of the reasons so many people find the doctrine of providence implausible in the contemporary world is that we're not sure whether an abstract affirmation of God's absolute power is bad news or good news.

The story of the binding of Isaac in Genesis 22 reveals God's providence not as a general claim about divine control of history, but specifically as God's

---

24. *Church Dogmatics,* III.3, p. 31.

determination to provide for the covenant. This story must be read in light of the preceding stories of Abraham, in which he is depicted as a willing follower of God but one who is ultimately unable to rely on God's provision. In the face of perceived threats from both the Egyptian Pharaoh and King Abimelech, Abraham schemes to protect himself by passing off his wife, Sarah, as his sister, thus betraying her to their amorous advances. In the face of Sarah's barrenness, Abraham schemes with her to produce progeny through Hagar. In each instance God provides for the covenant and saves Abraham from the destructive consequences of his actions. So when we reach Genesis 22 and read that "After these things, God tested Abraham," we realize that this test strikes at the heart of Abraham's unwillingness to trust God with the covenant. The God who has provided for Abraham now threatens to take away that provision. Abraham and Isaac journey to Mount Moriah. On the way Isaac asks, "Father . . . where is the lamb for a burnt offering?" Abraham answers in faith (or is it simply another scheme?), "God himself will provide." They reach the mountain, the knife is taken, the angel speaks, Isaac is returned, and a ram is provided for a sacrifice. "So Abraham called that place, 'The Lord will provide'; as it is said to this day, 'On the mount of the Lord it shall be provided'" (Gen. 22:14). In the biblical world, to affirm divine providence is above all else to learn to live not by human scheming but by trust in God's provision.

Such trust is not always easy, since life is filled with struggle, suffering, and evil. Reflection on the patterns of divine provision in Scripture leads us to the conclusion that God ordinarily chooses not to prevent evil and suffering but to redeem it. Why God works this way remains mysterious, though the pattern is clear. Joseph's brothers are not prevented from selling him into slavery, but this injustice is redeemed as Joseph becomes an advisor to Pharaoh and preserves both Egypt and Israel from famine. The Israelites do not avoid slavery and oppression in Egypt but they are redeemed when Moses leads them across the Red Sea. Job is not protected from suffering but his cries are answered and his righteousness is vindicated. This pattern of suffering and redemption reaches its climax in Jesus' own suffering and death which are redeemed in the resurrection in such a way that all of our suffering is now drawn into and redeemed by this eschatological triumph. Reading our sufferings in figurative relation to cross and resurrection does not dissolve the significance of earthly events, but it does challenge the finality and ultimacy of the tragic.[25] The practice of figuration puts worldly events into a context in which their pattern of meaning is derived from earlier patterns of divine pro-

---

25. Erich Auerbach, *Mimesis* (Princeton: Princeton University Press, 1953), p. 317.

vision as well as an eschatological hope of ultimate fulfillment. Thus, to the extent one believes exodus and Sinai, cross and resurrection to be paradigmatic patterns of divine activity, no earthly event can be finally and utterly tragic. Tragedy is real but penultimate.

This leads us to the third way in which we must revise our discourse of providence. The doctrine of providence is first and foremost a practical doctrine, oriented to action more so than theory. The story of Jesus and the man born blind in John's Gospel helpfully displays this shift from theory to practice. "As [Jesus] walked along, he saw a man blind from birth. His disciples asked him, 'Rabbi, who sinned, this man or his parents, that he was born blind?' Jesus answered, 'Neither this man nor his parents sinned; he was born blind so that God's works might be revealed in him. We must work the works of him who sent me while it is day; night is coming when no one can work'" (John 9:1-4). The disciples come to Jesus seeking a causal explanation for suffering, assuming that God caused the man's blindness as a punishment for sin. Such an assumption would make God's governance of the world visible, rational, and justifiable at the level of each particular event. Jesus begins by denying that it was sin (the man's or his parents') that caused the blindness. In so doing, he refuses to dignify our desire for the kind of orderly world in which no suffering occurs that is not deserved. The matter is clearly more complicated. Jesus does not point back to a divinely determined cause, nor does he even entertain the wrongly formulated question; rather, he points forward to a divinely appointed end: "he was born blind so that God's works might be revealed in him." In so doing, Jesus urges us to reshape the questions we ask in the face of suffering. The real issue may not be determining "why" something happened but rather what kind of response is necessary to participate in God's redemptive work, to sustain hope, to uphold one another in a world that is unpredictable and even tragic, though only in a penultimate way. "We must work the works of him who sent me," Jesus says. While these words may at first seem to be a weak editorial seam (tacked on by John in a way that does not naturally follow from the previous story), we may rightly read this as Jesus redirecting the disciples away from the safe, theoretical conversation about the cause of suffering and toward the dangerous practical work of embodying God's provision and redemption while there is still time.

Providence calls forth action that is made possible precisely by the assurance that God will provide. We might say that providence is a way of giving time a story that invites a certain kind of politics. Trust in divine provision makes possible risky ventures of vulnerable love because we trust that the end of the story is in God's hands and not ours. We have been freed from the pressure of making history turn out right and thus have been set free to live the generosity, peacefulness, and hospitality that correspond to God's gracious and plentiful provision.

Providence Disfigured

> Temporal power, to build a good world,
> To keep order, as the world knows order.
> Those who put their faith in worldly order
> Not controlled by the order of God,
> In confident ignorance, but arrest disorder,
> Make it fast, breed fatal disease,
> Degrade what they exalt.[26]

Thomas Becket in *Murder in the Cathedral*

Lamentably, in modernity providence has often been disfigured to serve another politics. While Christians have generally lost interest in providence as a way of interpreting and understanding history, the rhetoric of providence has been enlisted persuasively in the service of power and wealth, as an apologetic for imperialism and capitalism. Specifically, providence has become an affirmation of a divine order that underwrites the pursuit of self-interest as altruistic and the exertion of national power as divinely sanctioned.

Both the defense of capitalism in Adam Smith and the nineteenth-century justifications of European and American imperialism threatened to reduce providence to a divine rubber stamp on human ideologies — whatever is, is God's will; whoever wins is God's winner. Providence as a claim about divine activity was abstracted from the narratives of Israel and church and thus abstracted from the form of life that seeks to correspond to the divine initiative. In the process providence was refigured to place the divine imprimatur on human endeavors, themselves conceived apart from the claim and call of God. John Milbank has persuasively argued that the rise of political economy in the eighteenth and nineteenth centuries can be read as a "finitizing" of providence. "Political economy . . . seeks to supplement science as making with a science of providence, or a social theodicy. . . . This does not, however, amount to the reintroduction of the traditional providence of Catholic orthodoxy. Such a providence was ultimately unknown and could only be dimly apprehended. This providence can be *exactly*

---

26. Eliot, *Murder in the Cathedral,* p. 30.

known about, and it is invoked at the level of finite causality."[27] Visible causality and apologetic theodicy are taken up in discussions of politics and economy and are finitized — not in a way that eliminates God, but rather in a way that invokes God as the absentee landlord whose master plan justifies the emerging models of the nation and the market. The design of God written into the creation became in the eighteenth and nineteenth centuries not just an undergirding for *natural science,* by creating the assumption of rational and universal laws of nature, but also for *social science,* by providing a theodicy that would theologically sanction the rise of the market and the extension of the nation despite the apparently unchristian capitulation to self-interest, national interest, and acquisitiveness.

Providence as a theodicy for the marketplace appeared in the form of the "invisible hand" of Adam Smith. In *The Wealth of Nations* he writes of the businessman:

> By preferring the support of domestic to that of foreign industry, he intends only his own security; and by directing that industry in such a manner as its produce may be of the greatest value, he intends only his own gain, and he is in this, as in many other cases, led by an invisible hand to promote an end which was no part of his intention. Nor is it always the worse for the society that it was not part of it. By pursuing his own interest he frequently promotes that of the society more effectually than when he really intends to promote it.[28]

At work here is a providence of God (or of nature) that does not include a direct or particular providence in which God somehow participates in history. Rather, God so orders the means of economic provision that the pursuit of one's own good has the serendipitous effect of doing good to others.[29] Smith justifies the social struggle that is endemic to capitalism by appealing to a providential theodicy that would vindicate the injustices created by the emerging political economy. The rise of political economy spelled the end of classic Christian affirmations of providence, not by making God irrelevant to the social order but by making God so intrinsic to the economic struggle as to silence theological critique of the market.

Providence was "disfigured" in modernity not only as it became an apol-

---

27. John Milbank, *Theology and Social Theory: Beyond Secular Reason* (Cambridge, Mass.: Blackwell, 1991), p. 29.

28. Adam Smith, *The Wealth of Nations,* The Modern Library (New York: Random House, 1947), p. 423.

29. See Milbank, *Theology and Social Theory,* pp. 39-40.

ogetic for capitalism but also as it served the interests of nineteenth- and early-twentieth-century imperialisms. Most notably, the American rhetoric of "manifest destiny" accompanied the nation's expansion into the western frontier in the mid-1800s. This appeal to providence served to justify the destruction of Native Americans who were seen as incapable of self-governance and thus unable to become participants in the democratic project of the United States. Further, it justified the annexing of their tribal lands. And for some, the providential imperial destiny of the United States did not stop at the Pacific but extended westward to the Philippines. In a now notorious speech before the U.S. Senate, Senator Albert Beveridge urged Congress in 1900 to continue the war it had begun in the Philippines and to claim the territory as an act of obedience to God. "MR. PRESIDENT," he began, "the times call for candor. The Philippines are ours forever, 'territory belonging to the United States,' as the Constitution calls them. And just beyond the Philippines are China's illimitable markets. We will not retreat from either. . . . We will not renounce our part in the mission of our race, trustee, under God, of the civilization of the world. And we will move forward to our work, not howling out regrets like slaves whipped to their burdens but with gratitude for a task worthy of our strength and thanksgiving to Almighty God that He has marked us as His chosen people, henceforth to lead in the regeneration of the world."[30] Tellingly, Beveridge links economic interest with divine duty. He goes on to imply that this is not only duty but destiny. "This is the divine mission of America. . . . Blind indeed is he who sees not the hand of God in events so vast, so harmonious, so benign."[31] Race, nation, wealth, and God's providential hand all interweave seamlessly in Beveridge's vision, producing a harmonious and benign plan for American imperialism.

Practicing Providence: The Politics of Provision

Peace, and be at peace with your thoughts and visions.
These things had to come to you and you to accept them.
This is your share of the eternal burden,
The perpetual glory. This is one moment,

---

30. Senator Albert J. Beveridge, "In Support of an American Empire," *Record,* 56th Congress, I Session, 1900, pp. 704-12, available online at http://www.mtholyoke.edu/acad/intrel/ajb72.htm, accessed May 24, 2005.

31. Beveridge, "In Support."

But know that another
Shall pierce you with a sudden painful joy
When the figure of God's purpose is made complete.[32]

Thomas Becket in *Murder in the Cathedral*

As we have seen, to speak of providence and politics in the same sentence can be a dangerous thing. Yet how can we avoid reducing providence to a divine imprimatur on the interests of race, class, tribe, or nation? If we are to be faithful in our discourse of providence, we must refrain from making providence commensurate with our causes and instead seek to make our ways correspond to God's gracious provision. So Barth reminds us: "As God sees to His creature, and cares for it, in order that it may not cease as the object of His love, He requires of man the action corresponding to this care and providence."[33] It is this "corresponding action" that we seek when we speak of the practice and politics of providence.

Jesus articulates this correspondence in the Sermon on the Mount when he assures his hearers of God's providential care. "I tell you, do not worry about your life, what you will eat or what you will drink, or about your body, what you will wear. . . . Look at the birds of the air. . . . Consider the lilies of the field" (Matt. 6:25-33; Luke 12:22-27). If God feeds the birds and clothes the lilies, surely he will feed and clothe you as well, Jesus tells them. "Therefore do not worry, saying, 'What will we eat?' or 'What will we drink?' or 'What will we wear?' For it is the Gentiles who strive for all these things; and indeed your heavenly Father knows that you need all these things" (Matt. 6:31-32). The Gentiles, those who do not yet know God's covenantal provision, worry about these things but it should not be so for God's people. Immediately following these words of comfort is the injunction, "But strive first for the kingdom of God and his righteousness, and all these things will be given to you as well" (Matt. 6:33). God's provision calls forth a distinct pattern of life that Jesus calls "the kingdom of God." And what does this pattern of life look like? Both Matthew and Luke situate this teaching adjacent to teachings about wealth. Matthew's gospel places this assurance of providential care directly after the injunctions, "Do not store up for yourselves treasures on earth," and "you cannot serve God and wealth" (Matt. 6:19, 24). Luke places the passage between the parable of the rich fool and the sharp command to "sell your possessions, and give alms" (Luke 12:33). What we do with our money, includ-

---

32. Eliot, *Murder in the Cathedral*, p. 69.

33. Karl Barth, *Church Dogmatics*, III/4, trans. A. T. Mackay, T. H. L. Parker, Harold Knight, Henry A. Kennedy, John Marks (Edinburgh: T&T Clark, 1961), p. 517.

ing our ability to take the risk of generosity, has a lot to do with how we understand the source of our provision.

The question of how, and to what extent, divine providence calls forth a distinct pattern of life (that is, a distinctive politics) energized an argument between H. Richard Niebuhr and his brother Reinhold in March and April of 1932. The context was the Japanese invasion of China, and the question was American involvement. What is most interesting for our purposes is the way the brothers frame the issues of war and peace, action and inaction, theologically. They rightly avoid an argument over the relative merits of just war versus pacifism. Rather, they recognize that what constitutes faithful action in response to violence has everything to do with how we conceive of God's activity in the world and God's lordship over history. In short, if God continues to exercise lordship even in the midst of evil, then patient "inactivity" (of a certain kind) can be justified. But if God has retreated to the edges of history and left the world to resolve its own conflicts, then the best we can do is achieve relative peace and relative justice as we act in ways that always fall short of the extra-historical ideal.

In the first of the three essays that make up the 1932 exchange, H. Richard makes a case for "the grace of doing nothing," that is, for a hopeful patience in the face of aggression. The "meaningful inactivity" he proposes seeks not so much to change history through intervention as to prepare, through repentance, for the inexorable coming of God's reign.[34] H. Richard maintains that God is active in all things, and thus "the fact that men can do nothing constructive is no indication of the fact that nothing constructive is being done."[35] God is working through all historical actions and events to bring the "mundane process" of history to its "inevitably good outcome."[36] But as H. Richard acknowledges in the closing line of his essay, "if there is no God, or if God is up in heaven and not in time itself," then patient self-analysis, repentance, and a "reconstruction of habits" constitute "a very foolish inactivity."[37]

Reinhold responds by arguing for the necessity of coercion as a means of justice in a political arena where love is impossible and patience is impractical. Reinhold writes, "I do not share his [H. Richard's] conviction that a pure love ethic can ever be made the basis of a civilization. . . . The ethical and spir-

---

34. H. Richard Niebuhr, "The Grace of Doing Nothing," *Christian Century* (March 23, 1932): 378-80; reprinted in Wayne Boulton, Thomas D. Kennedy, and Allen Verhey, eds., *From Christ to the World* (Grand Rapids: Eerdmans, 1994), pp. 419-22.

35. Niebuhr, "The Grace of Doing Nothing," p. 420.

36. Niebuhr, "The Grace of Doing Nothing," p. 421.

37. Niebuhr, "The Grace of Doing Nothing," pp. 421-22.

itual note of love and repentance can do no more than qualify the social struggle in history. It will never abolish it."[38] For Reinhold the social struggle in history is not part of God's mysterious work, but is a very human struggle that requires the very human response of coercive action. Reinhold understands that ultimately his argument with his brother is about God's activity in history, that is, about providence and eschatology. "What makes my brother's particular kind of eschatology impossible for me," Reinhold writes, "is that he identifies everything that is occurring in history (the drift toward disaster, another world war, and possibly a world revolution) with the counsels of God, and then suddenly, by a leap of faith, comes to the conclusion that the same God, who uses brutalities and forces, against which man must maintain conscientious scruples, will finally establish an ideal society in which pure love will reign."[39] In contrast, Reinhold asserts that "the history of mankind is a perennial tragedy" which "is why it is inevitable that religious imagination should set goals *beyond* history."[40] "My brother," Reinhold tells us, "does not like these goals above and beyond history. He wants religion and social idealism to deal with history."[41] But Reinhold argues that this is a misunderstanding of the historical process, and that rather than facing the inevitable conflict between "a pure gospel ethic" and a "realistic interpretation of the facts of history," H. Richard has avoided the problem by "leaving the field of social theory entirely and resorting to eschatology."[42] Reinhold tellingly contrasts eschatology with the social and the historical, revealing the disjunction in his own thought between divine action and human history.

H. Richard responds with his own challenge: "The fundamental question seems to me to be whether 'the history of mankind is a perennial tragedy' which can derive meaning only from a goal which lies beyond history, as my brother maintains, or whether the 'eschatological' faith, to which I seek to adhere, is justifiable."[43] For H. Richard "God . . . is always in history; he is the structure of things, the source of all meaning, the 'I am that I am,' that which is that it is. He is the rock against which we beat in vain, that which bruises

38. Reinhold Niebuhr, "Must We Do Nothing?," *Christian Century* (March 30, 1933): 415-17; reprinted in Wayne Boulton, Thomas D. Kennedy, and Allen Verhey, eds., *From Christ to the World* (Grand Rapids: Eerdmans, 1994), pp. 422-25.

39. Niebuhr, "Must We Do Nothing?" p. 424.

40. Niebuhr, "Must We Do Nothing?" p. 425, emphasis added.

41. Niebuhr, "Must We Do Nothing?" p. 425.

42. Niebuhr, "Must We Do Nothing?" p. 424.

43. H. Richard Niebuhr, "The Only Way into the Kingdom of God," *Christian Century* (April 6, 1932): 447; reprinted in Wayne Boulton, Thomas D. Kennedy, and Allen Verhey, eds., *From Christ to the World* (Grand Rapids: Eerdmans, 1994), p. 426.

and overwhelms us when we seek to impose our wishes, contrary to his, upon him."[44] Thus, "Man's task is not that of building Utopias but that of eliminating weeds and tilling the soil so that the Kingdom of God can grow."[45] "The grace of doing nothing" turns out not to be *nothing* but to be an active waiting and preparing. Yet being able to engage in this kind of action is difficult in a world that prizes the quick and effective solution.

How do we learn to practice the patient waiting that is appropriate to our affirmation of divine providence? I would suggest that we need to understand the importance of liturgical practice. For instance, this kind of active waiting and preparing is practiced throughout the liturgical season of Advent. As we remember Christ's coming, we prepare for his return and situate ourselves in that time between the times, when the reign of God has begun in our midst but has not been consummated in the world. So we learn the hard lessons of waiting through liturgical practice, through Scripture lessons that yearn toward the future, and through the simple (but hard) practice of singing Advent hymns while the world (that is, the shopping mall) bombards us with Christmas carols.

Liturgy provides the forum in which we enact and thus come to understand rightly God's presence in history. Providence as a concept abstracted from Scripture and liturgy becomes a cipher onto which we can easily project our own ideologies and agendas. As we saw above, modern accounts of providence tended toward abstract affirmations of divine power rather than full-blown trinitarian accounts of divine activity. Providence gets reduced to an affirmation of God's sovereignty as such rather than the particular ways in which God has chosen to display this sovereignty in the life, death, and resurrection of Jesus. Keeping providence figuratively grounded in Scripture and practically grounded in the liturgy can help constrain our distorted appeals to divine favor.

The celebration of the Eucharist provides for Christians the central liturgical enactment of divine provision and thereby the central means of reshaping our perception of time from commodity to gift. Here at the table Christ's own body and blood become our sustenance. The bread and wine are offered freely, figuring the manna Israel received in the desert, and the gathered people become guests at a great feast which they do not deserve but learn to receive with joy. Barth has asked about the Sabbath day, "Is not this irruption the true time from which alone he [the Christian] can have other time?"[46] We

---

44. Niebuhr, "The Only Way into the Kingdom of God," p. 426.

45. Niebuhr, "The Only Way into the Kingdom of God," p. 427.

46. Karl Barth, *Church Dogmatics*, III.4, ed. G. W. Bromiley and T. F. Torrance, trans. A. T. Mackay, T. H. L. Parker, Harold Knight, Henry A. Kennedy, John Marks (Edinburgh: T&T Clark, 1961), p. 51.

might more specifically ask this of the Eucharist. Is this not the time when the Christian community participates, if only for a moment, in the "joyful consummation" of all things, that makes it possible for us to live all other time? Is this celebration of thanksgiving not the "true time" that orders all other time?

The Eucharist is a celebration of plenitude; it is a recognition of God's provision. It is a challenge to all politics of scarcity. Here at this table the truth about God's world is told: there is enough. We need not hoard out of fear that there will be too little. We need not fight to get what others have. There is enough. God will provide. God will redeem. And so we are made bold to live the risks of peacemaking, generosity, and hospitality, knowing that our extension of ourselves to others, our open hand that refuses to cling, our peaceful waiting will be met with provision, and that such actions will finally be narratable as participation in the great story of God's redemption of time itself.

Rosenzweig's Liturgical Reasoning as Response to Augustine's Temporal Aporias

Steven Kepnes

Augustine opens Book Eleven of his *Confessions* with a query about God's eternity and our temporality. "Lord, since eternity is Yours, are You ignorant of what I say to you? Or do You see in time, what passes in time?" (187).[1] This is a question that not only asks about God's relation to us as temporal beings, but begs the question of our relation to God as an eternal being and our relation to eternity. Without fully answering these questions, Augustine moves further in his thoughts about temporality and makes us realize that as difficult as it is to contemplate eternity, we also are far from comprehending what we mean by time. "What, then, is time? If no one asks me I know; If I wish to explain it to one that asks, I know not" (194). Augustine describes the reality of time as a moment that passes before we can apprehend it. The present moment passes in an instant into the past. And the past is irretrievable precisely because it is past. The future that lies in front of us includes infinite possibilities, so it, too, is beyond our grasp. As if the immediate past and future are not enough to befuddle us, we have no knowledge of our own origins, our birth, and we equally can have no knowledge of our death. This problem is magnified when we think of the ultimate origins of life and its final end.

In this brief series of reflections, I will argue that Torah and Jewish liturgy work together to mold Israel's experience of time. Looking at the first chapter of Genesis we see how time is fashioned in the beginning in such a way that the festivals and its liturgies are included in the very fabric of creation. I use the third part of Franz Rosenzweig's *Der Stern der Erlösung* (1921; *The Star of*

---

1. All Augustine quotes in this essay are taken from *The Confessions of Saint Augustine*, trans. Edward Pusey (New York: Macmillan, 1961).

Redemption)[2] to argue that Jewish liturgy provides an avenue to convert the Jewish past into cultural memory and the Jewish future to messianic expectation. In addition, the liturgy of Shabbat works upon profane time to develop a sense of another quality for time as holy time. Shabbat constitutes a kind of mediation or bridge through which God's eternity and human temporality meet. Shabbat therefore provides one answer to Augustine's question about the human connection to eternal time.

At the end of the eleventh chapter of the *Confessions*, Augustine offers us the Psalm, whose beginning, middle, and end we internalize through recitation, as a model for knowledge of the totality of time. I interpret this to suggest that the liturgical singing of the Psalms may be viewed as a kind of extension of the Psalm into religious theatre that gives the Jew a sense of a beginning, middle, and end to the experience of time and opens Jews to eternal time.

The Genesis of Time in Torah

Through an exercise in "textual reasoning"[3] with the text of Genesis 1, we can see that the Torah, at its beginning, takes up issues of temporality. Genesis 1 suggests that along with the creation of the heavens and the earth, the creation of space, came the creation of the most elementary unit of time, the day. "And there was evening and there was morning: One Day." The units of space that we are given in creation, heaven and earth, are so large that we shudder at the impossibility of comprehending them. Yet the unit of time that we are given, one day, is of human proportions — nighttime and daytime, taken together: that is something that we can get our minds around. So perhaps Torah, in its opening verses, has an answer for Augustine. What is time? How can we think it? Think of night and day, think in terms of the unit: One day. Beyond the unit of the day, Genesis continues to give more details about the creation of time by describing the creation of the celestial bodies: the sun, and the moon. "Let there be lights in the vault of the heavens to divide the day from the night." And we even are given their purpose.

2. Except where indicated, German and English quotes from Rosenzweig taken from, respectively, *Der Stern der Erlösung* (The Hague: Martinus Nijhoff, 1921, repr. 1976) and *The Star of Redemption*, trans. William Hallo (Notre Dame, Ind.: University of Notre Dame Press, 1985).

3. For more extensive description of the methods and goals of textual reasoning see the online *Journal of Textual Reasoning* I:1 http://etext.lib.virginia.edu/journals/tr/. See also Peter Ochs and Nancy Levene, eds., *Textual Reasonings: Jewish Philosophy and Text Study at the End of the Twentieth Century* (Grand Rapids: Eerdmans, 2002).

"And they shall be signs for the *moadim,* the fixed times and for days and years" (1:14). Now we have two more divisions in time: years and fixed times *(moadim),* festival seasons, or simply "festivals." Genesis shows that the Torah is not a book of astronomy or physics, but a narrative of what Rosenzweig called the relationships between God, world, and person. This brings us to focus on the meaning of the celestial bodies for the world and humans. That meaning is that these bodies mark not only divisions in time, day, season, year, but qualitative gradations in time — sacred time and its opposite, profane time.

However, as creation is finished, another unit of time emerges, the week, and a very special day is created, the day of Shabbat. The seventh day sets a pattern that is already somewhat removed from the celestial bodies of nature. The seventh day is a quarter of the temporal period established by the lunar cycle. But the division into fourths is relatively arbitrary and divisions into halves or no division at all might be equally conceivable. The division into weeks suggests that there is a fundamental separation between profane and sacred — a separation that, when blessed, signifies holy time. In Genesis 2, holy time is correlated with the completion of work and with rest. This rest suggests a kind of still time that is out of the natural cycles of time that the moon demarcates. The time of Shabbat is associated in other references to it in the Torah with the highest level of holy time which is eternal time — God's time before and after time.

Thus we see in the first chapters of Genesis that the Torah provides us with tools to divide, order, and even stop time. The Torah suggests that there is an intricate relationship between time and the cosmos, but there is also a relationship between time and God.

Yet with the expulsion of Adam and Eve from the Garden of Eden another quality of time emerges: the time of exile and the time of history. If Eden represents union with creation and with God, if Eden represents a kind of continual experience of gradations of holy time and rest, exile represents the pervasive experience of profane time. This is a time of disorder, struggle, and work. With the Book of Exodus, profane time takes on a "history-like" quality. Here another quality of time emerges as the time in which the trials, tribulations, and accomplishments of human social and political achievement predominate over the time of the cycles of nature. Here, the time of events of meeting between humans and God takes center-stage, and the central stories of time become the story of God's intervention in time in events of revelation and redemption.

With history-like time, the seasonal festivals that mark the cycles of nature from Spring to Summer to Autumn take on additional meaning as markers of the historical events of Israel's slavery and redemption in Egypt, her desert wanderings and the reception of the Torah at Sinai.

Rosenzweig and the Time of Modernity

In the modern world, we see the ascendancy of secular history and the scientific notion of time as a linear string of discrete and unique moments. Secular time significantly narrows the range of temporal qualities to the monotony of clock time. In secular time, the sun and moon and the cycles of nature that they rule become irrelevant to human lives. In secular time, there are no divine interruptions. There is no return to earlier time and no experience of future time. No stopping of time. No purification of time. No new beginning or final end. No eternal time. It is one damn moment after the other. Secular time leaves us with Augustine's questions and *aporiai*. We are left only with the experience of time as a fleeting, ungraspable present moment that is destined to be encased in an irretrievable past. We are left with the exacting time of electric clocks that cut up time into ever smaller units. The scientific theory of the Big Bang locks us into the past, as our telescopes allow us only to see the time between the Big Bang and the now. We are thus deprived of future time and we are also robbed of the time of people — the time of relationships, the time of epic events, the time of exile and hope for a transformed and redeemed future.

Out of the emptiness and monotony of what he calls the "historical enlightenment" (p. 99) Rosenzweig seeks a temporality that includes the possibility of miracles (p. 93). It is out of the situation of the impoverishment of time that Rosenzweig reintroduces us to Jewish liturgy as the bridge to the time of relation between God, world, and humans. The most dramatic portrait of the increased possibilities for temporal experience that I know comes out of a letter that Rosenzweig wrote to members of the German Jewish adult education center called the *Lehrhaus* in November of 1924. Allow me here to confess that I have been transfixed by this letter, and since reading it over twenty years ago have continually returned to its words as one of the most significant portraits of the power of liturgy.

> All the days of the year Balaam's talking ass may be a mere fairy tale but not on the Sabbath wherein this portion is read in the synagogue, when it speaks to me out of the open Torah. But if not a fairy tale what then? I cannot say right now; if I should think about it today, when it is past, and try to say what it is, I should probably only utter the platitude that it is a fairy tale.

But on that day, in that very hour, it is, well, certainly not a fairy tale, but that which is communicated to me, provided I am able to fulfill the command of the hour, namely to open my ears.[4]

Here, Rosenzweig acknowledges what all of us as heirs to the Enlightenment know to be true: that we can no longer simply take the Torah as God's revelation to Moses from Sinai. As most Jews walk and work in the secularized world, they cannot but think of a story of a talking ass as a nice story, as a fairy tale. But then Rosenzweig opens up another possibility. While Jews are in the synagogue, on Shabbat, and in the context of the communal and liturgical reading of the Torah, another avenue, a unique order of reality is opened wherein suddenly, yes, some Jews cannot only imagine the ass speaking, but they hear her speak. And she is speaking not only to Balaam, but she is speaking to them.

Rosenzweig's experience of liturgy recalls to mind Victor Turner's notion that ritual creates a kind of "liminal" space between fantasy and reality.[5] Liturgy transpires in a kind of pretend or dream space, a space that is set aside from secular time and thereby open to sacred and holy time. When Jews are opened to sacred time they are opened to a different form of relationship to the natural world, one in which donkeys can speak. When Jews are open to sacred time, the past is no longer past and the future no longer inaccessible.

Rosenzweig argues that history, for the Jews, never tells the story of events that are lost to the past. Rather, they exist in memory and remain "eternally present." He turns to the liturgy of the Passover Haggadah: "Every single member of this community is bound to regard the Exodus from Egypt as if he himself had been one of those to go out" (1985, p. 304). Thus, it is through a liturgical retelling on the night of Passover that the Jewish people make their way back to their past and are able to re-present their past as present. And it is liturgy which brings the future redemption to the present by presenting images of the redeemed present and experiences of its peaceful and harmonious qualities. It is liturgy through which the Jewish people's sense of their eternity unfolds and develops in their consciousness.

---

4. Franz Rosenzweig, *Briefe und Tagebücher* I:2, ed. Rachel Rosenzweig and Edith Rosenzweig-Scheinmann (The Hague: Martinus Nijhoff, 1979). Translated by Nahum Glatzer in *Franz Rosenzweig: His Life and Thought* (New York: Schocken, 1970), p. 246.

5. Victor Turner, "Betwixt and Between: The Liminal Period in Rites de Passage," in *Reader in Comparative Religion: An Anthropological Approach*, 4th ed., ed. W. Lessa and E. Voigt (San Francisco: Harper and Row, 1979), pp. 234-43.

The Liturgical Calendar

In one of his most memorable phrases of Part Three, indeed of the entire *Star*, Rosenzweig speaks of the liturgy in this way: Liturgy "is the reflector which focuses the sunbeams of eternity in the small circle of the year" (p. 308). Eternity shoots out beams of light. And those beams are captured and concentrated in liturgy. So the liturgical calendar creates a form into which eternity is invited. So as time takes the shape of a circle, with neither beginning nor end, the tenses of past, present, and future lose their fixed character. Through the calendar, what is past is not lost and what is future can be grasped. The annual calendar provides markers in the sea of undifferentiated time that gives time shape and punctuation. The liturgical calendar is correlated to the natural rhythms of time given by night and day, months and seasons. It therefore allows for the renewal of time in festivals of the New Year and the arrival of spring.

Shabbat

In *The Star of Redemption*, Rosenzweig shows how the most important festivals and holy days of the liturgical year calendar each contribute to the Jewish sense of time, reviewing the liturgies of Shabbat; the three pilgrimage festivals of Sukkot, Pesach, and Shavuot; and the high holy days of Rosh Hashanah and Yom Kippur. We do not have space to cover all of this material here, and thus we will focus on Rosenzweig's "liturgical reasoning" on the meaning of Shabbat. We do this at least in part because Rosenzweig follows Jewish tradition in asserting that the holiday of all holidays is Shabbat. Upon it the spiritual year finds its foundation, regulation, and sense of wholeness.

The Sabbath accomplishes all this through its prohibitions against work and its commandments to rest and be refreshed and its successive liturgical readings from the Torah. These are apportioned to each week so that the entire five books are finished in a year's time. Through the liturgical reading of portions of the Torah, the *Parashah Ha-Shavuah*, the Jews move through the week with the text and time of the Torah. The *Parashah Ha-Shavuah* marks each week with the episodes, characters and laws of the different Torah portions for that week. At the same time, the consistency of the Shabbat ritual and liturgy, which envelops the *Parashah* with its sameness, provides the year with a regularized spiritual base:

> In the circle of weekly portions, which, in the course of one year, cover all of the Torah, the spiritual year is paced out, and the paces of this course are the

Sabbaths. By and large, every Sabbath is just like any other, but the difference in the portions from the Scriptures distinguishes each from each, and this difference shows that they are not final in themselves, but only parts of a higher order of the year. For only in the year do the differentiating elements of the individual parts again fuse into a whole. (p. 310)

Following Rosenzweig's theme of the calendar as cyclical time, we could say that the weekly Shabbat Torah readings make time over into the form of the scroll. The circular form of the scroll implies that there is no beginning and end to the Torah. At the end of the annual cycle of reading the Torah, Deuteronomy is finished and followed by Genesis. Thus one could read Genesis as coming after Deuteronomy and commenting upon it. Genesis' creation accounts could then be seen as occurring *after* revelation as a portrait of the hoped-for redemption.

Rosenzweig comments that Shabbat provides a peaceful and stable counterpoint to the other festivals that take the Jews back through the "anguish and bliss" (p. 311) of Jewish historical time. Shabbat provides an "even flow" of peace out of time through which "whirlpools of the soul are created" (p. 311). These "whirlpools of the soul" provide a constant communal resource for Jews to receive God's love. Like the created world that Shabbat celebrates, Shabbat itself is "always there, wholly there, before anything at all happens in it" (p. 311). However, just as God did not create the world once and for all, but must renew the creation daily, so Jews cannot observe Shabbat only once a year but must observe and renew Shabbat weekly. This parallel suggests that the "work," the "service," the *avodah* that Jews perform to make Shabbat a day of rest parallels the creative work which God performs in making the world.

The work of "making Shabbat," which humans do, involves a combination of domestic and liturgical preparations in the profane time before Shabbat that allows Shabbat to be a time of rest. These preparations include domestic chores like preparing meals in advance so cooking is not done on Shabbat, setting out special cutlery and candlesticks and arranging for lighting. The preparations also include learning the Shabbat Torah *Parashah* and studying the exegetes. What these preparations mean is that when Shabbat is ushered in through synagogue prayer and the saying of the Kiddush prayer over wine and bread in the home, profane time can be brought to a stop and life can be lived in a different quality of time. The time of Shabbat can foreground holiness, family, and community, study of Torah and rest. Participation in liturgical events in the synagogue and home make the field of relations between humans, God, and world come alive. The liturgical time of Shabbat is time unobstructed by secular aims of acquisition and goals of productive work. And this, Rosenzweig suggests, "lends reality to the year" (p. 310).[6]

Since the central theme of Shabbat is the celebration of the creation of the world and humans as good, this means that Shabbat is the celebration of created life. Shabbat prescribes the enjoyment of the senses through taste, sight, touch, and hearing. Sexual relations between spouses are encouraged, as are eating, singing, dancing, and social interactions. Rosenzweig recognizes that central to Shabbat are the three meals: evening, Shabbat day, and afternoon. These meals, eaten by families and their guests in homes, create a sense of *yedidut* or *communitas* by simultaneously satisfying the human bodily need for food and spiritual need for community: "The sweet and fully ripened fruit of humanity craves the community of man with man in the very act of renewing the life of the body" (p. 316). Emphasizing basic bodily needs and celebrating the natural creation, Shabbat has what we might call a "pagan" quality to it. It expresses a pagan sense of satisfaction in the goodness and completeness of the created world. Shabbat's temporal direction is toward the past, when the world was created as good. It recalls images of Eden and of Eve's joy in seeing, touching, and tasting the fruit of the tree in the middle of the Garden.

Although Shabbat celebrates the natural world of creation and thereby has something of the pagan in it, it remains a festival of monotheism. This means that Shabbat also celebrates the role of the transcendent God in creation and the relationship between God and the world and humans. Rosenzweig notes that almost all of the temporal periods, the day, the month, the season, the year, correspond to divisions of time that derive from movements of the earth and moon in nature. The week, however, aside from its weak relation to the phases of the moon, corresponds to a somewhat arbitrary division of time into groups of seven days. The seventh day of the week, as a day of rest for humans from work, is more of a marker for human culture than for nature. It signifies the imposition of human time on natural time. It also signifies the imposition of the divine on nature as it suggests that nature, as it is created, is not complete until it is supplied with the super-natural element of holiness that God and then humans supply for it.

---

6. A better translation for the term "reality" would be "existence," as the German is *Dasein*. Thus, in her new translation of the *Star* Gallie has "Shabbat grants existence to the year." *The Star of Redemption,* trans. Barbara Gallie (Madison: University of Wisconsin Press, 2005), p. 329.

Augustine and Rosenzweig on the Temporality of the Psalm

As rich and satisfying as the Shabbat rest is, Jews do not live in its Edenic time of creation and the time of the rest that signifies the completion of creation in holiness. The Jewish people also live in and through the cycles of their historical existence from Exodus, to Sinai, to wilderness wandering. It is the task of the three "pilgrimage festivals" — Passover, Shavuot, and Sukkot — to introduce every new generation into this history and into its central event of the revelation at Sinai. Rosenzweig speaks of these three festivals together as the "feasts of Revelation," since the high point and purpose of the three festivals is the celebration of the revelation of the Torah at Sinai. However, Rosenzweig also notes that each festival touches other theological themes, namely creation and redemption. Through these festivals the notions of creation, revelation, and redemption receive interpretations geared to the historical experience of the Jewish people. Yet the history that is told here, because it is touched by holiness, is not a fully secular history. This is a history that is intensified and elevated through poetic narration and images that attempt to relate salvific and revelatory experiences that happened to the people Israel in the past. This past is never truly past but allows Jews in other times and places to participate in it. It is a holy history retold and re-experienced through liturgical narrative. Rosenzweig likes to refer to this history as "eternal history" (p. 317). With this expression he means that the events of this history are accessible to every Jew in the present. Rosenzweig underscores that this means that the festivals of revelation are not simply "holidays of remembrance," for "the history in them is a fully compact present" (p. 336) that is "born anew" in each new generation.

Although we do not have space to review the liturgies of the three pilgrimage festivals in depth, it is noteworthy that Rosenzweig underscores the importance of one liturgical event that is common to the three festivals. That event is the Hallel service which includes the communal chanting of Psalms 113–118. Rosenzweig's discussion of the chanting of the Psalms is particularly interesting for our attempt to correlate Rosenzweig and Augustine's thoughts on time. For the height of chapter 11 in the *Confessions* includes an analysis of the resources of the recitation of the Psalm to address the *aporiai* of time. Given this parallel we will conclude with a comparison of Augustine and Rosenzweig on time and the Psalm.

At the end of chapter 11, Augustine points to the recitation of a Psalm as a model for the comprehension of the various levels of temporality and of the relationship between humans and God. The Psalm provides Augustine with a device to imagine the unity of time, a way in which to accomplish

what seems to be impossible, to extend the present out into the past and future in such a way that the fleeting present becomes what he calls a "long
present":

> I am about to repeat a Psalm that I know. Before I begin, my expectation is
> extended over the whole; but when I have begun, how much so ever of it I
> shall separate off into the past, is extended along my memory; thus the life
> of this action of mine is divided between my memory as to what I have re-
> peated, and expectation as to what I am about to repeat; but consideration
> is present with me, that through it what was future, may be conveyed over,
> so as to become past. (p. 204)

Augustine's suggestion — that the Psalm's unity is a model for the relatedness
of the past, present and future — provides a key to understand the temporal
unity of a human life. Our lives take shape as a kind of poem or narrative or
even an autobiographical "confession." In this view, we grasp our own temporal unity when our own past becomes the beginning of a story, our present
becomes the middle and our imagined future, the end of the story. The narrative form is crucial to both Judaism and Christianity as it supplies a beginning, middle, and end to the collective life of the Jewish and Christian communities. Augustine goes further to suggest that the narrative form of the
Psalm, if enlarged, can encompass "the whole age of the sons of men" (p. 205).
Thus, the form of the Psalm allows for the telling of the vast human past and
the presentation of the expected future, and through this all the dimensions
of time are comprehended.

In Rosenzweig's discussion of the Hallel service, he gives us a greater sense
for how the temporal contours and scope and the spiritual power of the
Psalm can be enlarged. Where Augustine remains largely with the recitation
of the Psalm and its cognitive digestion in the individual mind, Rosenzweig
considers the Psalm as it is sung by the community in synagogue.[7] Here, the

---

7. I have adopted a fairly traditional interpretation of Augustine's solution to the aporias of
time that stresses the individual and cognitive dimension of the recitation of the Psalm. This interpretation stays very close to the eleventh chapter of the *Confessions* and does not use other
writings of Augustine on textual interpretation, liturgy, and Christian community to provide a
larger interpretive context. I realize that recent Augustine interpreters, like Rowan Williams,
have shown that Augustine's concerns go beyond narrow individual and purely philosophical
concerns. Chad Pennington has specifically attempted to provide a view of Augustine as a
postliberal thinker that could serve to bring Rosenzweig much closer to Augustine. For purposes of emphasis and differentiation in this relatively brief essay I use the more traditional interpretation of Augustine. The reader should know however that a broader reading of Augustine is possible and available. See Chad Pennington, *Transforming Postliberal Theology* (London:

Psalm is taken up into the community and enlarged through the communal chant, through gesture, and sacred space. The liturgical chanting of the Psalm gives Augustine's meditative mental recitation a communal and sensual embodiment. The liturgical chanting of the Psalm suggests that the experience of the deepest dimensions of time requires the participation of the community and the body. Rosenzweig points us to the culmination of the Hallel service in the festival liturgy, in which Psalm 118 is chanted:

Hodu Adonai ki tov; ki lolam hasdo
Give thanks to the Lord, for he is good,
For his mercy endures forever.

Rosenzweig suggests that the Psalm allows for the expression of the event of redemption as both "not-yet-happened" and "yet to happen" (p. 250). The Psalm gives voice to the world and to the community in words of praise and thanks. In Psalm 19, we hear the world speak: "The Heavens declare the glory of God and the sky declares his handiwork." Rosenzweig argues that even when the Psalm speaks in the voice of the individual that voice represents the whole community. And the central task of the Psalm is to praise God. "Therefore I will give thanks unto you, O God. And will sing praises unto your name" (Psalm 18:50). The great temple and then the synagogue provide space for these voices to come together liturgically and harmonize in what Rosenzweig calls the *"Gemeinsamkeit des Gesanges,"* the "community of the chant" (p. 232). The community of the chant provides the unity of the human soul and world under God that will occur in the future redemption. In the Hallel service, Rosenzweig finds a kind of theatre of the future redemption in which the unity of world, human soul and God is dramatized and performed. Since the future is known only in anticipation and waiting, the Hallel provides a modality of waiting for redemption in which redemption is enacted. The culminating refrain of the Hallel in Psalm 118, "Praise God for he is good" provides a responsive refrain to the theme words of Genesis 1: *"ki tov,"* "it is good." In redemption, all realize that the goodness of creation is an outgrowth of the goodness of God. Rosenzweig suggests that we understand this answering refrain as a conclusion: "For he is good," or "Because he is good." God is praised because he loves the human and ensouls her. God is praised

---

T&T Clark, 2005). See also R. A. Markus, *Signs and Meanings: World and Text in Ancient Christianity* (Liverpool: Liverpool University Press, 1996); Brian Stock, *Augustine the Reader: Meditation, Self-Knowledge, and the Ethics of Interpretation* (Cambridge, Mass.: Belknap Press of Harvard University Press, 1996); and Randi Rashkover, "Cultivating Theology: Overcoming America's Skepticism about Religious Rationality," *Cross Currents* 55:2.

because he created and revealed. He is to be praised because he redeems. And he redeems because he is good.

Where Psalms 113 through 117 of the Hallel celebrate creation of the world in the past and the revelation of God's love in the present, Rosenzweig sees Psalm 118 as an anticipation of a future redemption. Indeed, the most important role of liturgy for Rosenzweig is to point toward and enact the future redemption. Liturgy for Rosenzweig is finally a theater of the redeemed which is full of harmony, opulence, and celestial images. Unlike most of rabbinic literature which eschews theology and is dominated by legal discussion, Jewish liturgy is full of God language and direct theological address. In contrast to Jewish historical experience which is full of suffering, liturgy is full of joy. Where the yeshiva or school environment encourages Jews to argue, dispute, and disagree, liturgical theater requires singing in unison and ordered refrain. The stage direction of liturgy requires decorum and respect. At the peak moment of praying the central prayer of all worship services, in the *kedushah* or holiness section of the *Amidah* (standing prayer), worshippers are instructed to rise up on their toes to mimic the actions of the angels when they acknowledge God's holiness. Given the rest of Jewish experience, it may seem almost comical to have Jews taking on the behaviors of angels. Rosenzweig's answer to the curious harmony and celestial quality of Jewish liturgy is that at its height liturgy is truly not of this world. It is intended to take place after time, after redemption, in the time of eternity. Thus, in Rosenzweig's view, liturgy intends to cross over the ultimate temporal barrier that Augustine established in the opening of chapter 11 of the *Confessions,* the barrier between time and eternity.

In the culminating chant of Psalm 118 of the Hallel, worshippers are thus looking back from eternity to redemption. In this time, all humans and the world enchant the "root-sentence of redemption" (p. 231), *Adonai ki tov.* God is good. With the union of "the voice of the human soul" with "the voice of the world" (p. 232) Rosenzweig says that the liturgy establishes "a great fugue." The purpose of this community is solely to praise, thank, and acknowledge *Ki lolam hasdo* — that the mercy of the Lord endures forever.

PART III

LITURGICAL SCROLLING

Eternity in History: Rolling the Scroll

Robert Gibbs

I will be focusing on an anachronistic practice: rolling the Torah scroll from beginning to end in the course of one year. It is anachronistic, most of all, because today we read books, not scrolls, and no one makes a liturgy of turning the pages of a book. (The computer age, ironically, has taught us all how to scroll again.) Because it is normal practice for Jews to pray with a prayerbook and to read even those prayers that are well-known, the *reading* of the scroll itself is not our focus. And the clue that I will offer here is that we are looking at the reading or narrating process, and not primarily at the narrated events. It is as though the *way* we tell the historical events, the process of rolling a scroll and reading in sequence, is the key to our experience of history.

And ultimately, the question that orients me in this essay is the question of how history matters for our vision of eternity. My focus is on Jewish liturgy and Franz Rosenzweig's interpretation of those practices in his magnum opus, *The Star of Redemption*. I am sure you have heard the old saws: That Judaism "invented" linear history and that earlier cultures knew only circular time; or, oppositely, that Judaism dwells in a timeless space beyond history, immune to historical slings and arrows. Rosenzweig, by the way, is normally associated with the latter position. The topic, moreover, smacks of the most basic metaphysical sort of question: How does eternity relate to history? The answer here lies not in a configuration of concepts or ideas, but in a liturgical practice, rolling a scroll. The challenge is to live in time in a different fashion, to think about lived time as a place where eternity enters history. Our point of departure, however, is to revise our approach to these terms. Time is not primarily a present moment, but is extended and dislocated in favor of a future. Eternity is not an object of thought, nor is history a sequence of events given in objective time. Rather, time arises and is structured through social practices — temporality is a social performance. Eternity, then, will also be a specific mode of social interaction. And history, too, is never independent from the practices of narrating history.

In Rosenzweig's work the study of liturgy arises as a dramatic and important departure from two previous stages of study: first, thinking; and second, speech-thinking. That is, he turns to liturgy as a medium for exploring the truth in ways that he could not access by studying either how we think or how we speak to each other. While thought is in its own way timeless, speech-thinking takes time very seriously. I have to await your answer to my question, and my own response to you takes time. The way that our relations with others take time offers us important insight into how we live in time, insight unavailable to thinking that has as its subject logical and mathematical relations. But if time is required to have a conversation or to sing together, as time is required to tell a story, then what further addition to our temporality can we gain from the study of liturgy? (Alternatively, if we study rabbinic and scriptural texts in textual reasoning, what will we gain in liturgical reasoning?)

What speech-thinking is unable to deliver is a way for eternity to enter into our temporality, and the fruit of that entrance is visionary — it is a glimpse of God, or at least of the configuration of relations with God. Rosenzweig also writes of this third part of his work as the verification of what we experience in speech-thinking. By that he is not offering a matter of confirmation, but rather a making true of the world, of humanity and of our relations with God. That is, in the communal practice the community "rights" or "trues" itself and the world, and in truing the cosmos, the community sees the truth. At the first level, then, we need communal liturgy in order to right our cosmos, to see beyond our speaking experience — to enact redemption. At the second level, however, we need to study liturgy, and not just ways of speaking, because the sociological dimension of communal practices can show something about the full sociality of temporality and about the promise that certain forms of sociality can envision redemption, eternalizing our temporal existence.

The Hour: Repetition and the Social Production of Time

Again, what concerns us here is not how we experience time in speech, but rather how we construct our social temporality. If eternity enters time, then it enters by becoming a change in our temporality — a change from the passing on and away of the moment and also from the sequence past–present–future. Not only is our time not lived as disconnected seconds, as uniform mathematic units, but it is not simply the flight of the arrow, the flow of the river.

Societies build temporal structures, in part to resist that passing away or flight of time. Society discovers rhythm, that is, repetitions. Rosenzweig understands temporal repetition by looking at the notion of the hour (*die Stunde* in German), because not only does the hour repeat, but it has discursive extension, that is, it lasts a while, and then repeats. The alternatives are: (1) a kind of eternity that lasts forever, or is not in time at all, (2) a temporality of moments that are sheer instants, one after another; and (3) a sequence of repeating instants, each disconnected from its neighbors. Perhaps we can recognize the hour as fidelity to narrativity, but Rosenzweig would add that truth itself takes time, and an instant or even a string of repeating instants does not allow time to extend. Hence, the clock, and later the calendar, are ways for time to run a course, and yet not to run off. Closing the circle allows truth to occur, whereas an incessant banging of repetitive instants allows only for some merely instantaneous truth.

Rosenzweig writes in the introduction to Part III of the *Star,*

> The new we seek must be a *nunc stans,* not a vanishing moment thus, but a standing one. Such a standing now is called, in contrast to the moment, an hour [*Stunde*]. Because it is standing, the hour can already contain within itself the multiplicity of old and new, the fullness of moments. Its end can discharge back into its beginning, because it has a middle, indeed many middle moments between its beginning and its end. With beginning, middle, and end it can become that which the mere sequence of individual and ever new moments never can, a recoiling circle. In itself it can now be full of moments and yet ever equal to itself again. When an hour is up, there begins not only "a new" hour, much as a new moment relieves the old one. Rather, there begins 'again an' hour. This re-commencement, however would not be possible for the hour if it were merely a sequence of moments — such as it indeed is in its middle. It is possible only because the hour has beginning and end. Only the striking of the bells establishes the hour, not the ticking of the pendulum. For the hour is a wholly human institution. (pp. 322-23/290)[1]

Perhaps most interesting here is the sense of beginning, middle, and end. Middle is what gives body to time, what allows something to happen (indeed, the matter of truth); but by coinciding beginning and end allow the cycle to

---

1. Parenthetical citations throughout this essay are to Franz Rosenzweig, first the German, then the equivalent English; all translations, however, are mine. *Der Stern der Erlösung,* in *Franz Rosenzweig: Der Mensch und sein Werk: Gesammelte Schriften,* Vol. 2 (The Hague: Martinus Nijhoff, 1979). Translated by William W. Hallo as *The Star of Redemption* (Boston: Beacon Press, 1971).

recycle, to repeat itself again. Each hour is the same story, and not just one identical instant. Humanity creates the hour, overcoming the flight of time, and producing a temporality that already partakes of eternity. Countable time is not, then, the same as mathematical, homogeneous time. For the latter is perhaps derived from social time, but social time is built out of differences within the hour. Think of any hour spent in a class or, even worse, in a lecture and how time is lived in such disparate shapes and qualities.

The Week: Redemption and Justice for All

In an even more bold manner, the week structures our experience of time because on the seventh day we stop our work. Here the end bears a specific mark of reflection, of completion, and is not just a transition to a new start. Rosenzweig accepts Hermann Cohen's reading, which emphasizes the social justice dimension of the Shabbat (contained in the Deuteronomy version of the commandment). The week is the "hour" of humanity — the repetition that has extension and allows our time to lead eternity into time.

> Thus the week with its day of rest is the proper sign of human freedom. Scripture thus explains the sign by its purpose and not its basis. The week is the true "hour" of all the times of the common human life, posited for people alone, set free from the orbit of the earth and thus altogether law for the earth and the changing times of its service. . . . But how then does the power to force eternity to accept the invitation reside in prayer? . . . Because time which is prepared for the visit of eternity is not the individual's time, not mine, yours or his secret time: it is everyone's time. Day, week, year belong to everyone in common, are grounded in the world's orbit of the earth which patiently bears them all and in the law of labor on earth which is common to all. The clock's chiming of the hour is for every ear. The time that the cult prepares is for no one without all of the others. . . . (pp. 324-25/291)

Rest is the first key feature of this new "hour." Rest signifies completion and freedom — that people are not to be reduced to laborers. Here the temporal cycle comes to its end in a moment without a future task, without the imperfection of an ongoing project. Second, the Shabbat extends this rest to all the people in the community (including women and slaves, and even including animals) — and so signifies a profound equality or redemption of all. Moreover, we have a chiming clock (a public time) that is the mark of the inclusivity. Public time, thus, is quite different from scientific time — and the time that is everyone's allows everyone the vision of the end. Indeed, the vision of redemption is a common vision, and so must be one of ultimate completion of the end of time, of universal redemption.

So if the hour allows the cycling of temporality in the first stage of overcoming first the incessant identical instants of mathematical time, and then the existential flowing on and off of time, then the week creates the experience of universal redemption — at least one might rather say the experience of the vision of that temporality. The week is an invention, a social construction, and all of our temporality depends on its pattern — work and rest. Beginning, middle, and end. But the end is now a vision of the ultimate end: of humanity redeemed together.

Rosenzweig has moved in the study of lived temporality beyond the speech-thinking of past-present-future, creation-revelation-redemption. Both the social reality (communal, public time) and the level of awareness that is a vision of a redeemed world exceed the experience of speaking and singing together. Here is a proleptic messianic moment used to punctuate our temporality: not a mere disconnection or interruption, but rather an ever-turning wheel or cycle that leads to completion as well as to beginning again. Yet the social reality of that temporality is not produced merely by taking a day off; instead, there is a practice of praying together.

The Year: Liturgy and Rolling the Scroll

Indeed, we are almost at the place where we can see the specific contribution of liturgy, and specifically of the odd practice of rolling the scroll. While the hour may be prevalent in various cultures, and even the notion of the week is not exclusive to the Jews, the Shabbat service is a distinctly Jewish practice. Rosenzweig's own argument in interpreting liturgy is to focus on the way that each stage of practices instigates the sequence creation–revelation–redemption. He argues that the liturgies create common consciousness of the sequence (and the cycle) of temporality, pointing forward in the vision of the end.

The Jewish year itself is created from weeks (as well as months). And while a year seems a natural and thus a universal unit of temporality, the year built from weeks is built out of Sabbaths, out of a sequence of both identical and somehow differentiated weeks. For Rosenzweig, the key to that differentiation is that the Sabbaths each have their own portion of the Torah. Over the length of one year, the Torah is read from beginning to end. (There are various ancillary readings, as well as special readings for special days, and there are also traditions of triennial Torah readings, but the most common practice today is the annual cycle which serves as the backbone of public reading of the Torah.) The weeks thus have their own portion of Torah, different from last week's and from next's, but also the same as last year's week at this time.

Rosenzweig writes:

> . . . In which the spiritual year is grounded, the recurrence in its recurrence, of the Sabbath. In the cycle of weekly portions, which in the course of one year, run through the whole of the Torah, the spiritual year is paced out, and the paces of this course are the Sabbaths. By and large, every Sabbath is like every other, but the change in the portions of Scripture distinguishes each from each, and this lets us know that there is not a last portion, but that they are only individual parts of a higher order, of the year. For in the year the individual parts first again fuse into a whole. The Sabbath bestows existence [*Dasein*] on the year. This existence must be recreated week by week. The spiritual year must always completely begin in the weekly portions of the running week. It knows, so to speak, only what is found in this week's portion, but it will become a year first through that, so that each week is only a fleeting moment. It is first in the course of Sabbaths that the year rounds to a garland. The very regularity in the course of the Sabbaths, the very fact that, aside from the weekly portions, one Sabbath is just like the other makes them the *cornerstones* of the year. (pp. 344/310)

If the hour is a story of beginning, middle, and end, and the week is a story that leads to a completion, then a year must be a yet longer story, made up, again, of many middles, as well as an end that turns again into a beginning. To structure the middles is the task of the cycle of Shabbats, or rather the cycle of Shabbat readings. For like the hours, each week is the same as every other — except through the sequence of Torah portions. With that sequence, we not only receive the narrative (and law, and poetry) that constitutes the whole of the Torah, we also become aware of the year in which our social temporality is lived. Our year is a human re-creation of the natural, and the act of signifying the year as meaningful, by which we make living the year as year explicit, is a sequence of public readings. Hence, the year is formed as a whole through this practice of moving through a sequence of portions.

A comment by Rosenzweig, however, refocuses us on the reality of the scroll in the liturgy.

> Only cultic objects, once formed, oppose every variation of their form; they are just no longer things like other things; they have become, as daring as the expression sounds, "living objects." The Torah and the Scroll of Esther are the only ancient books preserved till today exactly in their ancient form;

but through this rigorously preserved form, a Torah scroll is no longer a regular object. One might say, that the feelings associated with such a parchment scroll are more personal or at least equally as alive as those with what is in it. (pp. 396/357)

While the context of this comment is the way that an object through its liturgical use becomes both invariable and also a focus of distinctive feelings, what we wish to pause to notice here is the emphasis on the scroll *as scroll*. The scroll becomes a focus of feeling, and even vision, precisely as scroll, as a transformation of the object. But what strikes one here is the preference for the scroll over the text within it. The materiality, or perhaps the scroll-ness, of the Torah is the focus. And what is it that makes a scroll different from a book: that it is rolled and unrolled.

Thus we are at the very center of this paper: where we can look at the practice of rolling the scroll. Because the scroll is long, it is divided for its reading into portions. They are a course, a path, and they are rolled through in the time of a year. The narrative is built on the portions of Torah read, week by week, that make a year of the scroll. And at the end of the year, the scroll must be re-rolled. The rolling and re-rolling of the Torah is the image of this circle of our reading. Thus rolling the scroll (or if you prefer the computer verb, *scrolling*) is the time that is the performance of eternity. It always begins again, even when it has just finished. A year is the narrating time, just long enough to tell the story of the Torah. The time it takes to read through the scroll is the measure of the year.

The portion that is read, week by week, determines the year. But the actual public reading is performed during services, and the most important of these is the Shabbat morning service. Our central text is the following:

... in the morning [Shabbat service], is the consciousness of the chosenness of the People through the giving of the Torah and the consciousness that in this giving occurs the planting of eternal life in its midst. With the former (the consciousness of the chosenness), the one called up steps out of the congregation up to the book of revelation, with this one (the consciousness of eternal life), he turns his back to it and plunges again into the congregation. With this consciousness of eternal life, however, he crosses the threshold which distinguishes revelation, like creation, from redemption, even within Shabbat. (pp. 346-47/312)

Rosenzweig is citing two blessings, each recited by an individual in the midst of being called up to read the Torah scroll. Before reading the weekly portion of the Torah, the scroll itself is paraded through the congregation, and there are special songs and prayers that mark off this specific event. Then, usually, one person actually reads out the text from the scroll, and another oversees the reading. That overseer is granted a special honor and is called up out of the congregation to recite two blessings, one before and one after.

Before the reading the one who is called up recites:

> Blessed are you, Adonai our God, Ruler of the Universe, who has chosen us from all the peoples and given us his Torah. Blessed are you, Adonai, giver of the Torah.

And after the reading that same person says:

> Blessed are you, Adonai our God, Ruler of the Universe, who has given us the true Torah and implanted within us eternal life. Blessed are you, Adonai, giver of the Torah.

In our passage, Rosenzweig is interpreting this sequence; and while the first blessing produces the consciousness of being chosen, the second one offers the consciousness of eternal life. This latter blessing is cited by Rosenzweig five times. It is both his introduction to the book on eternal life, and its concluding sentence. It takes a prominent place in the final section of the whole *Star,* the Gate. It is the key to the most radical claim about eternity he makes: that the Jews have eternal life. To indicate the stakes of this notion for Rosenzweig: at the center of the star of redemption burns a fire, a fire of eternal life. The whole grand scheme of the work depends on this eternity of life, an eternal life, that is implanted within the Jewish community. But no claim has been more disturbing, because it seems blatantly dogmatic, exclusionary, metaphysical, and ethically dangerous. Only the Jews have eternal life. It means that they are immune to world history.

My strategy is not to regard Rosenzweig's claims about eternal life based on this blessing as a metaphysical dogma, but rather to think through the liturgical practice which requires this recitation in order to understand just what Rosenzweig invokes in exploring the concept of eternal life. The implanting of eternal life refers to the giving of the Torah — that is, the giving of the Torah is the way in which eternal life is implanted. But even that can quickly become a dogma, so let us take it one more step: The implanting of eternal life transpires in the weekly reading and rolling of the Torah. The two blessings bracket the practice of reading from the scroll, hence the consciousness of eternal life occurs in that action. In the first blessing, a person experience election as an elevation, a moment of being singled out to receive Torah.

But in the second blessing the person becomes part of the redemptive community, aware of eternal life as implanted in the giving of the law.

This choreography and liturgy makes the rolling of the scroll, the procession through the scroll, week-by-week, the key practice of eternalizing time. By proclaiming these blessings, the one called up announces to the community that eternity is implanted in the performance of this liturgical practice. But the rolling of the scroll itself performs the cycling that is a symbol of eternality.

The Torah as Recounted History

The question that we need to reconsider, however, is, *What is the text that is read?* The portions of Torah do not lead up to the present time. This is not a *New York Times* bestseller that explains, say, how the U.S. got into Iraq. The story told is the "history" of the world up to the Patriarchs and Matriarchs, and then through the birth of the nation (drawn forth through the waters), the giving of the law, the wandering in the desert, and preparation for entering into the promised land. We know that that story is "our" story, but we are not the characters in it. It is set, even within its textual development, as a history of what happened long ago. The story told does not connect with the time of its telling — neither of the inscription nor of our own time. Indeed, the story told does not lead continuously into the time of the editing of the Torah, or if you are more traditional, to the time of its first public reading under Ezra.

Surely this account of the history of the world up through the birth of the Israelite nation works as a kind of history because it is unwilling to collapse the distance between its listeners/readers and the events being told. It is not merely that we now perceive a gap between us moderns and this ancient text: the text itself is built on a gap of time, one that is not bridged by the story. Rosenzweig's incessant insistence on reading Jewish holidays as following the sequence creation–revelation–redemption, shows that the cycling in *our* calendar has within it a cycle of a history of past events, events held in their pastness. Our cycle is experienced as weeks of portions of an earlier story — itself rolled up in a scroll. The way we experience eternity is not by a collapse of this historical gap. Rather, each year Noah survives the flood and later Israel crosses the sea on dry land, and each year it seems to be not about us (located in its narrative) and yet we participate in eternity by listening to it each year. That it takes a year to read the scroll, gives it a certain kind of narrativity, each station on the cycle has its own story, law, genealogy, etc., has its own bit of Torah, that itself is perplexing.

Noah survives year after year in the same week. Does it mean the same thing to us, year after year? No, of course not. But we do not substitute some other event (World War I), for instance. Always the same text at the same season, whatever is happening to us. Whatever has happened since last year. (Because what has "happened" is we have read to the end of Deuteronomy, re-rolled the scroll, and are preparing again for the going forth from Egypt.) The weekly portion is the template of our time, even though there is no connection.

But perhaps we have not quite grasped the Torah's own temporality. For the events that happen there are not governed by necessity but by freedom, and told by a specific kind of discontinuity. Hardly a chronicle, the Torah's sequence follows construction principles that I cannot begin to describe here. What we do see, however, is that people speak, and they act, and they are surprised by events. Perhaps they are even more surprised than we, because we have read the story just last year. But though our sequence of reading is fixed, our own lives are not governed by a necessity.

Historiography as Messianic Activity

The Hegelian historiography that Rosenzweig rebelled against was one of world-historical necessity. When Rosenzweig says the Jews are eternal, or rather have eternal life implanted within them, he is saying at least, that they do not participate in the dialectics and the necessities of world-history. For many people, this has meant that Rosenzweig thinks that Jews and Judaism have no history of any sort. But considering the cycling of the scroll, the lived temporality of a calendar, we might release Rosenzweig from this prison.

Jews experience their eternality, the eternal life, by reading each year the same portion, a portion which always has its own discontinuities within it and its sense of contingency. That reading alerts us to see our present moment as also one that is not fated or governed by the sway of world-history. Whether we are in Babylon, or Spain, under emperors, kings, or even President Bush, we persist in seeing our own time as bound to a template that resists a reduction to necessity. The Torah portion promises change and justice — and it does not stop short of criticizing the practices and ideas of its narrated time. Indeed, one can consult biblical historians who recognize the concerns of the redactors, and see the Torah text itself criticizing the prevalent ideas and practices at the time of its editing. The Torah portion breaks the spell of our present moment, and so makes us free due to the discontinuity between our own moment and the moment of which we read.

A discontinuous narrative, of criticism and of the demand for justice, told over the time of a year, produces a lived temporality in which discontinuity is recognizable. This is a temporality that is eternal precisely because the intrusion of the messianic demand for justice structures the week-by-week construction of the long story of the year. Progress is neither impossible nor inexorable, and the history of the world-epochs around us defines neither our times nor our moral compass. As Lévinas would claim interpreting Rosenzweig, being eternal means not being judged by history but being able to judge history.[2]

Standing in judgment of history, however, also offers insight into a final stage of the practice of rolling the scroll, because in Jewish practice each portion of Torah is matched to a second portion from the Bible, and this second portion is read publicly as the *haftarah*. This practice is not discussed by Rosenzweig, and so we are now extending his interpretation of lived time and eternal vision. While the first set of cycles is the cycle of the year as rolling the scroll (imagine it on the outside), and a cycle of portions of Torah in a large narrative frame from Creation to preparing to enter the Land (imagine it as an inner circle); there is inserted between the two cycles also an intermediary cycle. Originally, the rabbinic sages set up a triennial cycle of Torah passages, and early in the common era, the rabbis of Palestine established a series of secondary readings that matched the Torah portions. Those secondary readings came from the part of the Bible called Prophets [*nevi'im*]. The earlier sages had a marked preference for messianic texts, where they clearly inserted a later text with an end-time vision in order to hold apart the two circles of the Torah's story and of the rolling. Later, the Babylonian rabbis instituted a yearly cycle, and in addition chose the texts that are most familiar to us as the passages for *haftarot*.

A brief look at the set of texts includes a leftover smattering of messianic texts, and a large percentage of what we would probably call historical texts from Joshua, Judges, Samuel, and Kings. Now, what I propose is that we consider these events as a historiographic performance. Historical events from the period after the end of the Torah's narrative are plotted in relation to the Torah itself.

Then what happens to Jewish history, to the events between the narrated events of the Torah and the rollers today? The Bible (Tanakh) provides historical narratives up to the moment of restoration under Cyrus. The historical

---

2. Emmanuel Lévinas, "Between Two Worlds: The Way of Franz Rosenzweig," trans. Séan Hand, in *Difficult Freedom: Essays on Judaism* (Baltimore: Johns Hopkins University Press, 1990), pp. 199-201.

accounts within the Bible disagree on how to interpret the events (the conquest of the land, the institution of the monarchy, the destruction of both Northern and Southern Kingdom, and the exile). The sages, however, chose pieces of these texts to juxtapose, on Shabbat and on holidays, to the inner circle of Torah texts, often insisting on a historical piece to interrupt technical legal matters in the Torah.

I cannot here explore the specific juxtaposition of passages (for instance of the violent going forth from Egypt with Jeremiah's prophecy of Babylonian victory over Egypt) but one cannot help but notice a few things immediately: (1) The historical matters that the sages juxtapose still are distanced by several hundreds of years from the outer circle of the people who will read this cycle of *haftarot*. (2) Those past events are put to the task of reciprocally commenting on the inner circle of Torah texts. (3) That second level of texts often refers to a promise of messianic time — in part as a lever against a simple reading of the Torah text. Hence (4) the historical texts, often originally placed — at a distance — as a moment of criticism, then are institutionalized for a doubling of the gaps and redemptive possibility in relation to both the inner circle of the scroll and the outer circle of the rolling of the scroll.

But perhaps here we should copy a page from Rosenzweig and notice the blessings that are recited before and after reading the *haftarah*. I will look here only at the blessings before:

> Blessed are you, Adonai our God, Ruler of the Universe, who has chosen good prophets and found pleasure in their words, that were said in truth. Blessed are you, Adonai, who chooses Torah, Moses His servant, Israel His people, and prophets of truth and righteousness.

Again, before the reading the focus is on chosenness, but also here we have an emergence of the notion of truth. Truth, I would argue (again with a huge debt to Rosenzweig), arises precisely through the relation of the two cycles. Prophetic truth is the confirmation by a later event of an earlier prophecy. But just how the passage in the *haftarah* "confirms" the previous text is only half of the point. Truth will also extend into the outer circle, the time of the readers, the rollers of the scroll. Indeed, truth is not confirmed because the three line up as simple repetitions of the same event (or confirmation as direct application of the lessons from the Torah). On the contrary, the very opening up of the historical moment to a demand for a messianic justice, a disruption of not just one narrative circle, but of each in turn, is key to the "machine" of rolling. Truth is not adapting or applying an old lesson to our own time, or finding in our time the historical progress toward the messianic future. Truth requires the constellation and discontinuities between and within each cycle, making our own time loosen and unbind — freeing the current situation for a vision of messianic justice.

But this machine is not indifferent to history and its telling; rather, it depends on telling the story both of the Torah and of the latter prophets. We have explored a way of standing outside history. Jewish historiography became a social practice of placing a circle of remembering outside an inner and separated circle of the Torah scroll. In contrast to the book or especially to the encyclopedia of history in Hegel, the scroll, as rolled and read, accentuates the time of remembering, keeping the historian's work of remembering at a distance from what is remembered. That distance is accentuated by interspersing other historical matters, between the circles, not to mediate but to challenge both circles. In this practice *the circle* is not the perfection of unchangeableness, but is, when set within other circles, precisely the possibility for a messianic demand, interrupting both the past as story, and the present as the rolling of the scroll (as telling the story), enacted as a social memory that awaits its messianic future.

Studying Liturgy, Again

As I sat to revise this essay, I found myself lingering over a sense that what I wanted to contribute to this volume would again repeat things I have been exploring and interpreting from Franz Rosenzweig for many years now. I dared myself to persevere on two counts: first, that most readers of this volume will not be devoted readers of my various publications, and second, that indeed, in revising I saw again that I had learned new things in interpreting Rosenzweig. This is utterly appropriate for a scholar — to re-read and see afresh a familiar text, to find in it something new to say for others. But while this lingering seems a bit self-indulgent, it points to a key feature of this essay, and I expect of many of those you will read in this volume: we are engaging in a philosophical or theological exploration of liturgical practice. We are not a community praying together, but a community that speaks and writes to each other about praying together. Many of you did not know Rosenzweig intimately; none of you will be organized as a community that reads my work. Our communal activity is a form of study and conversation that is intrinsically different from the practices we study. That is normal for scholars, but it puts a specific tension between our practice here and its "subject."

If our activity is not identical to the practices we are exploring, is it then necessarily extrinsic? Is there a thinking, a study, that lies within the practices?

Surely there is often a self-consciousness, or a communal consciousness, that is articulated in liturgy — an articulation not only about God and belief, but also about what happens in prayer and other liturgies. If we are not praying together here, it is *not* reciprocally the case that the communities of prayer are not thinking. They are not unaware of the stakes of their own activities. If so, then, we may well see that scholars have greater need for liturgical reasoning (our scholarly practice) than liturgical communities do. It may be that what we discuss here can help deepen or reform liturgical understandings or practices, but the immediate benefit is for us, scholars of religion. Again, it is not that we are doing the thinking that the communities lack — rather they are doing practices that perform awareness that we seem to lack. And here the we is not just a few philosophers and theologians, but rather a wide swath of our academic world.

My own repetitions in this study are different in kind from those I examine in liturgies. And when history can play a vital role in inviting eternity into time, the liturgical use of historiography has little need for the register of reflection I have provided. The liturgy has no need to interpolate another circle of general theory or of philosophy of history. Rather, in contrast to my intervention, the Sages drew historical events into a cycle in order to create tensions between different events and to intensify criticism of what happened — what people have done — in history. The prophets demand justice and stand not against history as a whole, but as judges of particular events, judged in artificial contexts of other events — in order to propel us to be radical in our criticism of the present by beholding a vision of redemption. They could not dispense with the particularity of the past events, even as they forced them into eternalizing repetition.

The cycling readings project into our own reading/rolling moment a sense of breaking up of our time. We achieve eternity in asserting the repetitions of discontinuities, freed from the illusion that our own time is fated, that world-historical necessity dispenses what justice there is. Such a use of history for the opening up of our own future is a vital way to find eternity planted in our midst.

Holy Seeds: The *Trisagion* and the Liturgical Untilling of Time

Ben Quash

Therefore with Angels and Archangels, and with all the company of heaven, we laud and magnify thy glorious Name; evermore praising thee, and saying: Holy, holy, holy, Lord God of hosts, heaven and earth are full of thy glory: Glory be to thee, O Lord most High. Amen.

Book of Common Prayer

Introduction

The threefold *Sanctus* is now at the heart of the eucharistic prayer in virtually every mainstream Christian tradition. In the middle of the most holy prayer (the prayer of consecration), in the middle of the most sacred liturgy (the Eucharist), in the middle of the Christian Church's great cycling round of worship, these three "Holies" ring out — just as (in the form of the *kedushah*) they form a central and daily part of Jewish prayers.

In a Christian Eucharist the build-up to the eucharistic prayer includes confession and absolution of sins, attention to God's word in Scripture and sermon, and intercessory prayer — bringing the needs of a broken world to the altar. Out of this movement of self-examination, of being opened to divine self-communication, and of heightened attention to the natural and human world around them, the worshippers are prepared to "lift up their hearts" to God — and it is this summons to look heavenwards that initiates the eucharistic prayer proper, in a responsorial exchange between priest and people that also includes the recognition that "it is right to give the Lord thanks and praise." The priest then recites the main body of the prayer alone, and after their initial responses the members of the congregation join in again on just two further occasions — the great "Amen" at the conclusion of the prayer, and before that, at a point near the middle of the prayer, the *Sanctus.*

Immediately on either side of the *Sanctus* are recollections: preceding it, the recall of creation and God's great acts of faithfulness and deliverance in history; succeeding it, the recall of the night before Jesus died when he gathered his disciples for a final meal together and instituted the sacrament of the Eucharist. At the end of the prayer, with the invocation of the Holy Spirit having taken place (on the bread and wine, the people, or both), there is an anticipation of the eschatological fulfillment of all things — the uniting of heaven with earth of which the Eucharist is a foretaste.

In many churches, the particular significance of of the *Sanctus* is marked by the fact that priest and people will recite it while bowing reverently. Its specialness is also, perhaps, marked by the fact that its words are some of the few in the context of the prayer that are shared in by the whole gathered congregation, and by the fact that it is often sung (before the priest, resuming the prayer, reverts to ordinary spoken recitation). Some of the most beautiful pieces of church music are settings of the *Sanctus.*

A Christian might ask why the three "Holies" should have this place in the "holy of holies" of Christian liturgy, framed peculiarly as they are in the *anaphora* between the remembrance of God's mighty deeds, and the recounting of the institution narrative of the Last Supper. They do not immediately or obviously connect with what sits on either side of them — in fact they can seem to burst out like an irrepressible charismatic exclamation in the middle of more sober narrative structure. We have no record that Jesus himself used them as he sat at table with his disciples in the upper room. So why are they there? What compelling purpose did they seem to serve such that in the early centuries of the Church's life the *Trisagion* or threefold *Sanctus* sprang up in the heart of a number of eucharistic prayers and then spread until it had general currency from Syria and Egypt to Rome and the Western Empire?

This essay will suggest one answer to the question of what the *Trisagion* does in the eucharistic prayer — most especially, what it does to Christians and their politics; what resources it offers them for their political life. This will eventually lead us right back to its scriptural origins: both the highly and obviously political context in which the Thrice Holy sounds in the last book of the Christian Bible, the Book of Revelation, but also its earlier appearance in the Book of Isaiah. My aim is to show that the *Trisagion* is a holy "seed" that sows itself in the regular round of liturgical anticipation and celebration, and that it makes possible a distinctive and transformative perspective on the objects in which human beings invest value, and the uses to which they put their time in the service of their various projects and goals in the world.

The *Sanctus* and the Ends of the Earth

In the Book of Acts, Jesus' final words before his being taken up to heaven direct the hearers onward and outward: "You will be witnesses for me in Jerusalem, in all Judaea and Samaria, and to the ends of the earth" (1:8). In the two thousand years since then, human beings, Christian disciples or not, have spent much of their time, in many and various ways, trying to get to the ends of the earth — its margins, brinks and extremities. They have done everything they can to get to the bottom of things — and to the top, and to all the furthest edges. They have built roads; they have drilled shafts; they have crossed seas. They have plumbed these same seas to their very depths. Human beings have mapped the galaxy and walked on the moon.

Once upon a time, maps of the world had edges full of wild beasts and sea monsters; such maps had room for magnificent flights of the imagination and testified to the fact that the world had "margins." They thereby acknowledged possibilities that relativized people's usual assumptions about the world they thought they knew. Beyond the edges, beyond even the sea monsters, there was mystery: horizons off which you might fall and never be known of again. Since then, you might say, the world has been gradually shrinking, and as a result the modern person's horizons are not generally what their forebears' were. Modern, Western people do not really believe the earth has ends any more, because we do not really believe that there are limits to our power of access, even when we have to struggle a little bit first to get where we want to be. This tidying up and pinning down of the ends of the earth is attractive to human beings, who do not like the idea of horizons we can fall off. We spend much of our time and energy combatting our fear of edges by increasing our knowledge, power, and territorial conquest. Karl Rahner described this characteristically modern development as follows, when discussing the last two thousand years as the epoch "that saw the beginning of the history of mankind's self-appropriation through deliberate deeds, of history's conscious, active self-heightening":

> in a rapid acceleration, man developed from a being both secure in nature and directly at its mercy to one who inhabits an environment he himself has created, . . . who has transformed his numinous environment into one he

has rationally planned, making it a demythologized building-site for his own plans.[1]

The modern mind rejoices in the idea that the world around us is in our control. We are free to choose what boundaries we will draw for the world we choose to inhabit; free to map out the invented ends of the earth which we substitute for the former ones we seem to have eliminated. We are the masters of our own horizons, and these horizons are therefore always in principle revisable by us at will. They are not real ends of the earth; they are a game we play with ourselves. All the time, under the surface, we know that we have eliminated any real horizon to human expansion and control. We have fulfilled all that Jesus' parting words seemed to envision for us.

And yet this is exactly where the eucharistic *Sanctus* and its scriptural background in the visions of Isaiah and the seer of Revelation (whose visions we will look at shortly) show that we have missed the point. Because the *Sanctus*'s reminder to us of the heavenly courts and the supremacy of God *opens up* this self-enclosure, and announces to us an earth which has ends, boundaries and limits.

The *Sanctus* shows (and in this respect it is a counterpart to the *sursum corda* with which the eucharistic prayer begins — the point at which the worshippers' hearts are "lifted up" to the heavenly places) that the earth that we think we know has limits, and limits which it does not set for itself. It has limits which *God* sets. They are limits where God stands *beyond* as well as within the world; as its free creator; free to hide or reveal himself; free to ascend or descend beyond its furthest extremes. The *Sanctus* asks us to see the earth we thought we knew with fresh eyes, as under the lordship of its Creator and Redeemer, who has all dominion and power over it and the lives of mortal beings within it. It shows that there is a horizon we cannot eliminate — the most real and important of any horizon; the earth's realest end-point: the point where divine and human encounter one another. The Christian conviction is that life not oriented to *this* end is life not oriented at all.

This is our starting point: a point about the earth's limits in relation to the limitlessness of the divine freedom which constitutes the earth and gives it its definite possibilities. I now want to develop this point, to show how this relativisation of the earth's claims to self-mastery (a relativisation accom-

---

1. Karl Rahner, *Grundkurs des Glaubens: Einführung in den Begriff des Christentums* (Freiburg: Herder, 1976), p. 172; translation by Graham Harrison in Hans Urs von Balthasar, *Theo-Drama: Theological Dramatic Theory*, vol. IV, *The Action* (San Francisco: Ignatius Press, 1994), p. 438.

plished by the positive affirmation of the One who made it and will judge and redeem it) need not be seen as a denigration of the earth's possibilities, but can be the most truthful and positive way to affirm the earth *as well*. Because truthful, it can offer the best resources for living non-self-destructively in this world.

The *Trisagion* will help to show this, for it points the worshipper who utters it beyond the ends of the earth, and combats those ideologies which thirst for an impossibly total control of the social and natural world, and especially control of time. The *Trisagion*, used in worship as it is in the Christian eucharistic prayer, has an immense power of political resistance with genuine contemporary implications. In the following section, we go first to Scripture, however, to see its worshipful use not specifically in the Eucharist, but in the vision of the Book of Revelation, from which point it can nonetheless illuminate and inspire the weekly or even daily time Christians give to the tending of this seed.

Thrice-Holy, Slain, and Enthroned

> *After this I looked, and behold, a door standing open in heaven! And the first voice, which I had heard speaking to me like a trumpet, said, "Come up here, and I will show you what must take place after this." At once I was in the Spirit, and behold, a throne stood in heaven, with one seated on the throne. And he who sat there had the appearance of jasper and carnelian, and around the throne was a rainbow that had the appearance of an emerald. Around the throne were twenty-four thrones, and seated on the thrones were twenty-four elders, clothed in white garments, with golden crowns on their heads. From the throne came flashes of lightning, and rumblings and peals of thunder, and before the throne were burning seven torches of fire, which are the seven spirits of God, and before the throne there was as it were a sea of glass, like crystal.*
>
> *And around the throne, on each side of the throne, are four living creatures, full of eyes in front and behind: the first living creature like a lion, the second living creature like an ox, the third living creature with the face of a man, and the fourth living creature like an eagle in flight. And the four living creatures, each of them with six wings, are full of eyes all around and within, and day and night they never cease to say,*
>
> *"Holy, holy, holy, is the Lord God Almighty,*
> *who was and is and is to come!" (Revelation 4)*

In the Christian liturgical year, in the aftermath of the feast of the Ascension, the New Testament takes us up into heaven to witness a vision of extraordinary proportions. The divine throne is exposed at the very center of the heavenly circle of worship. Around the throne are the four living creatures and the twenty-four elders, representing the prayers and praises of the saints. They are singing what the Book of Revelation calls a "new song" — it is a song about Christ — and this song is taken up with variations by millions and millions of angels, and finally by the whole creation in heaven and on earth, and under the earth, and in the sea.

The early Christian person or people who experienced and recorded this apocalyptic vision were giving an answer to one of the questions of a lifetime: "To whom does the sovereignty of the world belong?" It is a question in response to which most people find themselves taking up some sort of position, even if their answer is only given somehow implicitly. The position that the Book of Revelation takes is beyond doubt: the earth is the Lord God's, and all that is in it. A huge price has been paid by God to preserve it: "by his *blood*," as the lesson puts it, "Jesus Christ has ransomed us for God."

The Book of Revelation made its claim, "The earth is the Lord's," against all appearances to the contrary. It made its claim in the brazen face of Roman imperial power, which straddled the whole world, and ruled people of "every tribe and tongue and people and nation," all of whom had to bow down to the emperor. The imperial claim was a claim to have absolute worldly authority. The Christians resisted the claim. And for this the Romans despised them and at intervals ruthlessly extinguished them. In the year 113 the governor Pliny reported to the Emperor Trajan that the Christians were meeting before sunrise, pledging themselves to refrain from theft, murder, and adultery, pledging not to break faith or loyalty, but more than this — despicably — they were worshipping Christ as God. We may imagine, perhaps, that they used songs like those we find in the text from Revelation:

> Worthy art thou to take the scroll and to open its seals, for thou wast slain and by thy blood didst ransom men for God . . . , and hast made men a kingdom and priests to our God, and they shall reign on earth. (5:9-10)

These people worshipped Christ — the provincial victim of a criminal execution — instead of bowing down to the emperor. The Romans were disgusted. And this is why the Book of Revelation is a deeply subversive, countercultural document. The acclamations of large numbers of people of every class, and the elders' acts of prostration, deliberately recall the honors that should be — and normally were — given to the Roman emperor. The seer shows these honors being offered to God and the Lamb.

It is not surprising, then, that on Pliny's orders — and those of many other governors like him — lapsed Christians had to show their true repentance by paying respect to images of the emperor and by cursing Christ. Many others were killed for *refusing* to do so. They died rather than commit idolatry — the worship of idols, which is bowing down to anything or anyone other than God.

The right attribution of holiness — on which both the song in Revelation and the *Sanctus* in Christian (and Jewish) liturgy insist — makes clear the political dimensions of the utterance of those three "Holies." As I indicated before, all people by their actions, their solidarities and their commitments take up some sort of position in relation to the question: "To whom does the sovereignty of the world belong?" To say "Holy, Holy, Holy" to the Lord God of Israel, to the God of Jesus Christ, is to take up a position with very definite features. It is to resist worship of anything less than the one true God as he is manifest in these Jewish and Christian traditions.

Our contemporary world is one in which millions and millions of people, of every tribe and tongue and people and nation, are prostrating themselves before an object of worship which they all have in common, and to which they sing passionately and wholeheartedly: "Worthy art thou!" The vision of the whole world united in worship is realized today as it has never been before. But it is the dark inverse of the vision of Revelation, because the loudest and most unified voices are not singing the praise of the Lamb with wounds of self-giving love — the wounds which are signs of a life lived for others, a love that embraced even death. The loudest voices praise the full flowering of a global market, which increases its grip from day to day, exerting its strength even now (as Nicholas Boyle has pointed out) through the proliferating tendrils of cables, television channels, and interconnected computers.[2]

Since 1945, writes Boyle, the economic interconnection of all human beings across the whole surface of the planet, "on earth, and under the earth, and in the sea," as Revelation might put it, has brought about "a shift, deep down, in the way we think about ourselves and our cultural and ethical activities."[3] Since 1945, the development of the global market has become the most overriding of economic facts. This cannot but have major implications for each individual. If we are paid in money, or in any of the market's products,

---

2. Nicholas Boyle, "Hegel and 'The End of History,'" *New Blackfriars* 76:891 (1995), 112.
3. Boyle, "Hegel and 'The End of History,'" 113.

we will eventually and inevitably, so it seems, be subjected to "the rule of participation in the market." Our activities — this is the rule of the market — will "be quantified, . . . broken down into measurable units, comparable with the units into which the behaviour of others, anywhere in the world, has [also] been broken down." We will be allowed "no standing in this new world order . . . that is not transparently related to [our] performance indicator, [our] input-output ratio." Meanwhile, as Boyle goes on to say, "[m]ore or less gradually every non-quantifiable . . . element" will find itself "leached out of the system of exchange." A shared day of rest, for example — once valued highly for the solidarity it represented, for being a collective acknowledgement of the Sabbath grace which makes possible all our endeavors — is now coming to be "redefined as a free lunch," which must be "paid for further down the line by somebody else."[4]

There used to be diverse ways of defining *who we are*. But now those who look for jobs enter a market in which the demand for accountability is reducing that diversity to what, following Boyle, we may call:

> [the] uniformity of different calculations in the same currency of somebody's costed time. . . . The concept of a vocation, of a job — or task — for life, that defines a large part of what a person is, loses its value, and is actively persecuted. We may still say "she is a printer," "he is a teacher" but what we mean, and what in future we shall increasingly say, is, "she is doing some printing, at the moment," "he is on a three-year teaching contract."[5]

Everyone and every activity in our society is now multiply and precisely quantified and valued: "productivity, efficiency, performance, cost/benefit . . . , credit and audience ratings, popularity polls." There has never been a world order which "knew so precisely what it valued and how much." And, as Boyle concludes, it is the market that is now the real repository of value and of truth.[6]

This is idolatry on a breathtaking scale. To quote Nicholas Lash, it is "the apparently final victory of what Karl Marx deplored as the 'universalization of the commodity form,' with price the only value and pleasure the only goal." And some of its most lurid effects are all too easy to see: "the degeneration of cities all over the world into wildernesses of poverty and squalor punctuated by fortresses of wealth; . . . the rape of non-renewable resources for short-term gain; . . . and, as the global context of it all, the cries of dying children in

---

4. Boyle, "Hegel and 'The End of History,'" 115.
5. Boyle, "Hegel and 'The End of History,'" 116.
6. Boyle, "Hegel and 'The End of History,'" 117.

that larger part of humankind whose subordination to our flourishing we sanitise with reference to 'our markets.'"[7]

The call of the *Trisagion,* seeded as it is in the vision of Revelation and in the regularity of the eucharistic liturgy, is a call to sing a "new song," and to live differently. Christians hear the call, both in passages of Scripture and in their amplification in the eucharistic liturgy, to respond in worship to the holy God, and thereby to be a holy people. If a person heeds this call, God promises vindication. He promises to restore his adulterous people to that joyful, innocent condition they knew long ago when they were the virgin spouse of God. He will rebuild Jerusalem. The Book of Revelation, like Isaiah before it, celebrates this promise.

Yet if Jerusalem is to be established again, watchmen are needed for the walls. "Watchmen," as it says in Isaiah, who "shall not be silent"; watchmen for "all of the day and for all of the night" (Isa. 62:6). God's will to restore people to freedom before him, to overturn the idols, needs people who will use their voices to sing his new song. God calls for confessors "who cannot keep silent but must speak of him; who commit themselves to his honour with clear and definite words; who are serviceable to him in and with these words; who are his declared and decided partisans."[8] These people alone will be privileged to learn the new song; and when they have learned it, they will have a voice given to them, and the task of using this voice, so that it may be heard for the sake of a wholly renewed world.

People make decisions about what to do with their lives, and these decisions are important to God and to their fellow human beings. People take up positions, and must judge whether theirs is the position of one who watches on the walls of Zion. Some people decide that the best witness is done from "the inside," by the influencing of the internal structures of the merchant banks, the management consultancies, the city law firms, or whatever. But the sheer power and extent of the idolatry are all too easy to underestimate, and it will take more than a little effort to resist it. And there are plenty of modern-day Plinys waiting to enforce the claims of the idols, and so to encourage us — implicitly — to curse the Lord. Meanwhile, some people assemble their own personal lifestyle from a range of so-called "alternative values" — a bit of environmentalism here, a touch of New Age spirituality there — and in this way seek to distance themselves from the dominance of materialism. But this way too risks a continuing entrapment in the ideology of the market by be-

---

7. Nicholas Lash, "Crisis and Tradition in *Veritatis Splendor,*" in *Studies in Christian Ethics* 7:2 (1994), 22.

8. Karl Barth, *Church Dogmatics* III.4 (Edinburgh: T&T Clark, 1961), p. 75.

ginning and ending with individual choice. Nicholas Boyle points this out. "The moral world, like the material world, [becomes] supremely represented as a shopping mall." It is now possible to stroll between the shelves and pick out whatever takes our fancy:

> [I]n this emporium of pluralism we can have what we want, and it is politically incorrect — that is, a restrictive, anti-market practice — to suggest that some commodities should not be put on sale.[9]

But "the good is not something that we *choose* to acknowledge; it is something that we *have* to acknowledge."[10] And a true value — the worthy object of our worship — is not something we have opted for; it is something that has claimed us with an unavoidable claim. Individual alternatives will do nothing to overthrow the rule of the market, or the fact that there are uncountable numbers of child prostitutes on the world's streets. *Jerusalem* is built and safeguarded by a people who are bound together in a common purpose. Christians who cooperate with God's work of bringing about a new world order come together as a *Church*. That's because the claim of the wounded Lamb — an unavoidable claim — is a claim that unites people corporately in worship and service. It teaches them to sing together — not each to his or her own tune. If Christians are to challenge the claim of the global market to express and exhaust the human world they need to make their commitment to the Church, and play their part in it. They need to join in with the *Trisagion*.

Isolationism is, of course, not an option. We cannot step outside the market — just as the early Christians could not step outside the Roman Empire. The early Christians had jobs, were paid in the currency of the Empire, and the same unavoidable embeddedness in many of the practices and structures of our environment is true of us. We are "embroiled" in our world. This is not just to be a cause of lamentation or complaint. It would be a betrayal of God's self-declared love for and patience with the world to seek to disengage from it, and a dangerous fantasy to suppose it was possible to retreat to some "pure" space of self-enclosed religious purity within it. We are responsible for how we live in the world, and responsible *for* the world. We are to serve its blessing.

On the other hand, as was the case for the early Christians, our embroiledness in the world may be an opportunity for challenging and transforming what we are embroiled in. The early Christians may have handled the currency of the Empire each day, but before any of that, before sunrise, they met as the people of God, as the Church. That was their true city, their real

---

9. Boyle, "Hegel and 'The End of History,'" 118.
10. Boyle, "Hegel and 'The End of History,'" 118; my emphasis.

"kingdom," their Jerusalem. Christians' present challenge, too, is to live and work in the world in such a way that the song we sing as people in the Church is so strong and beautiful that it relativizes and transforms other less sacred songs. By refusing to live by the market's values *alone,* by placing our vocational center of gravity in another place, in another framework of value and worship, by continuing to assert that there is another song that can be sung, we do more than we can imagine to show up the deficiencies of the market's claims — and serve the world better than the market can ever serve it.

The vision of God which Christians have is a vision of a wounded Lamb. He is a victorious conqueror and a Lion only as he is a slain Lamb, and only as such is the ultimate truth of things — which is concealed in the scroll — yielded to him. Those of us who follow the Lamb may take this as a reminder that what is finally true is yielded to those who carry wounds. Our knowledge is related to our living, and what we learn may be of value only if we live, like the Lamb, sacrificially. The Lamb's faithful and true witness is the model for our own.

A key part of the sacrifice of the Lamb, and a key part of what is signified by his wounds, is a readiness to accept in his person the *difference time makes.* The Lamb, Jesus Christ, suffers in time because he is ready to accompany it, and make space in it for resistance and opposition to himself. His wounds are the mark of the extraordinary generosity shown towards the "penultimate" by the "ultimate" (to echo Dietrich Bonhoeffer[11]). Jesus Christ does not force the hand of time. He abides with us, for the sake of our response, which though it can inflict wounds can also become the expression of a witness to, and a full relationship with, God, and so part of God's own gladness and glory.

I said above that the song "Holy, Holy, Holy" directed to God and evoked in the Book of Revelation as the "new song" of the redeemed has power to renew the world. What I now want to suggest is that its renewing power has at least in part to do with re-educating dwellers on earth about how to live well with delay; or, to put it another way, about how holiness is manifest in time-taking. How might the liturgical use of the *Sanctus,* day after day and week after week, be understood as educative in relation to human life in time? Part of the answer is that its very repetition points to the fact that the holy God accompanies time, and can be newly related to in each of its moments. His holiness can be praised in every new configuration of particular circumstances, historical and human. We are thus never to be impatient with the "extendedness" of time, seeking to wrest from it a once for all utterance that will put an end to the ongoing work of praise.

11. Cf. Dietrich Bonhoeffer, *Ethics* (London: SCM, 1955), pp. 79ff. (especially pp. 88-89).

Another part of the answer is that the holiness being hymned is, as we have just seen, sacrificial holiness, and one of the key things sacrificed by the holy ones (and above all the Lamb) is their time. They have learned to receive time as God's gift, rather than seeing it as something to be appropriated and deployed (without gratitude) for narrow human purposes. They are therefore readier to offer it back in thanksgiving *(eucharistically)*, in the service of ends that are God's.

It is at this point that I want to turn to the most ancient source of the triple Holy: Isaiah 6:3. This is because Isaiah, as I will argue, is supremely conscious of the temporal dimensions of the revelation of God's holiness (in a way wholly compatible with John of Patmos's use of the holies in Revelation), and the charge Isaiah receives from the thrice-holy God is itself an instruction in bearing sacrificially with delay. I intend to argue in the next section that this original Isaianic context can help Christians understand something of what they are importing into their worship in importing these words.

Isaiah and the Difference Time Makes: Fullness and Emptiness, Uncleanness and Purification

> *In the year that King Uzziah died I saw the Lord sitting upon a throne, high and lifted up; and the train of his robe filled the temple. Above him stood the seraphim. Each had six wings: with two he covered his face, and with two he covered his feet, and with two he flew. And one called to another and said:*
>
> > *"Holy, holy, holy is the LORD of hosts;*
> > *the whole earth is full of his glory!"*
>
> *And the foundations of the thresholds shook at the voice of him who called, and the house was filled with smoke. And I said: "Woe is me! For I am lost; for I am a man of unclean lips, and I dwell in the midst of a people of unclean lips; for my eyes have seen the King, the LORD of hosts!" Then one of the seraphim flew to me, having in his hand a burning coal that he had taken with tongs from the altar. And he touched my mouth and said: "Behold, this has touched your lips; your guilt is taken away, and your sin atoned for." And I heard the voice of the Lord saying, "Whom shall I send, and who will go for us?" Then I said, "Here am I! Send me."*
>
> *And [the LORD] said, "Go, and say to this people:*
> > *'Keep on hearing, but do not understand;*
> > *keep on seeing, but do not perceive.'*

Make the heart of this people dull,
  and their ears heavy,
  and blind their eyes;
lest they see with their eyes,
  and hear with their ears,
and understand with their hearts,
  and turn and be healed."
Then I said, "How long, O Lord?"
And he said:
  "Until cities lie waste
  without inhabitant,
and houses without people,
  and the land is a desolate waste,
and the LORD *removes people far away,*
  and vast is the emptiness in the midst of the land.
And though a tenth remain in it,
  it will be burned again,
like a terebinth or an oak,
  whose stump remains
  when it is felled."
The holy seed is its stump. (Isaiah 6)[12]

In this passage from Isaiah, the reader is startlingly confronted with the themes of uncleanness, the deafness and blindness of the people, delay before healing, the emptiness of the land, and burning. It is disturbing stuff.

The uncleanness of the people — their wickedness and vice — has been outlined in the foregoing chapters,[13] and especially in the series of "woes" ut-

---

12. It is worth signaling here that I am approaching this complex chapter in the Book of Isaiah mainly in a spirit which honours its final redaction. I choose here to relate to the text as it is related to in the devotions of its religious readers, and in its proclamation in worship. For this reason, the fact that the end of verse 13 is more than likely a later addition — a post-exilic gloss trying to elicit an element of hope from the metaphor used by the earlier redactor — is not something I intend to dwell on at any length. In fact, with Vriezen, I would say that "[a]lthough the close of 6:13 is a gloss, it is, seen from the whole of Isaiah's theology, essentially a correct addition" (T. C. Vriezen, "Essentials of the Theology of Isaiah" in B. W. Anderson and W. Harrelson, *Israel's Prophetic Heritage* [New York: Harper, 1962], p. 137). Modifications of the severe message of judgement in Isaiah appear in the idea of conversion (1:10-20; 30:15). "Although convinced on the basis of the knowledge of God's holiness that his people are ripe for judgement, Isaiah is nonetheless sure on the basis of the same might and glory of the holy God that after the day of judgement a new life for Israel and a new creation will be manifest" (Vriezen, "Essentials," p. 144).

13. Uncleanness is very much to the fore as a theme. Isaiah cries out: "I am a man of unclean

tered in chapter 5 (the word "woe" is uttered six times in the chapter[14]). Injustice and excessive consumption are especial marks of this present moral uncleanness. There is a vivid evocation of this wickedness in the parable of the vineyard: the wild grapes are the fruit of wickedness, despite every advantage given to the vineyard. The owner's decision is not to replant it, but to break it up and abandon it; it is almost as if the soil itself is tainted.

If the earth and the people are both unclean (the people's uncleanness powerfully signified in the uncleanness of their king — see footnote 13), what is to be done?

Two immediate answers offer themselves in the form of military destruction and the emptying out of the land. The description of the Lord of Hosts' signal to a nation afar off, and of the slick deadliness of their military machine, is chilling (Isaiah 5:26-30). In a sense, God is going to wage war on his people. And the consequence of this is going to be emptiness — "Until cities lie waste without inhabitant, and houses without people, and the land is a desolate waste, and the LORD removes people far away, and vast is the emptiness in the midst of the land" (6:11-12).

To be sure, not absolutely everyone is to be killed (there is, ambiguously, a stump). At the same time that the destruction is being promised, a seed is being planted for new growth — a seed planted in the soil of the prophet. The prophet himself is certainly having his identity reshaped — one minute a man of unclean lips, the next someone whose guilt is taken away and whose sin is forgiven, and who presses to offer himself for the Lord's purposes: "Here am I! Send me." Isaiah utters his own "woe" — the seventh after the six in the previous chapter. It is a woe on his own behalf. But it is the woe that triggers his remaking. (In the Book of Revelation, where the number seven continues its importance, the seventh trumpet in chapter 11 is the trumpet of consummation, whereby the kingdom of God is heralded, the temple opened and the ark seen; and the seventh mystic figure is the Lamb on Mount Zion along with the 144,000 redeemed and spotless ones. This moment in Isaiah's commissioning is one where he *should* have died, but instead he finds himself newly raised up.)

---

lips, and I dwell in the midst of a people of unclean lips!" The reference to King Uzziah may increase the associations of uncleanness, both because Uzziah entered the sanctuary of the Temple in a way that was unwarranted, and because he died of leprosy as a result (2 Chronicles 26). Isaiah now finds himself, likewise, in the holiest place in the Temple (in the presence of God), and is struck by his own uncleanness. (Though he does not die; on the contrary he is remade.)

14. It is often thought that the "woe" appearing later on in chapter 10 of Isaiah is a seventh one in this series that later became detached by the interpolation of the prophet's "memoir." I will read the text as it stands in order to see a Christian interpretative possibility in the appearance of the seventh woe on the prophet's own lips, right here in chapter 6.

So war and the emptying out of the land are not the only things going on here in the face of the uncleanness of the people. In Isaiah 6, alongside the uncleanness of the people we are confronted with burning holiness; and alongside the images of extraordinary emptiness ("vast . . . in the midst of the land") we are confronted with images of extraordinary fullness ("the whole earth is *full* of his glory"; "his train *filled* the temple"). How can the earth be filled with God's glory at the same time as being so empty? The key may be in the idea of burning (which fills the chapter just as the temple was filled with smoke). The smoke in the temple seems associated with the cloud of God's glory, as well as the holy incense of true worship. The seraphim are "burning ones." The coal one of them brings to touch Isaiah's lips is burning, perhaps with the same divine glory. And then we hear of burning in the darkest part of the description of promised destruction — even when only a tenth of the people remain, the land will "be burned again" (6:13). Are we expected to believe that this too is a form that the glory has taken? Would this explain how the empty land is also full — full of God's glory? If the "glory" in this passage appears in the form of burning, does the burning manifest itself both as judgment and as inspiration?

Hans Urs von Balthasar, in the deeply Johannine vein that is characteristic of his theology, reflects on the dynamic of the way that the divine concern to "gather" prompts at the same time a rejection of God and a separation from him. This may offer a way of casting light on the paradoxical conjunction of fullness and emptiness that we witness in Isaiah 6. Balthasar writes specifically of Christ's life and mission that "[t]he absolute 'gathering' that leads to the Cross inevitably involves an absolute separation: the Word that summons and gathers men collapses in death, darkness and the chaos of splintered freedom."[15] He then cites Gustav Siewerth:

This process, however, is the eternal design of the Trinity; it is the holy depth, the innermost sanctuary of the divine life, which could not reveal itself to sinful and finite creatures unless the latter were made ready [by the sacrifice of Christ].[16]

The fullness of the "depth" of God manifests itself in what seems to be an emptying (the emptying of Christ's very life; the emptying of all that is sinful in the land); and the emptying in question is read (in the light of the recognition of God's true "depth") as his concern to sanctify — though read only by

15. Balthasar, *Theo-Drama*, vol. IV, p. 436.
16. G. Siewerth, *Christentum und Tragik* (1934), p. 299; cited in Balthasar, *Theo-Drama*, vol. IV.

the sanctified. There is a process here of dividing in order to unite *(distinguer pour unir)* reminiscent of the first creation, when "what *seemed* to be 'gathered' was in fact a chaotic, undifferentiated amalgam,"[17] and needed to be separated out in order to bring order into the chaos and rightly relate things once again.

What Balthasar is exploring in his interpretation of this dynamic is the idea that God "has to campaign against recalcitrant human freedom for the sake of the coming kingdom."[18] Jesus Christ is victorious as he enacts this divine purpose through cross, descent into hell, and resurrection, but this does not mean that all his work is done. There is a delay. Some time-taking is required. "In making his provocative claim to have reconciled the world in God, Jesus never suggested that he was creating an earthly paradise":[19]

> [O]nly when "he delivers the kingdom to God the Father after destroying every rule and every authority and power . . . and puts all his enemies under his feet" (1 Corinthians 15:24f.) can he hand the perfected kingdom over to the Father. [In the meantime], this time of the end is the time of the most bitter struggle. . . .[20]

The struggle originates in the fact that God makes it impossible for the creature to ignore his summons. The comprehensiveness of the summons (represented for Balthasar by Christ's gesture of complete embrace, of gathering-in; and for Isaiah by the fullness of the Lord's presence, spilling out from the Temple to fill the whole land, the whole earth) means that the creature cannot remain neutral or detached in relation to God's call, and must take a stand somewhere. If we are not "for" this God who seeks to draw all creation into his fullness, we are already against him. Balthasar writes of Jesus, but in a way that can illuminate the apparent paradox we have noted in Isaiah, that:

> [i]n setting out to gather all men, Jesus . . . separates whatever is prepared to respond to his absolute summons from what resists it. So it comes about that his peace-bringing action ("he is our peace," Eph 2:14) introduces more division into the world than any other; not through fanaticism but because of an inherent logic: the very One who has come, "not to judge, but to save" utters that "word" that judges those who reject it.[21]

---

17. Balthasar, *Theo-Drama*, vol. IV, pp. 437-38.
18. Balthasar, *Theo-Drama*, vol. IV, p. 427.
19. Balthasar, *Theo-Drama*, vol. IV, p. 442.
20. Balthasar, *Theo-Drama*, vol. IV, p. 427.
21. Balthasar, *Theo-Drama*, vol. IV, p. 435.

Isaiah knows this experience — he even cries out in frustration at it: "How long, O Lord?" But the purpose of the summons is to attune humanity to the possibilities that lie beyond its own vitiated attempts to "gather" the world in its own power, or alternatively the attempts by individuals to "gather" their selfhood while abandoning the world. The parallels here with Isaiah's critique of the stratagems of his rulers should be evident: Judah's folly is to attempt to carve out its own destiny; the destinies of even the mightiest nations function only as instruments of the Lord God's "policy," and all human plans to the contrary are doomed to futility. Isaiah 7:8 forcibly reminds its hearers that behind each country is a city, and on the throne of that city a mere man, hence the countries are no stronger than the plans of the men who rule them, and these are not the plans of God.

The divine summons traced by Balthasar and recognisable in Isaiah 6 and 7 is to something impossible to the human being except by God's sanctifying grace: "namely, to 'gather' at the same level as God and with God";[22] to relinquish a certain self-determination by being shattered and remade and by participating in the holiness of God. This is bound to provoke resistance:

> God's offer goes far beyond all mundane constructs of ethics and religion; it can only resign itself to man's No — for it seems absurd to man to transcend his own utmost possibilities by negating them.

Balthasar adds, in explicitly Christological words, that this rejection of "the greatest possible opportunity, this desire to exercise freedom on the basis of one's *own* source, is the sin that comes into full consciousness through the provocation offered by Jesus." It is the choice of empty human possibility provoked by the fullness of the divine offer, and emptying is its consequence.

> And so we are brought to the following formulation, extravagant though it may seem: mankind's self-destruction is the only foreseeable end to the world, left to itself, and the only end it deserves, insofar as it prefers to hoard what is its own (that is, power, mammon) rather than to gather with Christ. It has already decided its own fate.[23]

But the most important feature of the passage in Isaiah is its understanding of the importance of *time* in God's action towards his people. We may be horrified at the idea that God will somehow *cause* a people to be deaf to his message, blind to the vision of his glory; we may be mystified that at the same

---

22. Balthasar, *Theo-Drama*, vol. IV, p. 435.
23. Balthasar, *Theo-Drama*, vol. IV, p. 442.

time as shutting ears and making eyelids fat he should commission someone to speak for him. Why have speech now and hearing later? This theme of delay is concentrated in the "until" of verse 11, in answer to Isaiah's "How long, O Lord?" Perhaps, although terrible in its effects, the delay is meant to be instructive (and is, incidentally, a confirmation of the fact that the destruction of absolutely everyone is not what is intended by God: there will again be a hearing and a seeing when the burning is over, and so presumably people to hear and see). Perhaps it is instructive because of the way it inserts the people into temporality. They are not allowed to evade the complex consequences of being creaturely agents in time, and of having to wait for the fulfillment of their needs (their "completion").

There may even perhaps be a theology of Scripture contained here — in the disclosure that what is said at one point will often, in the purposes of God, be heard later. This theme runs like thread through the Book of Isaiah; we see it again in Isaiah 29:11-12: "The vision of all this has become for you like the words of a sealed document." Is the *difference time makes* a central part of what Jewish and Christian communities bring to their reading of Scripture — especially in their attention to the way that newly-arrived circumstances make it possible for Scripture to speak as it did not seem to speak before, and their attempt to articulate how this might have to do with a (strugglingly-discerned) divine will? A central part of the difference time makes to these communities of readers is the opportunity it gives them for discerning, struggling and coming to terms with God's instruction. This — the temporal process itself — can become an intrinsic part of God's work of gathering and sanctifying.

And could the liturgy be a training in exactly this patience, this learning to wait well, for the sake of conversion of heart, and transformation of social life? This is itself a form of *revaluing* that is intrinsic to the witness against the commodifications of the market we discussed above — witness, indeed, against precisely the commodification of *time,* through a learned ability to receive it as a gift and to make the sacrifices necessary to holy life in it. It is possible to have a thankful, receiving attitude to time, or a calculating, proprietorial attitude to it. As Sam Wells has put it:

> For many people, time is a commodity. It is treated like one of the most valuable things money can buy. People who are busy and important use commodity-language to describe time. They "buy" time, or "spend" time; they talk of "using" time, or even of "investing a great deal of time," or sometimes of "putting time aside"; they "save" time or "waste" time, "lose" time or "find" time. Not any old time: they are only interested in "quality"

time. All of these words treat time as a product, like something one could buy in the supermarket. Occasionally it is pointed out that "time is money." It is considered a very good thing in these circles to save time — though it is not always clear how one is to spend the time one has saved.

Another group of people would love to be busy and important, but for a variety of reasons they feel they are not. Yet because commodity-language is the way so many people speak of time, this second group are made to feel that because they are not in a hurry, they are "wasting" time, or "losing precious time" in life's race. For these people, time quickly becomes an enemy. Because the commodity-language does not fit, they often use battle-language. Time is "against" them, or "presses in on" them; it "weighs heavy" on their lives. They seem to be failing the "test" of time. The saddest language is that which speaks of "killing" time, since those who set out to kill time almost always lose the battle.[24]

Jesus Christ, Christians would say, gives us a new time: time "as a gift and as a friend." As gift "because it is God's time, not one's own," and as friend because there is nothing to fear from it. "Time is 'on our side.' One cannot buy time with God. One must learn to enjoy God's time."[25] This disposition of enjoyment is also sacrificial in that it has thankful offering at its heart. Joyfully, we offer the time we receive from God back to God, eucharistically, by the way we use it. When time is treated in this way, then "the Christian community can enjoy time with those who do not promise to make the world a better place." It can witness against the plans of kings by identifying with the faithful holy, the weak whom God chooses to shame the strong, for "God chose what is low and despised in the world, things that are not, to reduce to nothing things that are" (1 Corinthians 1:28). As Wells argues, when the Church is full of people who witness in this way, it is evidence that the Church is living in God's time. To which I would add: living eucharistically, in conformity with the example of the wounded Lamb. Every bit of time Christians spend with the vulnerable or the powerless is part of the Church's proclamation of the joyful expenditure of the cross. Priests who are "given time" for proclamation are "given time" for a ministry of this kind. It is utterly eucharistic.

Worship, too, is the joyous expenditure of time for thanksgiving, refusing to treat time or people "as commodities for one's own advancement":

---

24. Samuel Wells, *Transforming Fate into Destiny: The Theological Ethics of Stanley Hauerwas* (Carlisle: Paternoster Press, 1998), p. 148.

25. Wells, *Transforming Fate into Destiny,* p. 149.

[G]athering together in worship, Sunday by Sunday and many times besides, is a constant reminder to the Church that it is living in God's time, not its own. The Church gathers because worship is the most profound recognition of God's sovereignty over time: hence there is nothing better in life than to worship God with others who love him. And if it takes all the time in the world it does not matter — because it is God's time.[26]

This is part of the political force of worship: its power to relativize all other kinds of sovereignty, and the resources it offers for good citizenship of what (echoing the epistle to the Romans in Barthian vein) we might call the time of God's "patience" (Romans 9:22-23). The Church is helped to harness this political power by the heavenly song that has been planted at the heart of Christian worship's marking of time: "Holy, Holy, Holy Lord; God of power and might."

We are readier now to relate the texts from Isaiah that we have looked at in this section back to the Christian liturgical use of the "Holy, Holy, Holy" text.

The Eucharistic *Sanctus*

In the previous section, we suggested with Balthasar that the intensity of the presence of God's gathering holiness forces sin to break cover, and offers the possibility of a remaking of the world — though not without time taking its course; not without a certain "untilling" during which unholy resistances self-destructively play themselves out. The "glory," which fills the whole earth, amounts to God's salvation for his people if it is participated in — and this salvation, or remaking, affects both individuals and the land (or earth) as a whole. But it is a glory to which eyes can be closed and against which hearts can be hardened. It requires a certain "untilling" before its full realisation and room is made for this by God's patience.

In this section, I want to show how the sanctifying power of the divine presence is acknowledged in the "Holy, Holy, Holy" of the Christian Eucharist at the same time as there is an honouring of time and its necessary outworking, and in this way to show how an Isaianic connection (Isaianic context included) makes sense in the eucharistic usage.

When, as is evidenced in the third century onwards,[27] the early Christians began to use the *Trisagion* in the eucharistic prayer, it remained clear that it

---

26. Wells, *Transforming Fate into Destiny.*

27. Cf. B. Spinks, *The Sanctus in the Eucharistic Prayer* (Cambridge: Cambridge University Press, 1991), pp. 57-61.

was a song of heaven, uttered in the presence of celestial glory, to which the thanksgiving of mortals was being joined. For this reason, the *Mystagogical Catecheses* attributed to Cyril of Jerusalem (c. 348) remark that "we rehearse this hymn of praise handed down to us from the seraphim that we might join in hymns with the hosts of the world above."[28] It is viewed as a gathering song, as well as a sanctifying one, and in both respects it is strongly Isaianic in character. For this reason, as Bouyer comments, it properly follows upon the summary of the whole of creation that customarily precedes it. The whole of creation:

> is invited to join unanimously in the hymn of the Seraphim. All creation is, as it were, summed up in the heavenly Jerusalem, the festal assembly, the Church of the first-born whose names are written in heaven.[29]

The Isaianic language of fullness is also present, describing how the consecrated eucharistic elements must be filled with sanctifying power — and the Syriac tradition intensifies this imagery of "filling" by conjoining it with the fire imagery derived from Isaiah's coal. Ephrem writes:

> Come and see, O Solomon, what the Lord of thy father has done; for fire and spirit, not according to its nature, He has mingled and poured into the hands of His disciples. . . . In the bread and cup is fire and the Holy Spirit.[30]

The appropriateness of the three "Holies" to use in the eucharistic prayer — with all their scriptural resonances from their original context in the Book of Isaiah — will be apparent here. Isaiah shows us that by his glory God's holiness is revealed, and by his holiness humanity's sin is revealed as well as the grace to be saved from it:

> The experience of being set free to know the true deity of God and his own creatureliness comes to a Christian in hearing the word of Christ who is crucified for him. There is therefore good reason for the Christian church to sing the hymn of the seraphim before hearing the words of institution in the Eucharist, in order to praise the coming of him whose glory fills and sustains the whole world, and from whose grasp man cannot find any place

28. Cf. Spinks, *The Sanctus in the Eucharistic Prayer*, p. 63.

29. Louis Bouyer, *Eucharist* (South Bend, Ind.: University of Notre Dame Press, 1968), pp. 270-71; cited in Spinks, *The Sanctus in the Eucharistic Prayer*, p. 65.

30. *Adv. Scrutatores*, hymn X, Opp. III, pp. 23E, 24A; cited in Hans Lietzman, *Mass and Lord's Supper: A Study in the History of the Liturgy*, trans. Dorothea H. G. Reeve (Leiden: Brill, 1979), p. 456.

to hide. The Holy One is always ready to reveal his glory, but sustains and permeates the earth, to slay everything that is unholy, and to consummate his judgment.[31]

The eucharistic *Sanctus* may give us the resources we need to begin an answer to a question put very starkly by Balthasar in his meditation on the separating out of light and darkness under the provocation of God's summons in Christ, and humanity's recalcitrance in clinging to its own sin. Balthasar's question is this:

> Given this essentially self-enclosed world, how far is it possible to sow in it the seeds of an openness that comes from God and goes to him? Can immortal seeds be sown in earth that is "dead," that is, subject to death in all its dimensions? If man knows and seeks a freedom that refers only to himself (whether individually or socially), is it possible to implant in him an entirely different, God-given freedom with God as its goal?

The echoes of Isaiah 6 here in the talk of seeds and dead earth are almost certainly not accidental. On the contrary, there is every reason to contend that the liturgical use of the *Trisagion* is the seeding of just such an "openness that comes from God and goes to him." It is a reminder that there are "ends" to the earth; that the earth is not all there is. And this in turn has major implications for human life in time. For the openness required is not just spatial; it is temporal. The *Trisagion* points to an *eschatological* "until" which is perhaps discernible for Christians behind the reply to Isaiah's question "How long, O Lord?" It keeps the worshipper longing for what lies beyond the present, and firm in expectation of it — ready to be "untilled" even when the land is laid waste, and ready to resist premature attempts at the consummation or arresting of time which are the mark of a certain godless political ambition.

This will mean being ready to abide in time, waiting the day when the assurance of God's sovereignty hymned in the *Trisagion* is fully manifest. It will mean keeping the heart unhardened (to echo Isaiah — for whom the heart is the site of human plans and desires), especially when asked to trust in what it cannot see and what is promised to it in the word alone; even when it has no outward success to point to. Balthasar writes:

> The kingdom of God will never be externally demonstrable (Lk 17:21); it grows, invisibly, perpendicular to world history, and the latter's fruits are al-

---

31. Otto Kaiser, *Isaiah 1–12: A Commentary* (The Old Testament Library), (London: SCM, 1972), p. 79.

ready in God's barns. Man responds to this provocation by attempting to manufacture the kingdom of God on earth, with increasing means and methods of power; logically this power that resists the powerlessness of the Cross is bound to destroy itself.[32]

In our day, the possibility of concentrated power — at an earthly planetary level — has increased beyond all imagining. It has obvious military and technological dimensions. "The Hellenistic *oikoumene* and the Roman world empire were pale anticipations of what today can be achieved by the modern stockpiling of arms and modern propaganda."[33] It also has economic dimensions, which this essay has considered at greater length. The economic counterpart of the human desire to concentrate power and "manufacture" an unfettered earthly *dominium* is manifest in the grip of the market and the institutions which uphold the ambitious claims made on its behalf, with their pretensions to define all value and draw all people into a relationship of dependency on its systems of exchange. Beneath all these bids for power, and the desire to "manufacture the kingdom," there lies the desire to manage all "untils," to take time in hand, and force God's hand — no longer to have to ask "How Long?"; or else to provide one's own answer to the question.

The voice from heaven in the Book of Revelation makes it clear that the Christians under the Roman yoke conquered Satan "by the blood of the Lamb and by the word of their testimony, for they loved not their lives even unto death." The Church now has a role to play in the full working out of the Lamb's conquest. It may be that this involves new martyrdoms. At any rate it will involve something continuous with martyrdom, a sacrificial witness that is thoroughly eucharistic in character: the sacrifice of one's praise and the generous offering up of the time needed to do justice to this praising.[34] We are not the arbiters of how much time this has to take. Practice of the regular recitation of the *Trisagion* holds Christians in the conviction that the timing of the full working out of God's conquest, and the just expression of his praises, is a matter for God's patience and not the devices and desires of our own hearts.

---

32. Balthasar, *Theo-Drama*, vol. IV, p. 442.

33. Balthasar, *Theo-Drama*, vol. IV, p. 441.

34. The spirit which breathes in martyrdom and the spirit which breathes in everyday thankfulness are, after all, one and the same: a spirit of grateful acknowledgement.

PART IV

LITURGICAL IMPROVISATION

For Such a Time as This:
Esther and the Practices of Improvisation

Samuel Wells

The Book of Esther

The Book of Esther is a study in the politics of redemption. It begins with the Jewish people in a precarious condition that soon becomes calamitous. Yet salvation comes to the Jews. Every year Jews celebrate that extraordinary reversal in the feast of Purim. In this liturgical context, the story becomes a form of training for Jews in how to respond in the face of challenging or threatening circumstances. Elsewhere I have studied practices through which Christians faithfully respond to demanding circumstances by improvising on the scriptural tradition.[1] Here I seek to display how the Book of Esther, when restored to a liturgical context in Christian worship and catechesis, offers a training in improvisatory practices that constitute the politics of the Church. Such practices empower and inspire Christians to realize that their particular social location, family, education, experiences, talents, opportunities and personality are gifts to enable them to play a key role in rescuing and restoring God's people at "just such a time as this" (4:14).[2]

The Book of Esther is a burlesque of risk and reversal. Mordecai is a Jew who lives in the Persian capital, Susa. He seizes an opportunity created by the summary deposition of the queen, putting forward his adopted daughter Esther as a potential successor. Esther's unrivalled charms steal the heart of King Xerxes and she becomes queen. But meanwhile the king appoints an evil

---

1. Samuel Wells, *Improvisation: The Drama of Christian Ethics* (Grand Rapids: Brazos, 2004).

2. I would like to express my appreciation to Michael Beckett, whose book *Gospel in Esther* (Carlisle: Paternoster, 2002) drew my attention to the typological potential of the Book of Esther.

grand vizier called Haman who takes an insatiable dislike to the Jews. Bridling at Mordecai's disrespectful behavior, Haman uses it as a pretext to issue a decree to wipe out the whole Jewish people. Only Esther can save them. After some equivocation she risks her life to plead for her people's salvation, using plenty of sexual and psychological manipulation. She succeeds in persuading the king. Meanwhile Haman's recklessness leads to his downfall. On the day when they were due to be massacred, the Jews succeed in killing 75,000 of their enemies throughout the empire. The feast of Purim is inaugurated to commemorate the great reversal of fortunes. Mordecai becomes prime minister.

In Judaism the Book of Esther has a festival to itself. For Jews, Esther means carnival. "During the festival of Purim . . . reverence, sobriety, law and authority go into a slide. Farcical plays based on the Esther story, called *Purimshpiels,* are often performed which parody the otherwise accepted authority of teachers, rabbis, and long-revered texts. Purim is, moreover, a festival preoccupied with masquerade. People gather in costumes and masks to hear, amid a cacophony of noise-making, a public reading of the scroll."[3] In Christianity, by contrast, the book is almost invisible. In the Church of England's version of the Revised Common Lectionary, for example, amidst the threefold sets of Sunday readings across a three-year calendar, the Book of Esther appears only once, and then as an option.[4] There is no other reference to the book in any of the liturgical material of *Common Worship.* Martin Luther's long suspicion of the book, based on the apparent absence of God and the presence of dubious behavior — "I am so hostile to it that I wish it did not exist" — clearly runs deep in the Christian imagination.

Improvisation and Christian Ethics

In my book *Improvisation: The Drama of Christian Ethics* I compare Christian discipleship with the practices that make up improvisation in the theater. I

---

3. Timothy K. Beal, *The Book of Hiding: Gender, Ethnicity, Annihilation, and Esther* (New York: Routledge, 1997), p. 1.

4. *Common Worship: Services and Prayers for the Church of England* (London: Church House Publishing, 2000), p. 572. The other readings for the principal service for proper 21, Year B are Psalm 124, James 5:13-20, and Mark 9:38-50 ("whoever is not against us is for us"). Old Testament readings during Ordinary Time are either Related (following the New Testament readings) or Continuous (following their own sequence). A congregation that insisted on its Old Testament readings being linked to its New Testament readings might never read Esther together at all.

describe improvisation as a practice through which actors seek to develop trust in themselves and one another in order to conduct unscripted dramas without fear. While I acknowledge that performance is a fruitful way of understanding the relationship between the life of the Church and the text of Scripture, I suggest that it has certain shortcomings. I propose that the discipline of improvisation in the theater resolves these shortcomings while retaining the benefits of perceiving the Christian life in terms of performance. Improvisation offers a way for the Church to remain faithful to Scripture without assuming the Bible provides a script to dictate appropriate conduct in every eventuality. It does so by treating the Scripture not so much as a static command, locked in the past, but as a dynamic training school, shaping the character of disciples as they enter ever-new contexts.

The Church is like a body of actors committed to treating every new development in the drama as a gift that can help it render its identity and character with greater faithfulness and clarity. The Church, like the company of actors, is not able to destroy threatening "gifts" but must find ways of integrating them into the story without jeopardizing its character and identity. The purpose of the story is always friendship between God and his people. Thus improvisation is a significant way of harmonizing an approach to ethics that values creation — seeing all around us as a potential gift — while remaining alert to the transformation brought by Christ — recognizing that there is a purposive and normative story that shapes all our responses. Improvisation is particularly suited to contexts where a body of people are not in a position to set the agenda, but must imaginatively receive and "play" with dominant forces around them. Hence the significance of the Book of Esther.

In my treatment I go on to describe six aspects of improvisation in the theater and in each case to outline ways in which these aspects are replicated in Scripture and in the practice of the Church. I shall briefly summarize these six aspects of improvisation here.[5]

(1) *Forming habits* refers to the way improvisation is not about being spontaneous, witty, or clever in the moment, but about developing trust and practices over time so that in the moment one relies on habit rather than resorting to inspiration. Improvisers work hard to cultivate a condition of relaxed awareness, which is alert, attentive, engaged, aware of the dynamics of narrative, eager to explore situations in depth, open to the unknown, and confident and respectful toward the self and other actors. Likewise discipleship is about the formation of character, understanding of the nature and dimensions of the Christian story, trust in God and in fellow

---

5. Each of these aspects has a chapter devoted to it in my *Improvisation*.

disciples, and hope in the face of the unknown. These are all fostered defin-itively in worship.

(2) *Assessing status* addresses the element of power and role in every single interaction between people. The way one responds to a classroom teacher will be shaped by the status the teacher plays. If he or she speaks slowly, keeps the head still, never touches the face, makes a long "errrrm" sound between com-ments, and is comfortable with silence, he or she is playing high-status and will usually evoke respect but perhaps not love. If by contrast the movements are jerky, the hands frequently touch the face, the "erm" is brief, and apologies are many, this is a low-status player who may struggle to control the class. An expert status player will swap status at will to achieve the desired results, and will invariably be popular and effective. Status is not so much bestowed as chosen. Life is not simply a battle to be high-status. It is much more subtle than that. Adopting an apparently low status can be a very effective means of retaining the initiative. Conventional relationships such as that between mas-ter and servant illustrate the endless possibilities of manipulation in appar-ently fixed status roles. Such reflections may help Christians to appreciate the subtleties of their relationships to power and role and to deepen their under-standing of politics. The scriptures are full of status interactions and are fasci-nated by the status complexities of Israel, Jesus, and the Church.

(3) The heart of improvisation is the ability to keep the story going. *Ac-cepting* refers to any response that accepts the premise of another actor's "of-fer" — whether that offer be physical or verbal. *Blocking* refers to any re-sponse that denies the premise of that offer. Actors have to learn to say "yes" even when to do so seems impossible, improper, or dangerous. Beleaguered groups may identify blocking with faithful resistance: but blocking assumes the politics of violence, presupposes access to sufficient power to close the story, and denies the role of providence in resolving the story benevolently. Improvisation springs to life when the Church realizes it cannot and should not block society's offers indefinitely, and when Christians are inspired by the vision of a community committed to accepting all offers.

(4) Part of what it takes to keep the story going is to dismantle the power of apparently dominant forces. Such forces — including death, sin and time — appear to be "givens" that must simply be accepted. But the scriptural nar-rative constantly rejoices in the subverting and overcoming of these givens, fundamentally in the pattern of cross and resurrection, such that Christianity is founded on one given only — the gospel. Thus *questioning givens* becomes a key aspect of being a community of improvisation. Death seems to be a given, but the resurrection dismantles its givenness, and makes it "but the gate of life immortal." Sin seems to be a given, but again Easter makes Adam's

fall a "happy fault that brings so great a redemption." Time, in its relentless, shapeless persistence, seems to be a given. But in eschatological perspective, it need no longer be an enemy. Through story and liturgy, through being the medium in which the purpose of God is disclosed, it can be "on our side" — a friend.[6]

(5) If there is only one given, only one unvarying determinant, everything else in all creation is set free to become a gift. That is, nothing is profane: all is not only capable of being incorporated into the Church's story, but potentially profitable when introduced in this way. Thus actors — and the Church — do not simply accept the givens of society and the world and stoically try to fit their discipleship around such givens; instead they *over*accept these apparent givens by fitting them into a much larger story — the story of God's ongoing relationship with his people — and thus transform the fate of accepting givens into the destiny of *overaccepting gifts*. In my account of Christian ethics as improvisation, overaccepting becomes the key practice by which the Church seeks to relate to new and sometimes threatening elements or forces in society. In doing so it imitates the way God in Christ overaccepts wayward humanity through incarnation and overaccepts death through cross and resurrection.

(6) Finally, actors do reach a sense of the "ending" of the story. This is when discarded elements from earlier in the narrative begin to reappear, especially at moments when redeeming these discarded elements offers the resolution to what seemed insurmountable problems. This is called *reincorporation*. Reincorporation is central to the Church's understanding of the reign of God. Just as St. Laurence, when called upon to assemble the riches of the Church, filled the church in Rome with the poor, the blind and the lame, and told the Roman authorities that these were indeed the riches of the Church, so disciples today discover the ways of God when the people discarded from the story reappear as gifts. A key test of the faithfulness of any course of action is whether this is taking place. One influential writer describes improvisation as like walking backwards.[7] Instead of facing the daunting emptiness of an unknown future, the improviser walks backwards, seeing discarded material as a host of gifts enabling the continuance and resolution of troubling narratives. In similar vein, the Church sees the oppressed as the key to unlocking the door of God's future.

---

6. In my *Transforming Fate into Destiny: The Theological Ethics of Stanley Hauerwas* (Carlisle: Paternoster, 1998), pp. 141-50, I discuss the failed effort of modernity to turn time into a commodity ("spend" time, "save" time, "waste" time, "quality" time) and the way the Church can see time eschatologically as a friend and a gift.

7. Keith Johnstone, *Impro: Improvisation in the Theatre* (London: Methuen, 1981), p. 116.

Improvising on Exile

The following treatment considers ways in which the Book of Esther, rehearsed in liturgical context, constitutes a training school in the politics of redemption. The condition of exile is an ideal context in which to see that politics at work. Esther is all about how a minority people manage to gain the initiative against overwhelming odds. Improvisation is about how God's people, in new and challenging situations, display the virtues of discipleship and illuminate the glory of the gospel through trusting God, one another, and the practices they share. This is the politics of redemption. Under the following six headings we shall see that politics at work.

Accepting and Blocking

In the simplest terms the story portrays a contrast between two queens: Vashti, who blocks, and Esther, who accepts.

The story opens with King Ahasuerus' lavish hospitality, which displays "the great wealth of his kingdom and the splendour and pomp of his majesty" (1:4). We know nothing of Vashti except that she is the queen, that she is beautiful, and that she is giving a hen party to coincide with Ahasuerus' extravagant stag party. The eunuchs convey to her the king's invitation, or offer, to display her beauty before his drunken table. She refuses — blocks. Like many blocks, it is initially breathtaking. It shows courage. In the short term, it exposes the weakness of the king, for his will is simply disobeyed. But blocking without power is quickly steamrollered. Not only is Vashti deposed as queen, but her actions threaten the room for maneuver held by every woman in this patriarchal culture: now it is formally decreed "that every man should be master in his own house" (1:22).

Here is a stark portrayal of one approach to exile. There is nothing to suggest Vashti is a Jew. But as a woman who finds herself a pawn in a male game she offers a vivid analogy for the vulnerability of the Jews in the Persian Empire. They may choose to block; they may choose to assert their own customs and traditions in the face of a culture that might humiliate or mistreat them from time to time. But they risk Vashti's fate — disappearing from the story before the end of the first chapter.[8]

---

8. The weakness of Vashti's approach is brought out well by Michael V. Fox, *Character and Ideology in the Book of Esther* (Columbia, S.C.: University of South Carolina Press, 1991), pp. 24-26. See also my *Transforming Fate into Destiny: The Theological Ethics of Stanley Hauerwas* (Carlisle: Paternoster, 1998).

Mordecai, by contrast, encourages Esther to pursue a different path. The king is on the lookout for young virgins to replace Vashti as queen. It is not just that Esther enters a path that Vashti found intolerable; it is also vital that, as a Jew, this means she accepts an approach that involves eating with gentiles, concubinage, and intermarriage. The life of the harem again provides a metaphor for the condition of exile: a life of constant compromise, uncertain length, complete subservience, and dubious integrity. The opening of the narrative makes clear that the story of the Persian Empire is one in which the Jews have a peripheral part. This is a story about what seems to be the whole world, and the Jewish people are a tiny presence among the nations. Blocking is therefore not a sustainable option for people without power, but neither is blocking the only strategy open to them.

Esther thus emerges out of this gigantic context as one who graciously accepts. She accepts Mordecai's initiative; she accepts Hegai the eunuch's favor; she accepts twelve months of cosmetic treatment; she even at the moment before entering the king's chamber asks for nothing except what Hegai advises. Likewise Mordecai and Esther have accepted exile; they have not gone back to Jerusalem; they have not taken the approach of Daniel and his companions but have "kept the story going."[9] The result is that Esther is "admired by all who [see] her" (2:15), including Ahasuerus, and becomes queen.[10]

Yet just when all is well, Mordecai blocks Haman. He can accept the customs of the Medes and the Persians, but he cannot accept the lordship of a descendant of Agag, king of the Amalekites, whom Saul had failed to kill, thus bringing about the Lord's rejection of Saul as king of Israel (1 Samuel 15).[11] This block, however understandable in the light of the ancient tradition, brings about the edict that threatens genocide for the Jews. Thus Mordecai initially accepts but then catastrophically blocks. Perhaps it is impossible for the Jews in exile to accept indefinitely, if they are to continue to be a people that treasure their story. Perhaps the structure of the story is such that it is up to the woman (doubly exiled through being a Jew and a member of a harem)

---

9. This resembles what John Howard Yoder calls "revolutionary subordination." In Yoder's words, "'Subordination' is itself the Christian form of rebellion. It is the way we share in God's patience with a system we basically reject." *The Politics of Jesus,* 2d. ed. (Grand Rapids: Eerdmans, 1994), p. 200 n. 10.

10. Fox helpfully points out that the narrator also "accepts." The narrator "perceives how women can be used as toys in the sexual games of the powerful, but he does not condemn the harem setup so harshly. He takes it for granted as he does all the peculiarities of the gentile state. Both are fields of obstacle and danger — but also opportunity — for the Jews who find themselves thrust into them" (*Character and Ideology,* p. 36).

11. See the discussion in Fox, *Character and Ideology,* pp. 42-45.

to resolve by overaccepting the problems created by her male cousin's inability to accept.[12] It is Mordecai's initial encouragement of Esther to accept the vacancy created by Vashti's block that creates the possibility that Esther can later overaccept to incorporate even Mordecai's own block. Indeed Esther's continuing willingness to accept resolves the problems that derive from Vashti's blocking of King Ahasuerus and Mordecai's blocking of Haman. She literally keeps the story going.

Assessing Status

The narrator of the Book of Esther is fascinated by status relationships. Perhaps the pivotal moment in the story comes when the king asks Haman, "What shall be done for the man whom the king wants to honor?" (6:6). This moment crystallizes the host of status reversals that characterise the narrative.

The story begins with the status reversal of Ahasuerus and Vashti. He is the all-powerful, the magnificent — but she is able to humiliate him. This is contrasted with a series of banquets in which Esther is the host, and thus the benefactor of the king, but also the one seeking a favor, and thus the one in deep need.[13] Then there are the scheming of Mordecai and the compliance of Esther: it seems that he is the brains and she is the beauty — but later it is his misjudgment that puts the Jews in jeopardy and her scheming that rescues them. It is he that pleads with her, and she that gives orders to him (4:9-17). The most complex pairing is the stubborn Mordecai and the ruthless Haman. Haman is infuriated by Mordecai's refusal to bow down and honor him. But it is ironically through Haman's own hasty arrogance that Mordecai comes to receive abundant honors, none more poignant than the sight of Haman himself leading the king's horse on which Mordecai proudly sits (6:11). The climax of the relationship comes in Haman himself being impaled on the vast stake he had set up to dispose of Mordecai. This is the only status relationship in the book that is not characterized by the interplay of permanent social

---

12. This would be a line followed by many feminist readings of the story. See, for example, Beal, *The Book of Hiding*.

13. Fox puts it well: "The world-ruler banishes a wife he cannot control, only to take on later a new one who controls him completely" (*Character and Ideology*, p. 24). Fox also points out that the Vashti-Ahasuerus-Esther triangle develops into an elaborate question of who "comes" to whom. Vashti refuses to come to Ahasuerus's banquet, and then is refused permission ever to come before him again; Esther by contrast comes to Ahasuerus's banquet, and Ahasuerus comes not once but twice to Esther's banquets. (69)

roles, and thus it has more dynamism than the others, which concentrate on subverting conventional relationships. An ironic element is that Haman is finally executed for bowing down to a Jew — Esther — whereas his rage (and the Jews' peril) began when a Jew — Mordecai — refused to bow down to him. Haman begs his life from Esther — and loses — whereas Esther had moments earlier begged her life from Ahasuerus — and won.

There are only two main characters in the story that strive for all they are worth to be high-status: Ahasuerus and Haman. But these two characters exhibit all the weaknesses of high-status players. These weaknesses are worth noting. They assume that everyone else wants to be high-status like them — that they are winning a game that is the only game worth playing: thus they are blind to the machinations of Mordecai, who is an expert status player, adopting whichever status is necessary to achieve his goal — deliverance for the Jews.[14] High-status players are vulnerable to flattery, because they take it to be one of the perks or entitlements of their lofty status: thus Ahasuerus, "pleased" (1:21) that the affront to his dignity was a point of principle rather than a personal insult, is manipulated by his officials into issuing a ridiculous edict (1:22). High-status players seldom pay close attention to detail: thus not only is Ahasuerus cajoled by Haman into issuing an edict that commands the annihilation of a people (without the king realizing the people Haman had in mind were the Jews), but also only a short time later he has already forgotten that such an edict has ever been issued. High-status players are particularly vulnerable to charm, for charm is the definitive weapon of the expert status player, able to change status at will. Thus Esther leads the king on from one banquet to the next, intriguing him by delaying her request and encouraging any latent jealousy of Haman, so that by the time she articulates her petition Ahasuerus is positively salivating and bound to accede. When the matter becomes not merely one of his own benefaction but of damage to his honor (7:4) Esther has him completely in her power. Haman illustrates the weakness of high-status players in two further ways. He is obsessed by maintaining his status, and this blinds him to all other considerations: his determination to dispose of Mordecai is out of all proportion to Mordecai's crime, and means he takes his eye off other threats.[15] And he is mesmerized by his relationship to the king, the only player more high-status than he: when asked, "What shall be done for the man whom the king wants to honor?" (6:6), he cannot

14. For expert status players see Wells, *Improvisation*, pp. 87-89.

15. It also interferes with his concern to remain high-status. Fox notes that Haman hurries to the banquet (5:5), then hurries to honor Mordecai (6:10) and then hurries home in misery (6:12). Mordecai, on the other hand, never hurries (*Character and Ideology*, p. 80, quoting Gerleman).

think of anyone more high-status than himself, and thus he blunders into a catastrophic misjudgement. On the only occasion Haman adopts a low-status approach — in pleading with Esther (7:7-8) — he makes a hash of it.

By contrast, those people in the story not concerned — or able — to maintain high-status gain access to opportunity and perspective unavailable to the high-status players. First, the weak see things the powerful do not. For example, it is Mordecai at the king's gate who uncovers the plot to kill Ahasuerus; the king and his advisers know nothing of it. Likewise it is Mordecai that learns of the edict that calls on the people of all provinces to annihilate the Jews: Esther, now the queen of the whole empire, knows nothing of it. The ensuing debate between Mordecai and Esther (4:9-17) is to a large extent a debate about status. Mordecai pleads that Esther cease seeing status as an end in itself and begin to use her skills as a status player for the service of a much greater cause — the deliverance of the Jews (4:14). Second, those forced to live by their wits forge a certain solidarity. The weak have friends the powerful do not. The eunuchs play a significant role in the narrative: they have a conventional low-status role, in contrast to the Jews' provisional low-status condition. One can see Bigthan and Teresh (the eunuchs who block by plotting to assassinate the king) as types of Vashti, and Hegai and Harbona (who accept all offers and yet make timely interventions at key moments, such as suggesting Haman be impaled on the pole prepared for Mordecai in 7:9) as types of Esther.[16] Without the cooperation of the messenger-eunuchs, Esther and Mordecai could not have communicated. Third and fundamentally, low-status players learn to use their imagination in order not to be overshadowed by fate. Mordecai's plea brings about a transformation in Esther that enables her thereafter constantly to be using her imagination to avert the apparent necessities of her and her people's situation.

The Book of Esther trains its readers to be expert status players. If you are going to survive in the face of hostile neighbors, sometimes threatening your obliteration and the extinction of your people, you need to use all the tactics available to those that have set aside the preservation of their own status.[17] This includes imagination. It includes charm (which is called manipulation by those who find they dislike its effects). It includes solidarity with other oppressed peoples. And it includes opportunism — an alertness to capitalizing on surprising turns of events, with an eye not to one's own glorification, but to the greater cause. Charm, solidarity, imagination, and opportunism are in-

16. Carol Bechtel, *Esther: A Bible Commentary for Teaching and Preaching* (Louisville: Westminster John Knox, 2001), pp. 12-13, drew my attention to the significance of the eunuchs.

17. For more on tactics see Wells, *Improvisation*, pp. 95-98.

tegral to the politics of redemption in the Book of Esther. They are the tactics of the weak.

Questioning Givens

The joy of the story is the overturning of the irreversible edict against the Jews, and the assertion of a new "given", spoken by Haman's advisers and his wife Zeresh: "If Mordecai, before whom your downfall has begun, is of the Jewish people, you will not prevail against him, but will surely fall before him" (6:13).

There are three kinds of givens that mount up together against the Jews. One is the given of the opening political context. The Jews are a small minority in the Persian Empire, and are potentially vulnerable.[18] A second given is the given of the laws of the Medes and the Persians, and in particular the decree "giving orders to destroy, to kill, and to annihilate all Jews, young and old, women and children, in one day, the thirteenth day of the twelfth month, which is the month of Adar, and to plunder their goods" (3:13). Such a law could not be revoked.[19] And with Haman at the helm, there is no doubt that it will be executed thoroughly. The looming date of the thirteenth day of Adar is perhaps the most significant given in the story. A third given is the social code of the period. The palace has a particular code of conduct. For example, as Esther points out to Mordecai, gaining the ear of the king is no simple matter: "All the king's servants and the people of the king's provinces know that if any man or woman goes to the king inside the inner court without being called, there is but one law — all alike are to be put to death. Only if the king holds out the golden sceptre to someone, may that person live" (4:11). In addition, the wider social code assumes a number of static relationships such as the low status of women.

These givens seem overwhelming. That is the force of the story. That is why the liturgical reading of the Book of Esther is such a significant training school for the politics of redemption. However well one knows the story, one shares the Jews' dismay at their plight: "Mordecai tore his clothes and put on sackcloth and ashes . . . there was great mourning among the Jews, with fast-

---

18. Fox notes that the narrator mentions that the king's edicts were sent "to all the royal provinces, to every province in its own script and to every people in its own language" (1:22) — indicating the general respect for ethnic diversity in the Persian Empire (*Character and Ideology*, p. 23).

19. Many commentators point out that there is no other historical corroboration for this, but it is nonetheless a given that is essential to the story.

ing and weeping and lamenting" (4:1-3). And yet brick by brick, this mountainous wall teetering ready to collapse over the Jews, is somehow dismantled. The process of dismantling establishes which factors really are givens, and which, finally, prove not to be.

There are five aspects to this undermining of givens. First, the whole story is written in a burlesque style. There is extravagance in every quarter: a colossal empire of 127 provinces, a 180-day banquet for the officials, a seven-day banquet for residents of the citadel of Susa, a decree for the whole empire on domestic politics, a yearlong preparation for the king's bedchamber, a massacre of the entire Jewish population of the empire, and so on. This is spatial and temporal excess on a grand scale. The exaggerated, sometimes absurd, proportions bend the boundaries of possibility, creating a narrative in which wonders may take place. The empire is clearly so large that it cannot be judged by any normal standards: the king undoubtedly has staggering power. He has so much power that only God can provide any analogy. Perhaps this story is not what it seems. Perhaps the overwhelming proportions are an indication that this is some kind of parable about God's kingdom. The only precedent for description on such a grand (but nonetheless measured) scale is the creation narrative. Is the beginning of the Esther story a kind of new creation? Is the Esther story a mini-world, a kind of thought-experiment of a world with a different kind of creator from the Lord God of Israel?

Second, while the social and political systems seem rigid, the characters at the heart of them are mercurial. Ahasuerus commands the world but not his wife. He is persuaded into issuing a ridiculous decree. He faces an assassination plot but forgets about it. He accepts a gigantic bribe from Haman to issue a decree. He orders genocide but again forgets he has done so. He maintains the golden scepter custom but is seduced by Esther into becoming her plaything.[20] He is quite prepared to issue an edict in favor of the Jews that practically countermands the previous edict against them. He is happy to give his signet ring away to a favourite and allow him to write as he pleases in the name of the king (8:8). Meanwhile Haman jeopardizes his high office by a vendetta against Mordecai's people, and is so puffed up with his own position that he cannot see the danger that lies around him. In an empire based on the king's whim, few givens are genuinely secure. This is a savage critique of monarchy.

Third, in spite of the forces pitted against them, there are a number of things the weak can do. Jews can be part of the royal household. Mordecai can get close enough to public affairs to uncover a plot against the king's life. Es-

---

20. The way Esther wins over the king by touching the top of his held-out scepter is a moment of humor so broad it would be quite at home in a classical farce.

ther can become queen. She can use her wit and charm to gain the king's ear (while his scepter stands erect!). Together they can win the confidence of the eunuchs who are the oil in the joints of the royal household. Their hand contains no aces — but it does contain one or two jokers.

Fourth, the kingdom of givens may still be subverted by luck, surprise and accident. When the lot is drawn for the date of the destruction of the Jews, it falls out with the greatest delay possible — almost a whole year. The king has a sleepless night. He asks for the annals to be read to him (6:1). Haman completely misunderstands Ahasuerus' inquiry about the man the king wishes to honor. These are key turning points in the plot: and they fall outside the conventional logic of intention and action. If givens held sway, every action would have its intended consequence, within a clearly prescribed boundary. But actions have extraordinarily unforeseen consequences, and "all works together for good" for the Jews. An unseen hand is at work. It is this hand, rather than conventional patterns of cause and effect, that is the true given, and it is this hand that is celebrated in liturgically embodied narrative.

Fifth, the givens that present themselves in the story are superseded by other givens that emerge as the story proceeds. Mordecai advises Esther that "if you keep silence at such a time as this, relief and deliverance will rise for the Jews from another quarter" (4:14). This "quarter" is hotly debated: for the name of God is notoriously absent from the narrative.[21] But the point here is that Mordecai assumes that there will be help from another quarter. It is a given. Similarly the narrative truth of the Book of Esther is that, as Zeresh puts it to Haman, "If Mordecai, before whom your downfall has begun, is of the Jewish people, you will not prevail against him, but will surely fall before him" (6:13). This given is so self-evident that even gentiles perceive it.[22] The Jews will survive, even if they require help from another quarter. These are the real givens of the story.

Incorporating Gifts

Overaccepting means placing the small story of the presenting "offer" within a much larger narrative. For example, a prostitute may say to a pedestrian, "Would you like a good time?" and the pedestrian may overaccept by saying, "Would you like me to tell you about what it means to have a *really* good

---

21. See, for example, Fox, *Character and Ideology*, p. 63. But Fox sees no need to suggest what this other quarter might be.

22. See Fox's list of parallels (*Character and Ideology*, pp. 79-80).

time?" In discipleship terms, overaccepting means placing the "small story" of challenging or threatening circumstances into the larger story of what God is doing in the world. For example, when Jesus says, "Give therefore to the emperor the things that are the emperor's, and to God the things that are God's" (Matt. 22:21), he neither blocks nor accepts the proffered denarius but overaccepts it in the light of God's sovereignty.

The Book of Esther read in liturgical context is fundamentally a training school in overaccepting. Overaccepting is the key to the politics of redemption. In a context where blocking is impossible and accepting is intolerable, overaccepting unlocks the door of despair for the Jews. Overaccepting is fundamentally a form of nonviolence — most aptly demonstrated in the lives of those for whom violence is unlikely in any case to be a viable option. Mordecai's address to Esther thus echoes through the political training schools of oppressed peoples throughout the ages. "Do not think that in the king's palace you will escape any more than all the other Jews. For if you keep silence at such a time as this, relief and deliverance will rise for the Jews from another quarter, but you and your father's family will perish. Who knows? Perhaps you have come to royal dignity for just such a time as this" (4:13-14). Blocking is not an available option. If you tacitly accept, you and your father's house will perish.[23] Therefore, says Mordecai, overaccept. Take your femininity, your long training in the harem, your vulnerability, your membership of the Jewish people — the givens that may seem objectionable, unclean, and unjust — and treat them as gifts by incorporating them into the larger story of saving your people. Each of these apparent givens does indeed become a gift in the course of Esther's sequence of banquets for and petitions to the king. Esther, in a decisive moment, overaccepts not only her situation but also Mordecai's appeal. "Go" she says, "gather all the Jews to be found in Susa, and hold a fast on my behalf, and neither eat nor drink for three days, night or day. I and my maids will also fast as you do. After that I will go to the king, though it is against the law; and if I perish, I perish" (4:16). She overaccepts her Jewishness by asking for the joint action of the Jews in Susa in solidarity with her. She overaccepts her position as queen by recognizing that it is not an end in itself but a means to a much higher end; she overaccepts her cousin's petition by going further than he had dared ask. She overaccepts her whole story by perceiving that she has been placed on earth for exactly this moment. And she overaccepts even her own death by

---

23. Commentators are bewildered about whom Mordecai could be implying by the words "your father's house" in relation to the orphan Esther, but it seems to me to be quite clearly a euphemism for himself.

realizing that her fundamental choice is between a politics of redemption and a politics of violence.

Esther's decision in 4:16 is not the only act of overaccepting in the Book of Esther. There are two significant parodies of overaccepting. The first is Memucan's colossal overacceptance of Vashti's refusal to come before the king. Memucan takes Vashti's gesture as the pretext for a decree to pass throughout the empire. The second is Haman's vast overacceptance of Mordecai's refusal to bow down before him. Haman takes Mordecai's gesture as the pretext for the savage decree invoking the genocide of the entire Jewish people. These two parodies may be taken as analogues of the fall of Adam: all are punished for the sin of one. By contrast, Esther's decision is an analogue of Christ's turning towards Jerusalem and the way of the cross: one accepts danger and likely death for the sake of the salvation of the many.

The more uncomfortable aspect of overaccepting is the edict of the twenty-third day of Sivan. This decree cannot accept the earlier edict of the thirteenth day of Nisan, commanding the annihilation of the Jews; neither however, may it simply block that decree, because the laws of the Medes and the Persians "may never be altered" (1:19). Therefore it overaccepts the earlier edict. The language of the composition, content and publication of the second edict (8:9-14) mirrors closely the precise expression of the first edict (3:12-15).[24] The only differences are that the second edict is permissive whereas the first is prescriptive,[25] and that the couriers used to deliver the second edict are given much better transport ("mounted couriers riding on fast steeds bred from the royal herd," 8:10) than were the couriers for the first.

Overaccepting in the Book of Esther therefore has two political dimensions. It shows, first, how one oppressed people treat their own story as a small part of a much larger story, and how they treat their own disadvantages and humiliations as gifts for the manifestation of God's manner of intervention and for capitalizing on unforeseen opportunities that may arise. It shows, second, how even when a threatening force cannot be blocked, it may be mimicked, or parodied, in such a way that its power is dismantled. Whether the edict of 23 Sivan is a genuine overacceptance of the edict of 13 Nisan is a question at the heart of the political interpretation of the Book of Esther.

If overaccepting is about politics, it is just as significantly about time. Overaccepting is about fitting the smaller story of the context into the larger

24. Bechtel has a close study (*Esther,* pp. 72-76).

25. Bechtel makes a case for the second edict not including women and children (*Esther,* p. 75).

story of God and his people and the way he is redeeming the world. It is thus about aligning the practice of a community with the providential governance of God. When Zeresh says to her husband Haman, "If Mordecai, before whom your downfall has begun, is of the Jewish people, you will not prevail against him, but will surely fall before him" (6:13), she is expressing a profound understanding of how the relentless tide of providence overaccepts the desperate straits that the Jews appear to be facing. Nearer and nearer draws the time, the time that shall surely be. . . . But time is ultimately the friend of the Jews, because whether help comes "from another quarter," or whether those who oppose them will "surely fall," destiny is undoubtedly on their side. Haman will turn out, in God's hands, not to be a given oppressing the Jews but a gift that catalyzes their salvation. As Michel de Certeau points out, a tactic is the triumph of time over place. Tactics depend on agile use of time, through rapidity, rhythm, pertinent intervention, and delay.[26] Overaccepting is the practice of placing the apparently urgent time of the moment within the eternal pattern of God's time: it is political liberation through the medium of time.

This pattern of fitting time within the providence of God underlines the role of liturgy. Within the Anglican tradition, the practice of saying Morning and Evening Prayer frames the day. The tenses of the verbs in the canticles become highly significant. Every morning the congregation remembers that God "has come to his people and set them free." Every evening the congregation remember that their eyes "have seen your salvation" and that God "has filled the hungry with good things and sent the rich away empty." Yet in the morning they resolve again this very day to "hear his voice" and not to harden their hearts; and in the evening they look forward to the fulfillment of the promise made to "Abraham and his children for ever."[27] In all these ways the day is set in the context of salvation history and eschatological expectation. Likewise the eucharistic liturgy places the deep needs of God's people (the intercessions) between the acts of God (the readings and sermon) and the sharing of God's life in the eucharistic banquet. The Book of Esther frames its story by narrating eight banquets between the "universal" banquet of chapter one and the salvific banquet of chapter nine. Banquets become the quasi-liturgical way in which Esther overaccepts the elusiveness of time.

Just as the Book of Esther is a story of how the world is transformed

---

26. Michel de Certeau, *The Practice of Everyday Life,* trans. Stephen Rendall (Berkeley: University of California Press, 1984), pp. 35-39.

27. Text of the Benedictus, Venite, Magnificat, and Nunc Dimittis is taken from *Common Worship.*

through a series of banquets, so Christians may read world history as a series of transformations embodied in the liturgy of the Eucharist. The Church may be seen as a way of overaccepting the Jews: by no means denying their story but fitting them into a larger narrative. This need not be seen as an entirely supersessionist claim. For the Christian banquet, the Eucharist, is fundamentally a Jewish Passover meal. The liberation being described is the same liberation as celebrated in Exodus and Covenant. The God is the same God. The Eucharist is perhaps the most significant single practice of overaccepting. And it shows the politics of improvisation. For it does not obliterate the Passover meal; it does not deny it, or simply mimic it: it sets it in a new context, the context of the new covenant. Far from being a rival, replacement practice, Christians and Jews may come to see Passover and Eucharist as complementary practices affirming the solidarity of God's diverse people. Both Passover and Eucharist are banquets that enact God's liberation of the oppressed.[28]

Reincorporating the Lost

The Book of Esther is manifestly a story of how the Jews lived to fight another day. It makes no claim to be a "story of everything," a definitive story whose beginning echoes creation and whose ending anticipates God's last word. Thus of all the themes of improvisation, reincorporation is perhaps the least explicit. Nonetheless, three dimensions of reincorporation are evident.

The first concerns genuine moments of reincorporation in the narrative. The most significant instance is when the sleepless Ahasuerus calls for the annals to be read to him, and he hears how Mordecai saved his life (6:1-2). Here is a vital moment of reincorporation. Discarded material (Mordecai's discovery of the plot) is reintroduced into the narrative at an important juncture and transforms the situation. While no cause for this eventuality is given in the narrative other than benevolent coincidence, the moment of reincorporation characteristically restores a sense of justice and completeness. Likewise, when Mordecai suggests Esther may have "come to royal dignity for just such a time as this" (4:14), there is a disarming sense of completeness, in that Mordecai, like a man walking backwards, has composed a vision of the future out of the shelved elements of the past.[29] The restored vision of the future gives a

---

28. The painful reality is that the Church has so seldom failed to overaccept the Jews. But my argument is that this failure is not inherent in the Eucharist — on the contrary, transforming banquets offer a highly fruitful area for dialogue.

29. For more on the improviser as a "man walking backwards" see Samuel Wells, *Improvisation*, p. 148.

renewed meaning to the past. The final significant moment of reincorporation comes when Mordecai instructs the Jews throughout the empire "that
they should keep the fourteenth day of the month Adar and also the fifteenth
day of the same month, year by year, as the days on which the Jews gained relief from their enemies, and as the month that had been turned for them from
sorrow into gladness and from mourning into a holiday; that they should
make them days of feasting and gladness, days for sending gifts of food to one
another and presents to the poor" (9:21-22). Finally the poor find a place in
the story, as in Deuteronomy, as the living reminders of the vulnerability the
Jews had known.

The second kind of reincorporation is, rather like the second kind of
overaccepting noted above, a parody or ironic instance of the practice. The
narrator enjoys moments when destructive elements may be reintegrated into
the story as humorous or constructive twists. I have earlier noted how
Haman's bowing before the queen proves his downfall (7:8), as a wry echo of
Mordecai's earlier refusal to bow before Haman (3:2). In similar fashion the
narrator twice reintroduces the theme of advice from wife to husband.
Ahasuerus foolishly ignores the wisdom in Vashti's refusal to be humiliated
before the people of Susa. Yet, despite his decree that every man should be
ruler in his own house, he is later quite prepared to attend to the words of his
new wife Esther, as she sets out the predicament of the Jews. Meanwhile
Haman's wife Zeresh orders him to set up a stake on which to impale Mordecai — advice he might have been better not to take — and later speaks the
greatest wisdom in the book, when she says, "If Mordecai, before whom your
downfall has begun, is of the Jewish people, you will not prevail against him,
but will surely fall before him" (6:13).

The third kind of reincorporation, like the third kind of overaccepting
considered above, is the most uncomfortable. The relationship of Mordecai
and Haman echoes the relationship of Saul and Agag. The reluctance of Saul
to kill Agag led, it seems, not only to Saul's own downfall but also to the predicament of the Jews in the Book of Esther. Mordecai, as disadvantaged in
this story as Saul is privileged in 1 Samuel, is resolved not to make the same
mistake again. This can be the only narrative explanation for the savagery of
the slaughter described in 9:5-16.[30] This moment of reincorporation may be
seen as the reappearance in the story, not so much of a discarded element that
may become a gift, as of unfinished business that has become a threat.

---

30. If the number of Jews in the empire (or in the empire besides the returnees from Exile)
were estimated at 75,000, it would lend this uncomfortable part of the narrative a slightly
greater sense of balance and completeness.

Reincorporation thus appears, like overaccepting, to give a name to the point where a Jewish reading of the Book of Esther begins to part company with a Christian one.[31] For the traditional Jewish reading, accompanied by the ribaldry of the Purim festival and in the shadow of the Holocaust, there may be a lesson in the Book of Esther that some people cannot be reincorporated, that some events and threats cannot be overaccepted, but must be blocked at all costs. A Christian reading must begin by recognizing the stark extent to which Christians have historically taken roles like those of Ahasuerus and even Haman towards the Jews, and less starkly the degree to which this book has itself been a discarded element in the tradition ripe for reincorporation. But it must also struggle with the issues of whether the brutal concluding chapters of the book genuinely represent the qualities of overaccepting and reincorporation so evident in the rest of the narrative. In the politics of redemption, the Book of Esther trains oppressed minorities to look to discarded elements — and people — for decisive reintegration into the story to provide unexpected transformation in unpropitious circumstances. It helps people look to the past with hope rather than to the future with despair. But when it comes to those with positions of considerable political power and influence, the Book of Esther poses a question of whether some threatening people and groups (Agag, Haman's sons, and the Amalekites) can ever be seen as potential gifts.

Forming Habits

When it comes to forming habits the Book of Esther is more explicit than in any other aspect. The lessons are as follows.

Record the saving deeds of your people. The fact that the king has an accurate record of the events that saved his life is a vital element in the narrative. It is the first political lesson to record and remember those deeds and people who have saved you. This is the book's conclusion (9:32). Just as Deuteronomy implores its readers to recall the Passover and the Exodus, so the Book of Esther is an appeal to its readers to record and remember how the Jewish people were saved. This is a highly significant instance of the scriptural-liturgical practices that constitute a particular kind of political life that challenges, through a number of complex strategies and tactics, other modes of power.

31. It is not that these extra-scriptural categories stand in judgment over scriptural narrative: it is more that these particular terms help Christians articulate a misgiving that is already there.

Recording saving deeds means having a certain kind of attentiveness to time, and an attention to historical particulars. The scriptures are full of apparently insignificant particulars that later become part of the story of salvation. The Church is concerned with the politics of those particulars.

Read aloud and interactively the story of your salvation. The reading of "the Scroll" at the feast of Purim is a suitably riotous community event, with an atmosphere of pantomime to suit the burlesque plot and dimensions of the narrative. This is not a text for private meditation, but a script for public performance. Memory is not a matter of writing tablets of stone, but of a covenant inscribed on the heart. The Book of Esther is a circus of somersaults, but once it has grabbed your attention, it has a gift for everyone. In this, the Church has a great deal to learn from the life and practices of Jewish communities. Esther is interlaced with implications for an understanding of the "other" — the "other" woman in the court, the "other" race at the heart of the Empire. For a Christian to say "salvation is from the Jews" (John 4:22) means, among other things, that the Jews had it first, and that to work out what it means must involve attending to what it means to Jews.

Repeat again and again. The Book of Esther is a training school that works by being repeated again and again, at least annually. It is a rehearsal for reversal. It is to be repeated until its lessons become habits, its gestures become practices, its givens become trusted, and its transformation becomes expected.

Relish eating food together. The Book of Esther is all about banquets — lavish, sensuous, enticing, surprising, joyous.[32] The key to seeing the narrative as a training school in the politics of redemption is to realize that in this book, the banquet is the transforming moment. An invitation to a banquet is an invitation to a political reversal. And now it will at last be clear why I have insisted that the Book of Esther, read in liturgical context, is a training school for the politics of redemption. For the appropriate "liturgical context" is the banquet: the repeated, interactive, reading-and-performing rehearsal of reversal Christians call the Eucharist. This is the place and time where Christians recall that God has put down the mighty from their seats and exalted the humble and meek — and that God, the mighty, has come down from his seat and become humble and meek so that we, if we are humble and meek, might, through the power of his Spirit, become mighty. This is the place and time where Christians celebrate that greatest of all reversals, and where they re-

---

32. Fox identifies ten banquets: Ahasuerus's banquets for the officials, for the people of Susa, for Esther's enthronement, and with Haman; Vashti's banquet for the women of Susa; Esther's two banquets; the Jews' feasting at the counter decree; and the first and second feasts of Purim. He carefully interconnects these banquets with one another (*Character and Ideology,* p. 157; see also Bechtel, *Esther,* pp. 4-6).

enact the death and resurrection of Christ, the definitive reversal gently antic-ipated in the mission of Esther.

Reading Esther in the context of the Eucharist and particularly in the con-text of Purim highlights one significant query in relation to Christian liturgy. Why is it, particularly in the West, so obsessed with imposing order on chaos? Why is it so sober, so measured, so modest in its emotional engagement and inhibited in its passionate display? There is a place for the carefully planned banquet of the thoughtful Esther, and there is clearly little place for the mind-lessly extravagant 180-day banquet of the king: but does Christian liturgy speak sufficiently of the sheer joy of being released from the sentence of death — does eucharistic worship feel like discovering the fearsome edict has been overturned? Is there a sufficient sense that the world has been turned upside down, and now anything is possible with God? Perhaps, among more de-prived and oppressed peoples, it does. But maybe in the West the banquet feels disturbingly like one of a people who never believed the fearsome edict really applied to them. And this is the real heart of the Church's alienation from the Jews.

The politics of redemption is a politics in which the sorely oppressed, the faithful, the unjustly condemned, the meek and mourning are blessed; in which those who cannot fight find ample ways of opening their situations and lives to grace; in which evil does not reign, but is overturned by its own pretensions, by imagination, by opportunism, surprise, and coincidence; in which forgotten kindness is reincorporated and subjugated femininity is overaccepted. This is the witness of the Book of Esther: and it is a politics for our time. But more than anything else the Book of Esther is an invitation to a party, a riotous mixture of memory, reversal, transformation and laughter, a party that is repeated time and again until it is inscribed on heart and mind and hand and voice. And that repetition is a liturgical one. For Christians call that party the Eucharist.

The Ritual Is Not the Hunt:
The Seven Wedding Blessings,
Redemption, and Jewish Ritual as Fantasy

Shaul Magid

"Do passive indolent women make the best wives?"

Mary Wollstonecraft

Ritual studies occupies a major place in the contemporary study of religion. The anthropological and theoretical work of scholars such as Margaret Mead, Emile Durkheim, Sigmund Freud, Claude Lévi-Strauss, Victor Turner, and Clifford Geertz has placed the study of ritual at the center of understanding the emergence, development, and survival of culture.[1] More recently, historians of religion such as Catherine Bell and Jonathan Z. Smith have taken this initial research and applied it more specifically to religious ritual, that is, to acts that are performed within a framework of devotional practice and/or are determined by their practitioners to have some dimension of transcendent or supernatural meaning and significance.[2] These acts are humanly constructed,

---

1. See Emile Durkheim, *The Elementary Forms of Religious Life* (New York: Free Press, 1965), pp. 337-65; Claude Lévi-Strauss, *The Naked Man,* trans. J. and D. Weitman (New York: Harper & Row, 1981); Clifford Geertz, *The Interpretation of Cultures* (New York: Basic Books, 1973); Sigmund Freud, "Obsessive Acts and Religious Practices," in *The Standard Edition of the Complete Psychological Works of Sigmund Freud,* vol. 9, ed. J. Strachey (London: Hogarth, 1953), pp. 117-27; Victor Turner, *The Forest of Symbols: Aspects of Ndembu Ritual* (Ithaca: Cornell University Press, 1967).

2. See Catherine Bell, *Ritual Theory, Ritual Practice* (New York: Oxford University Press,

---

To JP, NB, NKL: a response. I want to thank Rabbi Dr. Aubrey Glazer with whom I studied and debated some of these texts during the spring and summer of 2004 in Toronto, Canada, immediately preceding his marriage to Elyssa Wortzman. His passion and insight are much appreciated. Any errors are solely my own.

and thus "historical," but the actors claim they point to an unhistoricized dimension of reality, a dimension unrealized and, in some cases, only accessed *through* ritual.

The application of ritual studies to Judaism from a theoretical perspective is in its early stages. A recent book by Ithamar Gruenwald is one of the first devoted exclusively to ritual theory and Judaism.[3] This essay has a much narrower focus. It is devoted to one section of one ritual and based on one lengthy homily and some subsequent comments by an early Hasidic master's interpretation of that ritual. My intention here is not to give a broad interpretation of Jewish ritual but only to illustrate how this particular ritual, interpreted through this Hasidic lens, supports the notion of ritual as unrealizable fantasy rather than a reflection of reality. Through such a lens we can see how this Hasidic master understands the tension created through the ritual — perhaps created by the ritual — displacing the resolution to some unknown (and perhaps unattainable) future.

The ritual in question is the Jewish marriage ceremony, a layered ritual consisting of two basic legal components (the betrothal, or *'erusin,* and the marriage, or *kiddushin*) and various non- or quasi-legal components that accompany the implementation of these two legal criteria.[4] More specifically, it focuses on the liturgical component of the marriage ritual, the seven blessings that accompany, and conclude, the ceremony.[5]

1992), esp. pp. 19-46 and 182-95; Bell, *Ritual: Perspectives and Dimensions* (New York: Oxford University Press, 1997); Ronald C. Grimes, *Readings in Ritual Studies* (New York: Prentice Hall, 1995); and Jonathan Z. Smith, *To Take Place: Toward Theory in Ritual* (Chicago: University of Chicago Press, 1987).

3. Ithamar Gruenwald, *Ritual and Ritual Theory in Ancient Israel* (Leiden: Brill, 2003). Cf. the review of Gruenwald by Jonathan Klawans in *AJS Review* 29-1 (April 2005), 163-65; Moshe Hallamish, "The Place of Kabbala in Ritual" [Hebrew] in *The Rituals of Israel: Sources and Development,* vol. 3, ed. D. Sperber (Jerusalem: Mossad Ha-Rav Kook, 1998), pp. 289-311; Moshe Idel, "Some Remarks on Ritual and Mysticism in Geronese Kabbala," *Journal of Jewish Thought and Philosophy* 3 (1993), 111-30; Len Goodman, "Rational Law/Ritual Law," and Moshe Sokol, "Mitzvah as Metaphor," both in *A People Apart: Chosenness and Ritual in Jewish Philosophical Thought,* ed. Daniel H. Frank (Albany: SUNY Press, 1993), pp. 109-228; Yakov Travis, "Kabbalistic Foundations of Jewish Spiritual Practice: Rabbi Ezra of Gerona on the Kabbalistic Meaning of the Mitzvot," Ph.D. dissertation, Brandeis University, 2002, pp. 108-46; and Elliot Wolfson, *Language, Eros, Being* (New York: Fordham University Press, 2005), pp. 246-55.

4. For an explication of the ritual and its legal components in the rabbinic period see Michael Satlow, *Jewish Marriage in Antiquity* (Princeton: Princeton University Press, 2001), pp. 162-77; and Judith Hauptman, *Re-Reading the Rabbis* (Boulder: Westview Press, 1998), esp. pp. 60-73.

5. The seven blessings are commonly called *sheva berakhot* but also called *birkhat ha-hatanim* ("the blessings of the bridegroom") since *halakhically* (legally) the whole ritual and

As is the case with many religious rituals, the Jewish wedding ceremony serves as a motif or metaphor for a more formative moment in the myth or history of that culture. In this case, the wedding is viewed as a metaphor for the theophany at Sinai (Exodus 19–21), imagining the covenant of Israel with God in heterosexually erotic terms.[6] The midrashic depiction of Sinai as the "wedding" of God and Israel results in the wedding ritual adopting the trappings of that event, e.g. the Torah as the vehicle of the covenant is embodied in the bridegroom and bride and the ritual space of the *chuppah* becomes Sinai. That is, the midrashic correlation is reciprocal: Sinai is a wedding and any common wedding becomes Sinai.

The liturgical component of the wedding ceremony includes a statement of intent of the bridegroom to consecrate the bride solely to him (in the traditional ceremony the bride is silent and is "acquired" by the bridegroom, an idea that will become significant later on) and the recitation of seven blessings recited by prominent guests or family members.[7] This essay will focus on

---

subsequent celebration serve to cheer the bridegroom. See R. Azaria Berzon, "Birkhat Hatanim," *Tehumin* (Alon Shvut, Israel, 1985), vol. 6, pp. 101-17. This legal foundation only strengthens Shneur Zalman's kabbalistic interpretation. On the seven blessings see Rabbi Shaul Yisraeli, "On the Blessings of the Groom and the Participation of Women in Them" [Hebrew], *Barka-i* 1 (Summer 1983): 163-66. In English see Joel B. Wolowolsky, "Women's Participation in Sheva Berakhot," *Modern Judaism* 12 (1992), 157-65.

6. See b. T. Taanit, 26b; Mekhilta d'Rebbe Yishmael, Yitro, B'Hodesh (Horowitz, Rabin, eds.) 214. Cf. Tosefta Baba Kama 7:4; Satlow, *Marriage*, pp. 50-57; Arthur Green, "The Song of Songs in Early Jewish Mysticism," *Orim: A Jewish Journal at Yale* 2 (1987), 49-63; Green, *Keter: The Crown of God in Early Jewish Mysticism* (Princeton: Princeton University Press, 1997), pp. 78-87; and Henry Glazer, "The Marriage as Metaphor in Jewish Theology: A Mirror of God's Nature and Its Relation to Israel" (New York: The Jewish Theological Seminary, 1997), pp. 30-46. The classic prophetic text describing the relationship between Israel and God as a wedding can be found in Jeremiah 2:2: "I accounted to your favor, The devotion of your youth, Your love as a bride — How you followed Me in the wilderness, in a land not sown."

7. The blessings read as follows: (1) Blessed are you, O Lord our God, King of the universe, who has created the fruit of the vine. (2) Blessed are you, O Lord our God . . . who has created all things to His glory. (3) Blessed are you, O Lord our God . . . who has created man (Adam). (4) Blessed are you, O Lord our God . . . who has made man in His image, after His likeness, and out of His very self. You have prepared unto him a perpetual fabric. Blessed are you, O Lord, who has created man. (5) May she who is barren (Zion) be exceedingly glad and rejoice with her children who are united in her midst and joy. Blessed are you, O Lord, who makes Zion glad through restoring her children. (6) May You gladden the beloved friends (the married couple) as You made glad Your creature (Adam) in the Garden of Eden in the ancient time. Blessed are You, O Lord our God, who gladdens the bridegroom and the bride. (7) Blessed are you, O Lord, King of the universe, who has created joy and gladness, bridegroom and bride, rejoicing, song, pleasure and delight, love and friendship, peace and fellowship. May there soon be heard in the streets of Jerusalem, the voice of joy and gladness, the voice of the bridegroom and the bride,

the seven blessings as interpreted by the early Hasidic Grand Rabbi Shneur Zalman of Liady, patriarch of the Hasidic dynasty known as Habad or Lubavitch.[8] I will attempt to show that his Hasidic/kabbalistic interpretation of the seven blessings illustrates that the religious ritual in question does not conform to reality but, in fact, acknowledges, by implication, that the act being ritualized (i.e., marriage) by definition fails to live up to the expectation of the ritual constructs, just as exile (the reality of Israel) shows that Sinai is a moment of covenantal reciprocity that fails to reflect the reality of the covenant established there. Hence this ritual is not, in fact, a devotional moment inaugurating a human decision (in this case, marriage) but illustrates that the event in question fails before it begins.[9]

In his essay "The Bare Facts of Ritual" Jonathan Z. Smith argues that rituals often present unrealistic and unrealizable portrayals of certain behaviors.[10] One example Smith employs is an elaborate sentimental depiction of a hunting ritual among Finnish tribes. The "hunting ritual" describes and enacts detailed ways in which the animal is addressed during the hunt and specifies certain ways it must be killed (bloodlessly, painlessly, and never when the animal is asleep or hibernating). The ritual and accompanying "liturgy" describe the passive role the hunter plays in the process, seeing himself as a vehicle for returning the animal to its "Supernatural Owner." In short, the ritual depicts an environmentally friendly and humanitarian rendering of the hunt. In reality, however, these same tribes do not conform to the ritual they practice. In the real hunt, the tribesmen kill in much more conventional ways, trapping and sometimes bludgeoning the animal to death, killing bears while they hibernate, and so forth. That is, they blatantly act in ways that contradict the ritual. How does one make sense of the obvious discrepancy between the ritual and the reality? Smith argues that (1) the practitioners of the ritual are acutely aware of the discrepancy between ritual and reality and are not apologetic about it; and (2) the discrepancy is the very origin and basis for the ritual:

---

the jubilant voice of bridegrooms from their nuptial canopies, and of the young from their feats of song. Blessed are you, O Lord, who gladdens the bridegroom and the bride.

8. The homily appears in his *Siddur Tefilot M Kol Ha-Shana* (hereinafter TMKHS; Brooklyn: Ozar Ha-Hasidism, 1981), pp. 125-36. For a popular and schematic history of the Chabad dynasty see Chaim Dalfin, *The Seven Chabad-Lubavitch Rebbes,* ed. Dov Baron (Lanham, Md.: Jason Aronson, 1998).

9. On the rabbinic notion of the "ideal marriage" see Satlow, *Marriage,* pp. 225-245. This includes rabbinic texts expressing the notion of the ideal spouse.

10. See Jonathan Z. Smith, "The Bare Facts of Ritual," in his *Imagining Religion: From Babylon to Jonestown* (Chicago: University of Chicago Press, 1982), pp. 53-65.

I would suggest, among other things, ritual represents the creation of a controlled environment where the variables (i.e., the accidents) of ordinary life may be displaced precisely because they are felt to be so overwhelmingly present and powerful. Ritual is a means of performing the way things ought to be in conscious tension to the way things are in such a way that this ritualized perfection is recollected in the ordinary, uncontrolled course of things. . . . [Ritual] relies . . . for its power on the perceived fact that, in actuality, such possibilities cannot be realized.[11]

On this reading, ritual does not reflect reality but contradicts it such that the shortcomings of reality (bludgeoning a bear to death while it is hibernating due to the real fear that otherwise the bear might kill you) are tempered by the projection of a more perfect humanitarian model enacted in the "ritual of the hunt." Rituals create controlled environments void of the dangers of reality, enabling a society to fantasize about how it would like to live (and how it believes it should live) while mired in the complexities of its own frail existence. Sacred space is part of that controlled environment. In housing the ritual it accentuates the distinction between the real and ideal. In describing the hunting ritual, Smith argues that the ritual that precedes the hunt is not an attempt to create a model that can be replicated in the hunt itself. In fact, the principle of the ritual is that "the ritual is unlike the hunt."[12] The world created by the ritual is not only distinct from the real, it creates a model that, given the nature of the presently "real," simply cannot exist. Smith suggests, "There is a 'gnostic' dimension to ritual. It provides the means for demonstrating what we know ought to have been done, what ought to have taken place . . . ritual thus provides an occasion for reflection on and rationalization of the fact that what ought to have been done was not, what ought to have taken place, did not."[13] I will argue that in Judaism, a religion that has a strong redemptive component, the non- or even anti-reality of this ritual is constructed as a prefiguring of a messianic future, projecting an ideal redemptive moment into the mundane and fallen state of human affairs. Thus the seventh blessing concerning a redeemed Jerusalem frames the previous six.

In his commentary to the siddur (the classic text of Jewish liturgy) Shneur Zalman offers a kabbalistic interpretation of the seven blessings that accompany the wedding ceremony. The blessings constitute the center of the liturgical part of the ritual, recited under the *chuppah* (the sacred space) while hold-

11. Smith, "The Bare Facts of Ritual," p. 63.
12. Smith, "The Bare Facts of Ritual," p. 64.
13. Smith, *To Take Place*, p. 109.

ing the cup of wine used to consecrate the marriage (the sacred object). The blessings celebrate three moments: the creation of the human being (Adam/ man) in God's image, the joy of marital union, and the commandment to procreate. They conclude with a blessing of the future joy of wedding celebrations in a redeemed Jerusalem when the collective covenant between God and Israel will mirror the particular covenant of the bride and the bridegroom.

Shneur Zalman uses the language of these blessings as an occasion to reflect on what is occurring in and through the marriage, drawing heavily on two motifs: the rabbinic utilization of the wedding as a metaphor for Sinai, and procreation (more specifically, the sexual act), the formal *telos* of the marriage ritual. Thus Sinai (i.e., Torah) and the sex act (in all its biological details) become reflections of one another. The rabbinic metaphor of Sinai/ *chuppah* is hyperliteralized and elevated to an ontological status. In his depiction of the ritual, Shneur Zalman constructs a reality far from the real and messy nature of human relationships. In fact, according to his reading, the ritual creates a reality that undermines the very possibility of any spousal relationship accomplishing the goals set out in the ritual. The ritual is framed as a future-oriented expectation; a fantasy of accomplishing something that cannot be accomplished in this world. As we will see, in his reading one of the functional purposes of marriage is the limitation and thus control of male sexual desire through the objectification of the pious wife ("the woman of valor" of Proverbs 31:10) who dutifully serves her husband, summarily submitting to her status as catalyst and object. This is not merely an ideal to aspire to; it is a fantasy that cannot exist because the de-eroticized passive wife is not the compelling object of sexual desire (the seductive maiden in Song of Songs stands in contrast to the "woman of valor who is a crown to her husband" in Proverbs 12:4).

Human Bodies as Torah: Sex as Interpretation

The beginning of this homily introduces the well-known rabbinic depiction of the wedding as the metaphor for Sinai.[14] In midrashic literature, this correlation serves as a covenantal frame whereby Sinai is viewed as an event founded on love, eros, and a binding commitment. It is not that Sinai is the origin of the rabbinic ritual of marriage but rather the rabbinic ritual of marriage binds God and Israel to their Sinai commitments. Shneur Zalman writes that at Sinai

---

14. For a discussion of this metaphor within kabbalistic exegesis, see Elliot Wolfson, *Circle in the Square* (Albany: SUNY Press, 1995), pp. 7-10.

sometimes Torah is the bridegroom and Israel the bride and sometimes Israel in the bridegroom and Torah the bride. "When one studies Torah to fix his soul *(l'tikun ha-nefesh)* the Torah is the bridegroom who emanates [downward] and the divine soul receives that light and is thus the bride. When one studies Torah for its own sake it is the opposite. Israel is the bridegroom who draws light from *eyn sof* to Torah and Torah receives it and is called the betrothed."[15] The interpretive frame here seems to be one of mutual reciprocity, each party serving to fulfill the needs of the other. This ostensible egalitarian (or proto-egalitarian) approach is problematized in what follows.[16]

Shneur Zalman's Hasidic/kabbalistic interpretation hyperliteralizes the rabbinic metaphor of Sinai/*chuppah,* viewing the bridegroom and bride as two dimensions of Torah — the written law (Tanakh) and the oral law (its rabbinic interpretation).[17] He frames this discussion by noticing a liturgical difference between the second and third blessing. The second blessing begins with the liturgical formula using the word "Blessed [art Thou]" *barukh,* while the third blessing begins with *barukh* and also concludes with the standard liturgical formula of *barukh.* The second blessing is uncharacteristic of standard liturgy (not having a concluding sentence beginning with *barukh*). He argues this unconventional blessing corresponds to Adam (the male) while the third more conventional blessing corresponds to Eve (the female). He explains:

The notion of bridegroom and bride hints at the written law and the oral law. The written law does not explain any mitzvah in its fullness but only

15. TMKHS, p. 125a. The notion of gender reversals between God and Israel is not uncommon in kabbalistic literature. See, for example, in Elliot Wolfson, *Circle in the Square* (Albany: SUNY Press, 1995), pp. 79-121; and Wolfson, *Language, Eros, Being* (New York: Fordham University Press, 2005), pp. 46-58 and 333-71. Specific to our concerns, we read "To be sure, kabbalists portray ritual, with a special focus on liturgical practices, in terms of gender transformations that render fluid the distinction between male and female — Jewish men are feminized so that the divine female may be masculinized and the antediluvian androgyny restored . . ." (*Language,* p. 49).

16. For a more apologetic approach to this whole question, focusing on the Chabad tradition that emerges from Schneur Zalman, see Naftali Lowenthal, "'Daughter/Wife of Hasid' — Or: 'Hasidic Woman'?" *Jewish Studies* 40 (2000), 21-28; and idem, "Women and the Dialectic of Spirituality in Hasidism," in *Within Hasidic Circles: Studies in Hasidism in Memory of Mordecai Wilensky,* ed. I. Etkes, D. Assaf, I. Bartal, and E. Reiner (Jerusalem: Bialik Institute, 1999), pp. 7-65 [English section]. More generally see Ada Rapoport-Albert, "On Women in Hasidism," in *Jewish History: Essays in Honor of Chimen Abramsky* (London: Halban, 1988).

17. In the rabbinic mind both were given at Sinai. See *Midrash Sifra* to Leviticus, "Behar Sinai." The rabbinic depiction of the status of the oral law as equal or superior to the written law is discussed in David Weiss-Halivni's *Midrash, Mishna, and Gemara: The Jewish Predilection for Justified Law* (Cambridge, Mass.: Harvard University Press, 1986).

hints at it in writing . . . the oral law is fully disclosed . . . this is a metaphor for the male and female. The egg is initially formed into an embryo through the male semen in the womb of the woman. The "whiteness" of the father [the seminal drop] is completely undifferentiated, white and without blemish. It has no distinguishable form. . . . When this drop is disclosed [through insemination] in the womb of the mother it takes on form and appendages like a head, feet, and arms [begin to grow]. So too the oral law is called *malkhut* which is the world of disclosure (*'alma d'etgalyah*).[18] It interprets and explains how each mitzvah is done. This is not the case with the written law where the mitzvot are in a state of concealment, like the seminal drop.[19]

There is an ostensibly seamless transition from the Torah (written and oral), alluding perhaps to the rabbinic midrash, arguing that both were given at Sinai, to sexual consummation or insemination and procreation as the *telos* of marriage refracted through the lens of the wedding liturgy. The ritual has two referents — first the act of procreation and second the metaphor of Sinai (Torah). Shneur Zalman merges these two and then reads one through the lens of the other. The ritual points to procreation through the vision of Sinai; the bodies are the texts that create "religion" (another Jew who is also an embodiment of Torah and the process by which Torah is extended) through their actions upon each other. Sinai/the *chuppah* is not only the place where the Torah is given — it is where it is (re)created. The *chuppah* is simultaneously Sinai and the nuptial bed. Revelation is sexualized and sex becomes the creative/revelatory act that produces Torah.

But of course this romantic image does not hold the reality of the gender life in traditional Judaism nor does it correspond to the biological make-up of the bodies engendered here. The prohibition of women to engage in Torah is specific to the oral law while a woman studying the written law is, for many jurists, permissible.[20] For the male, it is the oral law (Talmud) that dominates his devotional life; and it is he, and not she, who "explains and interprets" the life of mitzvot. Biologically it is the female's genitals that are concealed while

---

18. See Tikkunei Zohar, p. 17a.

19. TMKHS, p. 132c.

20. See, for example, R. Yehiel Michel Epstein, *Arukh Ha-Shulkhan* V: "Yoreh Deah," 246, and R. Israel Meir Ha-Kohen, *Likkutei Halakhot* (St. Petersburg, 1918) to b.T. Sotah 20a; and R. Moseh Feinstein, Igrot Moshe, "Yoreh Deah" (Brooklyn, 1973), 1:137, 2:102 and 3:73b. Cf. the sources in Shoshana Zloty, *And Your Children Shall Be Learned* (New York: Jason Aronson, 1993), esp. pp. 227ff.; and Norma Baum Joseph, "Jewish Education for Women: Rabbi Moshe Feinstein's Map of America," *American Jewish History* 83:2 (1995), 207-9.

the male organ is "disclosed," a biological fact that is not lost in the rabbinic or kabbalistic tradition.

The ritual is thus interpreted here as envisioning a world inverse from our own. Women embody that which is forbidden to them. Men are represented (the written law as the undifferentiated and concealed seminal drop) by that which is antithetical to their charge as arbiters of Jewish law and practice.[21] The creative and interpretive skill (here depicted biologically) is ostensibly taken away from men and given to women. The ritual that should inaugurate the devotional roles of each gender turns the social structure on its head. As Smith suggests, "the ritual is unlike the hunt."

The correlation between man/woman and written/oral law is expanded later in this homily. There, however, the engendering is bent somewhat. The feminine now becomes the Zaddik (the righteous male) who carries the will of God through his oral teaching.[22] The bride now transmorphs into Israel at Sinai and this homily now returns to what we cited at the outset — the feminine and masculine are fluid categories. The wedding canopy now becomes the mountain and the blessings invoke God as the male whose will is being inherited by the female (the bridegroom turned Zaddik). The question then is: when Israel (or the Zaddik) becomes the female, what becomes of the "real" woman who stands under the *chuppah?* Before answering that question we need to see how this transgendering occurs in our text.

> There is an advantage of the oral law over the written law in that the oral law reveals the will of God *(razon elyon).* From the written law [alone] we cannot know how to make phylacteries or *zizit* (ritual fringes). From the oral law the will of God becomes manifest without any addition or subtraction, as is known. It is also known that divine will is a contract of God Himself *(ba'al razon),* as it is written, *Open up your hand and sustain all of life, your will* (Psalm 145:17).[23] That is, *all of life (kol hai)* is the Zaddik, the life of

21. In fact, there are prohibitions regarding the study of the written law without its interpretive (oral law) tradition. See Frank Talmage, "'Keep Your Sons from Scripture': The Bible in Medieval Jewish Scholarship and Spirituality," in *Understanding Scripture: Explorations of Jewish and Christian Traditions of Interpretation,* ed. Clemens Thoma and Michael Wyschogrod (New Jersey: Stimulus Books, 1987), pp. 81-101.

22. The feminization of the male in his relationship to the (masculine) deity is common in classical kabbalistic literature and also has its correlate in Christian mystical literature. See Moshe Idel, "Sexual Metaphors and Praxis in Kabbala," in *Jewish Family: Metaphor and Memory,* ed. David Kraemer (New York: Oxford University Press, 1989), pp. 197-224.

23. The hyper-literal and awkward translation is intentional in an attempt to exhibit how it is being read by Schneur Zalman. A more idiomatic translation would be, *Open up your hand and sustain the world with your will.*

the world, the last dimension of all divine emanations [who carry your will]. From the Zaddik, the divine will is drawn from its source (who is God, unified and one and above all will and wisdom). As it is written, *May it be your will*, or *makers of His will*.[24] That is, the Zaddik *makes* divine will by means of contraction *(zimzumim)*. Therefore, one should understand that since the oral law draws divine will from its source, saying this is ritually clean *(kosher)* and this is pure *(tahor)*, this must also contain a dimension of the source of that will (i.e. God). This is not the case with the written law which does not reveal the will (of God) but it is concealed in wisdom *(hokhma)* hints and crowns.[25]

The "female" who embodies the oral law in the previous citation is now envisioned as the feminized (yet still male) Zaddik who carries the divine message in his teaching ("this is kosher, this is *tahor*"). The wedding ceremony moves back to Sinai where Israel is feminized in relation to a masculine deity.[26]

We find that the feminine is actually rooted in the masculine and the masculine is rooted in the feminine. It is only in their formation [as physical male or female] that they are transformed. By means of these parables you will know that the oral law is the foundation of the origin of [divine] will, which is in the realm of the masculine, and the written law is founded on the feminine. . . . This is why [the final blessing] concludes, "to bring joy to the bridegroom *with (′im)* the bride." That is, the essential joy is the joy of the bride who, in their roots, is the opposite. The female bride is thus above the place of the masculine emanation. This is the meaning of, *A wife of valor is a crown to her husband* . . . (Proverbs 12:4). The crown refers to the root of the husband. He is masculine now but feminine in his root.[27]

Shneur Zalman has given us two ways of understanding how the feminine (the oral law) is higher than the masculine but in both cases the lofty feminine is, in essence, masculine. In this first case, the feminine is a manifestation

24. This usually refers to angels. See b. T. Sota 39b. But see Abraham ibn Ezra to Psalm 33:4 where this locution is also connected to the Zaddik.

25. TMKHS, p. 134b.

26. The text continues to offer a reason why the female produces a male child and the male produces a female child. The point is to substantiate the seemingly counterintuitive notion of the female serving the male function of explicating Torah (the oral law). While an interesting comment about the fluidity of gender, it is not essential to my argument. See TMKHS, p. 134b (middle section).

27. See TMKHS, p. 134b.

of the male (Zaddik). It is the Zaddik, as arbiter of the oral law, who serves as the feminine carrier of the masculine God (the *ba'al razon*). Thus the perfection of the female is only when she/he becomes male. In the second case, the feminine (oral law) is higher than the masculine because in essence the feminine is masculine in its roots.[28] Thus it is the male who carries the divine will and it is the male who interpreters Torah. The woman, as rooted in the masculine, is thus closed, concealed, and ineffectual. What Shneur Zalman has done is to take any positive assessment of the feminine exemplified in the wedding blessings and make it a manifestation of the male. We must now turn to the question, What becomes of the flesh and blood female bride whose illustrious femininity has now been taken by her male partner?

The Expression and Diffusion of the Masculine and the Bride as Object

In the previous section we viewed how the male bridegroom is transgendered to become either the "female" Zaddik (in relation to God) or rooted in the "positive" femininity as interpreter of (the closed and concealed) written law.[29] In some sense, both cases point back to the relationship between the male and God/Torah; that is, both are dominated by the Sinai experience. Does the bride under the *chuppah* also experience a transgendered state? My answer is no. I suggest she is un-gendered. By that I do not mean that she loses gender completely but that she loses any sovereignty that positive engendering entails. She becomes the object through which the male can embody his erotic desire that he then turns away from her and toward God. As noted above, this homily is based on the incongruity between the second and third blessing of the seven wedding blessings. The second blessing opens with *"barukh"* but does not conclude with *"barukh"*; and the third blessing opens with *"barukh"* and concludes with *"barukh."* That is, it has a seal *(hatima)* creating an enclosed (and enclosing) whole. The third blessing thus embodies the earthly bride. She is the seal of her husband, the receptacle of his "bless-

---

28. The masculine root of the feminine is common in Lurianic Kabbala, the tradition that plays most prominently in Schneur Zalman's thinking. See, for example, Hayyim Vital, *Likkutei Torah* (Vilna, 1880), p. 21; and Wolfson, *Language*, p. 94. Cf. Charles Mopsik, *Les sexes des âmes* (Paris: Editions de l'éclat, 2003).

29. I am in agreement with Wolfson that the "female" Zaddik is not a "womanly man" but rather very much a man who has absorbed the roots of the feminine to serve in a particularly passive (yet still male) role. In fact, here it is only through his maleness as bridegroom that he can become the (feminized) Zaddik. See *Language*, p. 94 and especially note 327 page 465.

ing" and/or the object of his desire. Shneur Zalman uses this structure as a frame to discuss the nature of desire, pleasure, and joy *(simha)*. The expression of desire is facilitated through *zimzum* (contraction) initiating the downward flow of divine light (and human desire) toward its object — the world or the wife. In reference to God and Israel, this *zimzum* is a consequence of mitzvot. The performance of mitzvot arouses divine (male) desire that emanates into the world (via *zimzum*) as reward and thus pleasure for Israel. Sin prevents divine flow and is thus the source of pain.

> These are the divine decrees. Through mitzvot Israel is able to arouse God to act in ways that result in joy and kindness. Sins have the opposite effect. . . . By means of rigor *(gevurot)* and *zimzum* [the contraction of divine light] light descends to give pleasure and joy through the performance of mitzvot. . . . Metaphorically we can see that human pleasure is also dependant on will. If one does not have the desire to eat he will not experience pleasure whereas if he desires it, he will experience pleasure. . . . It is known that joy *(simha)* comes from pleasure, that is, the disclosure of that which is concealed in the essence of the source of the emanation.[30]

The connection between pleasure and will serves as the model of healthy relation. Pleasure remains dormant and concealed in either God or the human, and it is only through desire (that is, the manifestation of will to instantiate desire) that the act of *zimzum* and thus disclosure is evoked. While Shneur Zalman chooses to express this in the context of divine will, mitzvot, and human appetite,[31] we should remember this is all an interpretation of the wedding ceremony the teleology of which is the sexual encounter of the bridegroom and the bride. Thus eros is the conspicuously absent frame of reference, and the pleasure for food described here is likely a foil for sexual pleasure, a common trope in rabbinic and later mystical traditions.[32] Shneur Zalman continues:

> *Zimzum* can take on many forms and through this we can understand the seal. [For example] the signature/seal of writing is a limitation [denoting that] this is as far as *zimzum* can go. As long as something is not signed/sealed it can always change direction. One can also understand metaphori-

---

30. TMKHS, p. 135a.

31. On the kabbalistic connection between human appetite, pleasure, and sexuality see Joel Hecker, *Each Man Ate an Angel's Meal: Eating and Embodiment in the Zohar* (Detroit: Wayne State University Press, 2005).

32. For example, see Genesis Raba's reading of Genesis 39:6 that Potiphar gave Joseph everything "except his bread." The sages render "bread" *(lehem)* a euphemism (literally, "refined language") for sexual partner, in this case, Potiphar's wife.

cally that one can draw playfulness/Enjoyment *(sha'ashu'im)*[33] from its [concealed] essence without any limit or telos. This is like a person who enjoys a particular food. He can experience desire for the pleasure [in a particular food] to the point that he even eats that which is extraneous *(pesolet)* and bad *(ra)* in it. He can also experience pleasure from that [extraneous] matter because pleasure emanates from the roots of enjoyment that can be drawn down even in something that is not in and of itself pleasurable. A final seal is required so that the pleasure that is drawn from its roots in Enjoyment will have one particular destination. Any other destination should be despised and viewed as disgusting.[34]

And again:

The notion of "opening" *(petiha)* with *"barukh"* enables the source of emanation to contract itself so much that the pleasure will be disclosed from its concealed state. . . . But the seal is *malkhut,* as we explained, because once something is fully disclosed there is [also] extraneous [desire for pleasure]. In order that this extraneous pleasure not be drawn to something foreign, the pleasure must be directed toward one particular thing. . . . This is achieved by means of the seal in the blessing that is sealed with *"barukh."*[35]

In these two excerpts Shneur Zalman discloses his understanding of the difference between the second and third blessing and, by extension, the essential difference between bridegroom and bride and, more generally, he reveals the true vocation of the physical bride under the wedding canopy. The male here (represented by the kabbalistic understanding of the word "blessing" [*barukh*] as a sign of emanation) enters the wedding canopy with his desire still concealed but aroused and ready for disclosure. The ritual not only provides the context for him to begin the process of *zimzum* (enabling his innate desire to become manifest). The ritual, in fact, is constructed precisely for that purpose. Yet at the same time the ritual is envisioned as Sinai, a moment where he (aspiring to emulate the ideal type — the Zaddik) must be feminized to carry the message of divine will disclosed (i.e., the oral law). So the bridegroom must be male and female at the same moment. His maleness unfolds in his desire to emanate (here seminal emission is more than a metaphor; it is the biology of the metaphysics). Yet this desire, that is, maleness

---

33. On the erotic dimension of *sha'ashu'im* see Wolfson, *Circle in the Square*, pp. 125ff., and *Language*, pp. 274-82.

34. TMKHS, p. 135a.

35. TMKHS, p. 135b.

unhindered, can or perhaps invariably will lead to licentiousness and the un-controlled desire to experience pleasure even in those things that are forbidden (i.e., other women). So the physical bride, now stripped of her constructive femininity (this was transferred to the male as the Zaddik in the midrashic rendering of the *chuppah* as Sinai or in the notion of his roots being feminine),[36] plays the role of the seal *(hatima)*.[37] That is, she is the stopgap that prevents the overflow of his male desire. She says (by *not* saying, her silence will be discussed below) "here and nowhere else." In saying that she strips him of pure masculinity, she limits his maleness by making herself the sole object of his desire. The price is that she sacrifices her eros in order to limit his, and her sacrifice may, in turn, diffuse the arousal of his desire that it would be redirected to God. Put differently, he needs her as object to become the Zaddik but when she is merely object he cannot become the Zaddik.

This may also have at least two negative consequences in the real world of human relationships. First, she becomes the sole object of his eros by legal decree, thus she can also be a source of resentment and sexual frustration; and second, as a seal she loses her sense of independence and sovereignty that may very well be the source of her attraction (it is the unmarried maiden who is the object of desire in Song of Songs. The wife in Proverbs 31:10 is defined as the "wife of valor," faithful and serving).[38] The way I am reading Shneur Zalman's rendition of the seven wedding blessings, the bride may become the object of desire that is not that desirable — or, the very status of "wife" (wife of valor) may require her to sacrifice her desirability! Her objectification as a "wife of valor" may be the source of her de-eroticized status. And, it is this de-eroticized subservience that makes her role as the sole object of his desire problematic.[39] Why? Not only because it may blemish their intimate marital relationship (this

36. On this point Wolfson notes, ". . . but suffice it here to underscore that in kabbalistic lore the uroboric quality is also associated in a distinctive way with the feminine and particularly with the imaginal symbol of the *Shekhina*, but in this context the matter must be seen from an androcentric perspective; the positive aspects of femininity are valenced as masculine and the negative as feminine" (*Language*, p. 68).

37. On the functional dimension of the bride as a vehicle for her husband's devotion to God in the kabbalistic tradition, see Moshe Idel, "Female Beauty: A Chapter in the History of Jewish Mysticism," in *Within Hasidic Circles: Essays in Memory of Mordecai Wilensky*, pp. 317-34. Cf. Wolfson, *Language*, pp. 49-50.

38. On Song of Songs in Kabbala more generally see Arthur Green, "The Song of Songs in Early Jewish Mysticism," *Orim* 2 (1987), 49-63; and Elliot Wolfson, *Language*, pp. 334-71.

39. For another perspective on the fragmented nature of the feminine as it emerges from the masculine gaze see Moshe Idel, "The Beloved and the Concubine: The Woman in Jewish Mysticism" [Hebrew] in *Blessed That I Was Made a Woman? The Woman in Judaism from the Bible to the Present*, ed. D. Ariel, M. Lebovitz, and Y. Mazor (Tel Aviv: Sifrei Hamad, 1999), pp. 23-84.

may also be true) but because his own "desire" for God is to some extent a product of his ability to draw down pleasure from the roots of Enjoyment and feminize that in order to be a servant of God. If she does not continue to arouse that male desire in him, he will not have the requisite desire for God.[40]

One could argue that if (male) pleasure was not necessary for the process of feminization into a Zaddik, marriage would not a goal in the Jewish devotional life. But in this case, if he does not desire his wife, he cannot be a Zaddik because he will not draw from the repository of desire and pleasure, that is, there will be no will that can initiate the process of drawing down desire that can then be transferred to God. If he desires women other than his wife he will never be able to feminize that desire and direct it toward God — he will remain hopelessly in the realm of unhindered masculinity.[41] How then can the bride be both a passive seal and an erotic mate? This may be one of Shneur Zalman's dilemmas, and his metaphysical understanding of the wedding ritual may reflect that uncertainty. To return once again to Smith, "the ritual is not the hunt." Put differently, what may emerge from this is that the medieval Jewish rejection of Christian celibacy that colors earlier kabbalistic literature simply does not work here.[42] For the aspiring devotee, marriage may not be an adequate "Jewish" answer to Christian asceticism but there may also be no other alternative.

The Jewish wedding ceremony has all the necessary criteria of a religious ritual: sacred space *(chuppah)*,[43] liturgy (the seven blessings), a text (the

---

40. Thus we read in Zohar 1.228b that the *Shekhina* only dwells with a man who has an earthly woman. This is also likely drawing from the oft-cited story told by Rabbi Isaac of Acre (thirteenth century) about the man who waits his entire life for the princess to submit herself to him in the graveyard and through this desire he is transformed into a righteous man. One version of the story states, "and R. Isaac of Acre wrote there his account of the deeds of the ascetics, that he who does not desire a woman is like a donkey, or even less than one, the point being that from the objects of sensation one may apprehend the worship of God." See as cited in Elijah da Vidas, *Reshit Hokhma*, "Gate of Love" (Jerusalem, 1984), p. 426.

41. It does not go unnoticed that this is a wholly heterosexual model. And yet, the homoeroticism of Kabbala is also quite prevalent. On Kabbala and the heterosexual matrix see Yehuda Liebes, "Zohar and Eros" [Hebrew], *Alpayyim* 9 (1994): 67-115; and Moshe Idel, "Sexual Metaphors and Praxis in Kabbala," pp. 197-224. On homoeroticism and Kabbala see most recently Wolfson, *Language*, pp. 324-32; and Mopsik, *Les sexes des âmes*.

42. On the kabbalistic rejection of Christian celibacy, see Scholem, *Major Trends in Jewish Mysticism* (New York: Schocken Books, 1941), p. 235. Elliot Wolfson has challenged this generalization and argued that the focus on marriage as an act of spiritual significance does not reject the notion of celibacy *in toto* but attenuates the ascetic lifestyle by using, and transforming, the sexual act. See Wolfson, *Language*, pp. 255 and 363-71. Cf. David Biale, *Eros and the Jews: From Biblical Israel to Contemporary America* (New York: Basic Books, 1990), pp. 101-20.

43. The custom of the *chuppah* the way it is presently practiced is quite new to Jewish ritual,

ketuba or marriage agreement),[44] religious objects (wine), and historical memory (breaking the glass commemorating the destruction of Jerusalem). It is also reified to represent the quintessential moment in Jewish religious/ mythic history — the covenant between God and Israel forged at Sinai. But more than that, it conforms to Jonathan Z. Smith's theory of ritual as fantasy — it has an inverse relationship to reality. On Shneur Zalman's reading it reflects the male tension of reality, the erotic desire for the female and the desire for God as incompatible impulses that are, nonetheless, dependent upon one another. Judaism's decision not to institute celibacy as convention left the aspiring devotee of God with little other choice but to marry.[45] This may be a case where communal/tribal survival trumps devotional practice. Yet marriage, both in terms of its familial responsibilities and its evocation and simultaneous limiting of masculine desire, presents itself as a challenge as much as a blessing for the aspiring devotee of God.

Ritual Reversal: The Sinai "Wedding" as Betrothal, the Imperfection of Reality, and the Ritual as Fantastic Ideal

Just as Smith suggests with the Finnish hunters, I argue Shneur Zalman (and others like him) were quite aware of the tension between the edifying fantasy of Jewish ritual and the messy reality of lived existence. In our case, marriage

---

likely originating in the sixteenth century. See R. Moshe Isserles (Rama) to *Shulkhan Arukh,* "Ha-Ezer" 55:1. Cf. Samuel B. Freehof, "The Chuppah," in *In the Time of Harvest: Essays in Honor of Abba Hillel Silver,* ed. D. J. Silber (New York: Macmillan, 1963), pp. 186-93.

44. On the history of the *ketubah,* see Moshe Gaster, *The Ketubah* (New York: Herman Press, 1923); and Mordecai Akiva Friedman, *Jewish Marriage in Palestine,* vol. 1 (Tel Aviv and New York: JTS Press, 1980), pp. 1-47.

45. The question of asceticism and celibacy in classical Judaism is a topic of considerable debate. For some informative studies see David Berger, *The Jewish-Christian Debate in the High Middle Ages: A Critical Edition of the Nizzahon Vetus* (Philadelphia: JPS, 1979), esp. pp. 27ff.; David Weiss-Ha-Livni, "On the Supposed Anti-Asceticism of Simon the Just," *Jewish Quarterly Review* 58 (1968), 243-52; Steven Fraade, "Ascetical Aspects of Ancient Judaism," in *Jewish Spirituality I: From the Bible to the Middle Ages* (New York: Crossroad, 1986), pp. 253-88; Eliezer Diamond, *Holy Men and Hunger Artists: Fasting and Asceticism in Rabbinic Culture* (New York: Oxford University Press, 2003); and Elliot Wolfson, "Martyrdom, Esotericism, and Asceticism in Twelfth-Century Ashkenazi Pietism," in *Jews and Christians in Twelfth-Century Europe,* ed. J. Van Engen and M. Signer (Notre Dame: University of Notre Dame Press, 2001), pp. 171-220; idem, "Re/Membering the Covenant: Memory, Forgetfulness and the Construction of History in the Zohar," in *Jewish History and Jewish Memory: Festschrift for Yosef Hayim Yerushalmi,* ed. E. Carlebach, J. Efron and D. Myers (Hanover and London: University of New England Press, 1998), pp. 214-46; and Wolfson, *Language,* pp. 296-332.

depicted through the wedding ceremony (according to Shneur Zalman) and the reality of marriage as a lived phenomenon exist in perennial tension. This is not simply because human beings fail to live up to the standard of the ritual — it is because the ritual is constructed with deep contradictions that we, as humans, are constitutionally unable to resolve. Moreover, the ritual, as a product of human creativity (and as interpreted through the human imagination), is constructed in full awareness of its incongruity with reality. As Smith suggests, this may precisely be the point. That is, that ritual creates the "work" for the community to overcome this chasm but "it relies, as well, for its power on the perceived fact that, in actuality, such possibilities cannot be realized."[46] I have argued that Shneur Zalman's interpretation of this ritual puts this tension into stark relief and that this tension, to some degree, exposes a crack between the legal obligation to marry and the spiritual trauma it creates. First, he integrates the Sinai metaphor as ontology by envisioning the two marriage partners as embodiments of Torah. In one sense, this only raises the stakes. Marriage in principle becomes more than human relation, it becomes the center of one's spiritual existence and the criteria for one's devotional success. Yet the reality of marriage as envisioned by Shneur Zalman is far more complicated. Second, he takes the maiden and makes her a seal *(hatima)*, stripping her of her feminine allure (she no longer embodies the oral law — that is now "masculinized" and given to the Zaddik) and rendering her a functional object limiting male desire. Elliot Wolfson's assessment of the zoharic worldview seems appropriate here. ". . . It becomes abundantly obvious that the zoharic author is promoting a purely instrumentalist view of the woman as one who provides the space — and hence the symbolic significance of referring to a wife as the 'essence of the house' — in which the male can cohabit, discharge his seminal overflow, and thereby unite with the *Shekhina*."[47]

In this homily, the earthly bride occupies a category shared by food and mitzvot — all three are objects of relation but not partners in relation. They are vehicles to evoke male desire that is then to be redirected to divine worship. In reality, of course, this is not the case. Jewish marriages are no better or worse than marriages in other cultures. Women play important roles in the Jewish family and society. Even though the legal structure of the Jewish marriage requires the male to "acquire" the woman (from her father's house),[48] in reality women generally do have a voice, a constructive role, and sometimes

46. Smith, "The Bare Facts of Ritual," p. 63.

47. Wolfson, *Language*, p. 83.

48. See Mishna Kiddushin 1:1. See Michael Satlow, *Marriage*, pp. 68-92; and Judith Hauptman, *Re-Reading the Rabbis*, pp. 60-73.

considerable influence even against the will of their husbands or the society in which they live. Even the rabbis in the Talmudic period, not always known for their positive assessment of women, state regarding the Sinai event, "Go and inquire of the daughters of Israel whether they want to receive the Torah, for the way of men is to follow the opinion of women, as it says, *Thus it has been spoken to the House of Jacob* (Exodus 19:3), this refers to women, *and declare unto the sons of Israel,* this refers to men."[49] The zoharic metaphysics that is transplanted in Shneur Zalman's description of the Jewish wedding is simply not a reflection of what it ostensibly represents, not in our time and not in his time. So what is going on here?

Smith argues that rituals are artificially controlled environments constructed precisely because they cannot be fulfilled. They exhibit, among other things, the frustration a society feels toward the chasm between what they want to happen and what they know must happen. In the case of the Finnish hunters the ritual conveys the desire for a more edifying, humanitarian, and righteous hunt. The real hunt is otherwise. In Shneur Zalman's depiction of the Jewish wedding, the seven blessings offer us a window into the anxiety of evoking and then limiting sexual desire, having only an object to fulfill that desire. The erotic desire evoked through this "object," facilitated through the institution of marriage, must then be transformed through transgendering the bridegroom into a female (the Zaddik) and then into divine worship. The fantasy of the ritual is that somehow those three components (bride as seductress, bride as submissive stopgap, bridegroom as male and then female) can work without interference. The reality, as one can expect, is quite different.

Smith concludes his essay by suggesting that these tribesmen simply enact something they know can never exist and that ritual at most illustrates the tension of the real and the ideal. Judaism's emphasis on redemption enables it to simply project all unrealizable phenomena to a transformed future. In a shorter commentary on the seven blessings that follows this homily Shneur Zalman presents us with a juxtaposition of exile and redemption through the lens of betrothal and marriage and Sinai that clarifies some of the more opaque elements of the larger homily and further affirms its place in Smith's model of ritual. As we will see, here the ritual is not describing the

49. See Pirkei d'Rebbe Eliezer, Chapter 41. As to not overstate the point, see Judith Wegner, *Women as Chattel? The Status of Women in the Mishna* (New York: Oxford University Press, 1988). But even here one could argue that the rabbi's legal writings were also constructing a "fantasy" that never really existed and may have in fact been a reaction against the reality that was lived. Cf. Daniel Boyarin, "Women's Bodies and the Rise of the Rabbis," in *Jews and Gender: Studies in Contemporary Jewry* 16 (2000), 88-100.

actual marriage at all but pointing to (1) the fact that the wedding taking place is imperfect and (2) the wedding alluded to in the ritual is a future wedding in the time of redemption when the tension between the ideal and the real will be resolved and when the wife of valor can also be the virginal maiden.

The liturgical context of this discussion is based on noting the difference between the description of joy described in the sixth and seventh blessings. The sixth blessing concludes, "Blessed are you God, who brings joy to the bridegroom *and* the bride." The seventh blessing concludes, "Blessed are you God, who brings joy to the bridegroom *with* the bride." Shneur Zalman notes, "When it says, 'who brings joy to the bridegroom *and* the bride' it is referring to this time of exile. When it says, 'who brings joy to the bridegroom *with* the bride,' this refers to the future, that is, after 'the voice of the bridegroom and the bride will be heard' (part of the seventh blessing). However before the voice of the bridegroom and the bride will be heard [that is, before the bride speaks, ed.] we say, who brings joy to the bridegroom *and* the bride."[50] The ritual thus concludes by noting its incongruence with reality. The seal of the final blessing points to the tension between the ritual and the real. As the explanation continues it appears as if Shneur Zalman is offering a proto-feminist resolution to this tension.

> The difference between these two locutions [the conclusion of the sixth and seventh blessings] is that when one says "who brings joy to the bridegroom *and* the bride," the joy comes from the bride who is the repository of joy (*u'mimena 'ikar ha-simha*) and she brings joy to her bridegroom. But when we say, "who brings joy to the bridegroom *and* the bride," it is the bridegroom who brings joy to the bride.[51]

In the future, then, the bride reveals her concealed source of joy. Only then does she have a voice ("the voice of the bridegroom and the bride will be heard") and can be the source of joy, and perhaps eros, for her bridegroom. That is, only in the future will the bride be both beautiful maiden and subservient wife. The distinction between exile (now) and redemption (the future), between the tension and anxiety of the real and its resolution takes a strange turn. The real wedding, it turns out, is not a wedding at all but only a betrothal. This is because the twofold purpose of the ideal wedding — (1) the simultaneous objectification of the bride as erotic object and the nullification of the bride as erotic partner; and (2) the arousal of male eros and the

50. TMKHS, p. 138a.
51. TMKHS, p. 138a.

feminization of the bridegroom as a "female" (Zaddik) for God — is simply impossible to achieve and Shneur Zalman knows it. So now the wedding ritual no longer embodies the event taking place but points to an unknown future when the "wedding" will finally take place. Interestingly but predictably, this all comes from the imperfect state of the Sinai event.

> There is betrothal *('erusin)* and there is marriage *(kiddushin)*. "It is written, *Moses commanded us in the Torah, an inheritance (morasha) to the community of Jacob* (Deut. 33:4). Do not read, *inheritance (morasha)* but rather betrothal *(m'ursa)*."[52] And so it is written, *Go out and see King Solomon, daughters of Zion, whose mother crowned him on the day of his wedding (hatunato), on the day of his joy* (Song of Songs 3:11). This is all the theophany at Sinai which only has the status of a betrothal, which is called *hatunato.*[53] It is not a wedding *(kiddushin)* because *kiddushin* will only take place in the redemptive future, as it is written *For He who made you shall penetrate you, His name is the Lord of Hosts, The Holy One of Israel will redeem you* (Isaiah 54:5). . . .[54] The difference between betrothal and marriage is like the difference between internality and externality. Even though there was a revelation of the light of *eyn sof* at Sinai in the ten commandments the light was still [only] in an external state. . . . The internal nature of Torah, its concealed secret called 'explanations of the mitzvot' was not revealed at all at Sinai and will only be revealed in the future. . . .[55]

The Sinai event, now presented as the preliminary stage in the process of full "penetration" (the engaged couple allow themselves to express attraction to one another but not to engage in sexual penetration), becomes the setting for the wedding ritual as a ritual that points to the marriage but recognizes the impossibility of achieving its goals (the engaged can never consummate the union). The verse from Song of Songs, using the image of the crown *('atara)* is now drawn to another use of that term describing the "the wife of

---

52. Midrash Exodus Raba 33:7.

53. But see R. Shlomo Yizhaki (Rashi) on Song of Songs 1:2, who suggests that this song is the song sung by Israel when they are in the state of exile and mourning. R. Shalom Noah Barzofsky (a late-twentieth-century Hasidic master) reads Rashi to mean that the desire of the song is an expression of a desire that is evoked precisely when the individual feels distance from the lover (i.e. the distance between Israel and God in the state of exile). See Barzofsky, *Netivot Shalom* to Numbers (Jerusalem: Yeshivat beit Avraham M'Slonim, n.d.), p. 192.

54. The colloquial translation renders the Hebrew term *bo'alayakh* as "espouse." The term more literally mans "to penetrate" in a sexual way and I think this is the intention of its use in this homily.

55. TMKHS p. 138a.

valor" *('eshet hayel).* In Kabbala the *'atara,* the corona of the penis *(ateret yesod),* is used to describe the *malkhut* or the feminine.[56]

> But in the future it is written, *The wife of valor ('eshet hayel), the crown of her husband* (Proverbs 12:4). This crown represents *malkhut* who is a *wife of valor.* She will be the crown of her husband, who is *zeir anpin,*[57] and she will embody the verse, *whose mother crowned him on the day of his wedding (hatunato), on the day of his joy* (Song of Songs 3:11) during Sinai. In the future he will get this crown from *malkhut* [in Song of Songs he gets it from his mother!] who is called 'the one who receives' because the light of *malkhut* will rise above the realm of *zeir anpin. . . .*[58]

In the future, then, the bride will also be the maiden — she will come alive from her dormant state of silence (she will have a voice) and arouse his desire for God.[59] I suggest the giving of the voice to the bride is symbolic of her transformation (back) into the maiden; she now becomes "the good [submissive] wife" who is also the seductress. The silencing of the bride under the *chuppah* accompanies her wearing a veil, an idea that denotes a subservient social and sexual status in Islam. It should be no surprise that in many communities the ritual of the wedding ceremony begins by the bridegroom veiling the bride, silencing her and thus making her a "woman of valor."[60] This final excerpt brings this to a conclusion.

> This is what the liturgy means when it says, 'May it be soon that we hear in the forests of Jerusalem . . . the voice of happiness, the voice of the bride-

---

56. See Wolfson, *Through a Speculum That Shines* (Princeton: Princeton University Press, 1996), pp. 357-68; and idem. *Language,* pp. 72 and 73. On the raising of *Malkhut* to *Keter,* see Arthur Green, *Keter: The Crown of God in Early Jewish Mysticism* (Princeton: Princeton University Press, 1997), pp. 156-61; and more recently "*Shekhina,* the Virgin Mary and the Song of Songs: Reflections on a Kabbalistic Symbol in Historical Context," *AJS Review* 26 (2002), 1-52.

57. *Zeir Anpin* is a kabbalistic construct referring to cosmic man. Although it is more complicated than that, for the purposes of this text this general definition will suffice.

58. TMKHS, p. 138a.

59. The relationship between Song of Songs and Sinai is a significant part of this text, albeit it remains unexplained. On the rabbinic idea that Song of Songs was actually a description of Sinai, fortifying the marriage metaphor with divine covenant, see Saul Lieberman, "Mishnat Shir Ha-Shirim," in *Jewish Gnosticism, Merkavah Mysticism, and the Talmudic Tradition,* ed. Gershom Scholem (New York: JTS, 1960), pp. 118-26; Daniel Boyarin's critique of Lieberman in "Two Introductions to the Midrash of Shir Ha-Shirim" [Hebrew] in *Tarbiz* 56 (1987): 479-500; and Green, *Keter,* pp. 78-87.

60. The veil plays a prominent role in kabbalistic teaching, symbolic (and not so symbolic) of this state of concealment. See, for example, Wolfson, *Language,* pp. 224-33.

groom and the voice of the bride.'[61] In our present state of exile *malkhut* is only that which receives from her husband, 'she has no independent reality.' Hence, her prayer is called 'the prayer of silence' because the bride has no voice. . . . This is why the bridegroom says to the bride 'behold you are sanctified to me'[62] and the bride is silent and this very silence is the sanctification. It would seem she should also speak? . . . [She is silent] because in the present [state of exile] *malkhut*, who is called bride, is subjugated and nullified to her husband. Hence her voice is not heard, not in prayer and not in the wedding ritual. Her silence is her sanctification. However, in the future when *malkhut* rises to *keter* and she will be a crown for her husband (*'ateret ba'ala*) then she will influence *zeir anpin* and she will have an independent voice that emanates outward. . . . [The reason this is not now] is because marriage is all a state of betrothal, the light [drawn down] is only external light. . . .[63]

I mentioned above that one could read this whole homily from a proto-feminist perspective. I think this is a mistake for various reasons. First, the fact remains that Sinai, now rendered as betrothal and not marriage, remains binding. That is, the silencing of the woman in the ritual is a reflection of Sinai *(halakha)* and thus embodies the promise that in some future era women will attain a voice. In my view this is no consolation even as the final blessing gives us a prelude to her voice. In fact, this blessing can be interpreted as a tool of oppression since her silence can be viewed as the prerequisite for redemption and thus women are relegated to a passive role in order to further a process that may, at some undetermined future, result in their taking on an active role. One could say that redemption rests on her silence. This again brings us back to the ritual as fantasy as Shneur Zalman knows that although the bride symbolically remains silent during the ritual, that silence is broken the moment the couple begin their life as husband and wife.

Second, in the text cited above distinguishing between betrothal and marriage where we read that in the future the woman *(malkhut)* will rise to *keter*,[64] the example Shneur Zalman brings of the redeemed *malkhut* is not the woman (the bride) but the Zaddik (perhaps the pious bridegroom). "This can be understood by the fact that in the messianic future the angels will say 'Holy!' to the Zaddikim. This is because the roots of their souls are in *malkhut*

61. This is part of the seventh blessing.

62. This is the proclamation the bridegroom says to the bride to verbalize the acquisition, "Behold you are sanctified to me with this ring according to the laws of Moses and Israel."

63. TMKHS, p. 135b. Cf. Moses Nahmanides, *Commentary to the Torah* on Exodus 16:6.

64. On this see Tikkunei Zohar, p. 11b.

that will rise above [the angels] and dwell in *keter* that is called 'their origins.' Therefore the angels will say to them 'Holy!' "[65] It is not inconsequential that the example Shneur Zalman chooses to describe this reversal of gender positioning in the future is the (feminine) Zaddikim. The redeemed woman, or bride, is presented as a man who has successfully integrated the feminine as a source for his devotion to God. When *malkhut* is absorbed into *keter,* she takes the form of the male Zaddik.

Finally, there is an implied distinction made here between Proverbs 31:10, *A wife of valor who can find?* and Proverbs 12:4, *A wife of valor who is a crown to her husband.* The second verse appears to be the fantasy of the first. The first is included in the liturgy sung at the Friday night dinner table. The male thanks God for giving him a wife who has prepared such a beautiful meal. But perhaps the eros of Shabbat (in some communities the entire Song of Songs is recited as part of the Friday evening liturgy interestingly juxtaposing the *wife of valor* verses likely recited within the same hour!) is better captured in Proverbs 12:4, a desire not adequately fulfilled in Proverbs 31:10. If only, this reading suggests, the wife of valor in Proverbs 31:10 was the wife in Proverbs 12:4.

Closer to our concerns, I suggest the deflection to the future in the seventh blessing illustrates the tension between the real state of marital relationships and the ideal state of marriage as the ultimate metaphor for covenant. The wedding ceremony fails to embody this because it requires contradictory things of the bridegroom and the bride. Shneur Zalman downgrades the Sinai metaphor introduced by the rabbis to a betrothal, the arousal of desire that remains unfulfilled awaiting a redemptive future. Sinai now becomes a metaphor for exile rather than covenantal fulfillment. In traditional Jewish societies, the period of engagement is significant yet quite frustrating and precarious. The bride has been chosen but not yet consecrated to her husband. She is silenced by him (she is no longer in search of a husband) but not yet a vessel for his desire (there is no physical intimacy). She arouses the desire of her bridegroom yet she is not yet able to help transform that desire into a desire for devotion (feminizing him) because she is not yet a physical vessel for him. Betrothal, like Sinai, is a covenant not yet fulfilled.

In portraying the conventional "wedding" at Sinai as only a betrothal, Shneur Zalman addresses the tension between the ritual and reality. How can the bridegroom be a man for the bride and a "woman" for God? How can the

---

65. TMKHS, p. 138b. The correlation between the rise of *malkhut* to *keter* and the Zaddik is predictable given the zoharic tradition that Shneur Zalman was intimately familiar with. When *malkhut* becomes *keter* she is envisioned by Tikkunei Zohar as the crown on the head of the Zaddik.

bride be a "good [submissive] wife/*wife of valor*" and a seductive maiden? How can she seduce him, arousing his desire, if she is silenced? In truth, neither the bride nor the bridegroom can achieve the ends intended in the ritual, either for themselves or for each other. This is the point of the seventh blessing. Only in the seventh blessing does the ritual acknowledge the failure of the entire enterprise as the seventh blessing reveals how the ritual and the reality are incompatible. Only in the seventh blessing does the liturgy acknowledge that the survival of the institution of marriage is dependent on the belief in a future when it could actually work (or even take place!). The promise of the future, however, does not resolve the dilemma; it only puts it into starker relief. If there is no belief in redemption, would the Sinai covenant be worth it? If there is no belief that the bride could be both a *wife of valor* and a seductive maiden, would marriage be worth it? If the bride cannot be both a woman with a voice and a vessel for her husband's erotic devotion to God, the wedding/Sinai metaphor collapses. The futuristic and "fantastic" core of the ritual as understood by Shneur Zalman may tacitly acknowledge that, in the present, *she* cannot be both (woman of valor and maiden) and thus *he* cannot be both (male for her, female for God).

Marriage works and it does not work. It works because the bride functions to limit the expression of male eros ("here and NOWHERE else!") that is required for divine worship. It does not work because that very function requires her silence and the subsequent de-eroticization of her seductive status ("HERE and nowhere else!"). In short, real marriage is as broken as the Sinai tablets. Once again, Smith is correct: "the ritual is not the hunt," and, like the Finnish tribesmen (according to this reading of Shneur Zalman's homily), the Jewish wedding ritual is deeply conscious of that tension. Only the fantasy of the future can hold the present together — but the future does not make marriage in the real world any easier, albeit for other reasons it may still be necessary.[66]

---

66. For example, see Satlow, *Marriage*, pp. 3-41.

PART V

LITURGICAL SILENCE

Cosmic Speech and the Liturgy of Silence

Oliver Davies

In his writings on the liturgy, Maximus the Confessor speaks of two distinct kinds of silence. The first is "the silence of the unseen and unknown call of the deity much hymned in the innermost sanctuaries," while the second is "another silence that speaks rich in tone."[1] The latter, which appears to be a human "silence" invested in liturgical speech, summons the former, which is the divine silence. Although precise designation of meaning is difficult in this demanding passage from the *Mystagogy*, the reader is confronted with what appears to be an exchange of silence, or an echoing, perhaps, across a divine-human boundary. It is part of the giftedness of liturgical speech, it seems, to be porous to the approach of the divine silence, to be able even in some sense to "summon" that silence which is a "call," and which is "much hymned in the innermost sanctuaries." Indeed, perhaps the paradoxical meaning of this passage is that the priest can summon the divine silence through words and "the altar of the mind" since it is already there, as heart and ground of all that is distinctive about liturgical speech. Such a calling, such a summoning, would in that case not be the straining of human speech with its own limits: a wrestling or struggling with its boundedness in the face of its divine creator. Rather it would be the realization of human speech as liturgy: the embrace of its own ground as properly creaturely speech, which is to say a human way of speaking which knows itself to be founded in and responsible before a divine silence which, while prior, is also dynamically present, as call, as a waiting to be summoned, in the "innermost sanctuaries" of the human imagination.

Another way to put this is that liturgy must in a sense mediate, or make present to us, or allow us finally to discern and to hear, the silences of God. Si-

---

1. Maximus the Confessor, *Mystagogy*, Chapter Four.

lences can only be heard, after all, within contexts of listening and speaking. Unbordered silence is "wild" silence and, as such, is too elemental and pure to come into our field of cognition. "Wild" silence is pure possibility that escapes cognitive mediations.

It is this essay's thesis that a collocation of silences is at the semantic heart of liturgy. Liturgy *is* the meeting of silence with silence, and the span between the divine and human silence is the measure of the liturgical moment. But nothing in this story will be straightforward. Silence is not a univocal term; rather it is one which knows as many potentiations as there are contexts within which silence can be heard. Silence refracts, echoes, and reproduces, furthermore, in ways that test the mind and memory. Above all, silence can conceal itself, exhibiting strategies of denuding and disguise, becoming a presence within or beyond speech, before or after or during the uttering of the human word. Silence can, in a sense, be spoken and yet, at the same time, it can be the hoped-for within the speaking.

Speech, Silence, and World

The story of silence culminates in the words "My God, my God, why have you forsaken me?" which, according to the Gospels of Mark and Matthew, were uttered by Jesus on the cross.[2] This phrase, which is the opening verse of Psalm 22, gives expression to the psalmist's sense of abandonment by God, who does not answer his cries (v. 2). The question, which can be taken as expressive of Jesus' own sense of abandonment by the Father, is suggestive of two distinct contexts. The first is the motif of divine silence from a cosmic perspective as worked out in Old Testament sources, particularly the later prophets, and linked with the end time, while the second is the continuous divine conversation between Father and Son during Jesus' ministry on earth. The latter offers one of the principal frameworks around which the New Testament narrative is structured, or within which the fundamental shape of the *Heilsgeschichte* comes into view.[3]

---

2. Mark (15:34) and Matthew (27:46) cite what they believed to be the actual words of Jesus, before giving a Greek translation. In Matthew the address to God is in Hebrew, while the difficult question "Why have you forsaken me?" is in the more homely Aramaic. Mark renders the Hebrew *Eli* as the Aramaic *Eloi*. The appellation *Eli* and its Aramaic variant may refer to the merciful rather than the strict God. This is its sense at Numbers 12:13 and Psalm 118:27 (Strack and Billerbeck, *Kommentar zum Neuen Testament aus Talmud und Midrash,* Vol. I [Munich: Beck, 1922], 1042).

3. I have argued the following at greater length in *The Creativity of God: World, Eucharist, Reason* (Cambridge: Cambridge University Press, 2004), pp. 75-94.

But let us begin with the silence of God as a phenomenon of cosmic significance. If falling silent means personal death for the Psalmist, or for Job, then God's falling silent threatens cosmic annihilation: "If he should take back his spirit to himself, and gather to himself his breath, all flesh would perish together, and all mortals return to dust" (Job 34:14-15).[4] After all, Genesis 1:1–2:4 establishes that the world is created through the speech or breath of God. Indeed, it is the word *ruach*, meaning "breath" and "wind" as well as "Spirit" or "spirit," that sustains the link between God's speaking and the fabric of the world.[5] Inevitably, Christians have read these texts through implicit theories of language so deeply embedded in our thinking — because so fundamental to cognition — that we have failed to grasp just how radical and extraordinary the divine creation is. Even today, we tend to read the Hebrew scriptures through a lens of speech-act theory that emphasizes the performative functions of the divine speaking.[6] But what is being suggested in the interplay between spirit-wind-breath (cf. the homonymous *dabar* as both "word" and "thing") is a far more intimate relation between world and (divine) speech than we have generally been prepared to contemplate. These texts are telling us that the world is shaped and structured by the divine speaking-breath; it is not that the world is merely the product of God's speaking, but that that speaking informs its inner content and is the ground of God's continuing presence within the world.[7] The polyvalence of *ruach* as spirit, breath and wind is maintained at Ezekiel 37:1-14, and the Psalmist can say: "By the word of the Lord the heavens were made, and all their host by the breath of his mouth" (Ps. 33:6).[8] Against such a background, the fear that God will withdraw his breath, and become silent, is a natural consequence of the belief that the world exists by a free and sovereign act of divine speaking. It is this kind of theological cosmology which underlies the New Testament conviction that it is through Christ as the Word — and Wisdom — of God that

---

4. Speech is linked with life and the Holy Spirit in Job at 27:3-4 and 33:3-4 (cf. Gen. 2:7).

5. Cf. Gen. 1:2.

6. See, for instance, Oswald Bayer, *Gott als Autor. Zu einer poietologischen Theologie* (Tübingen: Mohr Siebeck, 1999).

7. It is instructive to note, for instance, the occasions when the wind is an instrument of the service of the divine will, as at Is. 27:8, Jer. 13:24 and Hos. 13:15. We need also to take account of the word *děmāmâ* at 1 Kings 19:11-12 (cf. Job 4:16), which is expressive of the presence of God, with its complex and unresolved resonances of "silence," "stillness," and "breath of wind."

8. The word *rûaḥ* derives from an earlier root, *rûḥ*, which also underlies the verbal form *rāwaḥ*, meaning "to be wide" or "spacious." It thus has a secondary historical association with spaciality, or "ce qui est aéré, donc spacieux" (see D. Lys, "Rûach. Le souffle dans l'Ancien Testament," *Études d'Histoire et de Philosophie Religieuses* 56 [Paris, 1962], p. 19. Opinion is divided on whether the motif of spaciality preceded that of breathing, or came after it).

all things were made and that it is he who "sustains all things by his powerful word" (Heb. 1:2-4).

The second context against which the Father's silence at the cross needs to be measured is that of the conversation between Father and Son that occurs at certain key points within the gospel narrative (the role of the Spirit in this is a matter to which we shall return). This again needs to be seen against an Old Testament background, for the "conversational" relationship between Father and Son is already prefigured in the Mosaic dialogue with God on Mt. Sinai in which Moses, alone among the Israelites, spoke *with* God "face to face" or "mouth to mouth."[9] The particularity of this relationship is signaled in Hebrew by the use of the verbal phrase *dabar 'im* which is reserved for the Sinai encounter and its analogues.[10] The Father's speaking with the Son that takes place at the baptism of Jesus, and which marks the beginning of Jesus' mission, is a significant intensification of the Mosaic dialogue, and distinct from it (though still in relation with it) by virtue of the fact that the dialogue not only reveals the presence of God but reveals also the dialogue that is in God. The "speaking-with" of Father and Son actually reveals that the divine voice is itself constituted as a speaking of God with God. What is revealed at the baptism, then, is a divine conversation, one which continues throughout the gospel narrative.

Of course, Jesus' whole life is marked as one of prayer, and thus as a way of speaking with God, but from the perspective of the Father's speaking with Jesus, the divine conversation can be divided broadly into two sections. The first is the baptism-Transfiguration nexus from the synoptic Gospels in which the Father affirms the Sonship of Jesus with a play both upon the adoption motif at Psalm 2:7 and the Suffering Servant motif from Isaiah 42:1. The second begins with events immediately prior to the Passion narrative, focusing in the Johannine tradition on an account of the raising of Lazarus, in which Jesus tells us that the Father has "heard" him. Here the suggestion is that the Father has answered Jesus' prayer of petition (John 11). With its allusion to "glory," the Lazarus passage already seems to anticipate the resurrection thematic of the Passion to follow.[11] The same is true of the pericope at John 12:27-30, in which Jesus struggles with the thought of his imminent death.

---

9. Cf. Exodus 33:11 ("face to face"), Deuteronomy 34:10 ("face to face"). The form "mouth to mouth" is found also at Jeremiah 32:4 and 34:3, where it refers to an uncomfortably intimate encounter of Zedekiah king of Judah with the king of Babylon.

10. For a further discussion of this theme, see my *A Theology of Compassion* (London: SCM Press, 2001), pp. 192-99.

11. "This illness does not lead to death; rather it is for God's glory, so that the Son of God may be glorified through it" (John 11:4).

When Jesus says, "Father, glorify your name," a voice from heaven replies, which some hear as thunder and others as the voice of an angel: "I have glorified it, and I will glorify it again" (v. 28). In both passages the issue of private and public speech is in play. In the former, Jesus adds: "I knew that you always hear me, but I have said this for the sake of the crowd standing here, so that they may believe that you sent me" (John 11:42), while in the latter he states to the gathered people, "This voice has come for your sake, not for mine" (12:30).

What we find here, therefore, is the convergence and intertwining of two traditions of conversation between Jesus and the Father. The synoptic Gospels stress the initiative of the Father and the humanity of Christ (and it will lead to the sense of abandonment on the cross in the Markan-Matthean version), while the Johannine tradition emphasizes Jesus' certainty that he has indeed been "heard" by the Father and that he hears the Father without recourse to the senses. The latter, of course, will culminate in Jesus' words from the Cross: "It is accomplished" (John 19:30). The delineation of a theology of the Cross predicated upon the phenomenon of silence which I am developing here will draw upon both these traditions of "divine conversation," taking from the synoptics a strong sense of Jesus' dependence upon the gratuitous speech of the Father and, from John, the belief that the resurrection itself is bound up with the Father's speaking with, or answering of, the Son. From John too I shall take the principle that the divine speech has an intrinsically cosmic dimension.

Silence and the Body of Christ

The two contexts against which the silence of the cross needs to be seen, the one cosmic and the other relational, can also in fact be understood as two distinct types of silence. In English we use the same word for both, but Russian, for instance, has different terms: *tishina* and *molchanie*.[12] The former might be used of the natural silence of the steppe, whereas the latter is an interruption or cessation of speech. The distinction is an important one, for *molchanie* is in effect a form of communication, for it is always subtended by speech, whereas *tishina* is a state of soundlessness and rest which speech disturbs or breaks. There is nothing in our general experience to make us see the

---

12. I have developed a more complete genealogy of silence in "Soundings: Towards a Theological Poetics of Silence," in O. Davies and D. Turner, eds., *Silence and the Word: Negative Theology and Incarnation* (Cambridge: Cambridge University Press, 2002), pp. 201-22.

cosmic (or natural) and the relational in a unified way; rather the world and the interpersonal seem to be altogether at odds. The "subjective" human is the domain of the relational or interrelational and the "objective" or natural world is a sphere of possibility to be acted upon by human agents and society. There are some exceptions to this, such as romanticism with its appeal to an underlying unity within things that overcomes the subjective-objective distinction and thus sets up a form of cosmic relationality. We can see something of this too in the descendants of romanticism in the modern world, such as Gaia theory and deep ecology. There are also aspects of contemporary physics which suggest that the subjective and objective may be far more intimately combined than might appear.[13] But the principal thrust of modern thought is toward emphasizing either the subjective-objective divide in the light of robust theories of the freedom of the will and human responsibility before our actions on the one hand or deconstructions of the divide from the perspective of the objective order of the world on the other. This currently takes the form in some quarters of a strong view of determinism based in the science of genetics.[14] There is for us a radical challenge therefore in the fact that the silence on the cross obliges us to make precisely this link between the cosmic and the relational.

The Genesis creation narrative already undermines the subjective-objective distinction by suggesting, as we have noted, that the cosmos itself is a kind of extension of the divine creativity, through the play of divine spirit and word. The world's objectivity can itself be a modality of divine presence to us. The world is itself a divine gift, a thematic which finds its fullest expression in the theology of the covenant. The link between cosmos and relation in Genesis cosmogony is further intensified in early Christian tradition by the development of a trinitarian matrix for the creation of the world. The ultimate unity of these two axes is implied in a number of passages from the New Testament that suggest the cosmic character of Christ as the Word of God through whom "all things came into being" (John 1:1-3).[15] For the world to be made through Christ is for the world to be conceived in a relational space and for it to be set in relation with us from its foundation. According to this perspective, exteriority, objects, world must in some sense be relationally ordered to us, however

---

13. For example, Nancey Murphy and George F. R. Ellis, *On the Moral Nature of the Universe* (Minneapolis: Fortress Press, 1996), and John Polkinghorne, ed., *The Work of Love: Creation as Kenosis* (Grand Rapids: Eerdmans, 2001).

14. See for instance Steven Pinker, *The Blank Slate* (New York: Penguin, 2002).

15. Other relevant passages are Colossians 1:15-16, Hebrews 1:2-4, Ephesians 1, and 1 Corinthians 8:6, while Matthew 11:19, 12:42, and 1 Corinthians 1:18-31 place Jesus in the content of the wisdom of God.

counter this seems to be to our experience that it is we as persons who observe these things, which are exterior to us, and that we cannot be addressed, in the full relational sense of that term, either by or through them.[16]

A reflection upon the silence of the cross, as recorded in Markan-Matthean tradition, is an invitation for us to look upon the world in a new way therefore and to see within it the unity of cosmos and relation. We should note the intensely christological character of this invitation, since it is Jesus alone who experiences the Father's silence. Although awareness of the giftedness of the world and the perpetual possibility of its destruction is everywhere implied in the Old Testament, the Israelites did not as such experience the divine silence, however much they may at times have lived in fear of it. It is the new intimacy or union between Jesus and the Father which creates the possibility of the Son's hearing of the Father's silence. For in a sense, only God can hear the cosmic silence of God, which is the silence of the creator, since the creature will vanish along with the world that is deconstituted with that divine silence. But at the same time, if that silence is divine judgment of the world, then it is only a creature who can undergo that judgment. Jesus' hearing of the Father's silence — as total cosmic destruction — precisely captures the deep paradox of the Incarnation. That paradox is intensified if we consider that the identity of the cosmic silence *(tishina)* for Jesus with a communicative or relational silence *(molchanie)* means that the destruction of the world is taken into the intimate inner-trinitarian relation itself. Through the polyvalence — or multivocity — of "silence" as both prior or exterior to speech (in its cosmic aspect) and as a moment within speech and thus continuation of the relation of speech (in its relational aspect), Trinity and world are brought together again and the alienation between them is repaired and healed.

A deeper understanding of this moment can be gained if we look again at the concept of voice and world. Scripture can be viewed as a collection of texts which make present to us the voices of those whose own speaking has been shaped by the divine voice. We "hear" God's *fiat* through the litany of narrative and praise which the author or authors of the opening chapters of Genesis constructed around it. We "hear" God's words from the burning bush through the intimate narrative of Moses' response to them. It is through Moses' ears that we catch God's speaking in the divine dialogue of Sinai. The

---

16. I have developed the concept that a Christian semiotic oscillates between the modes of reference and address more fully in "The Sign Redeemed: Towards a Christian Fundamental Semiotic," *Modern Theology* 19:2 (April 2003): 219-41. See also *The Creativity of God*, pp. 137-43. For a discussion of biblical exegesis and world semiotics in the patristic period, see for instance R. A. Markus, *Signs and Meaning: World and Text in Ancient Christianity* (Liverpool: Liverpool University Press, 1996).

Psalms are shaped by the divine speaking, direct and through the prophets, in judgment, exhortation, blessing and liberation of Israel. The Old Testament can itself be taken as being formed in the expectation of a definitive divine speaking which, for Christians, culminates in the uttering of the divine Word: itself a "speaking Word" who makes present on earth what is revealed to be a trinitarian discourse. Indeed, we can say that the central referent of Scripture is the divine speaking, and that it "refers" to that voice through the assembling of numerous texts, and layering of voices, which allow us, the reader, to enter into the expressivity and world of human voices which have been profoundly shaped and transformed by the divine utterance.

But a voice is produced through the vibration of air that is generated by a body. And the occurrence of the divine voice throughout the Old Testament, which is — in the accounts of it — concrete enough to be heard by human ears, raises the possibility, or the expectation of the possibility, or indeed the sense of loss or absence, of a divine body from which the voice comes. If the divine presence takes the form of a *voice,* then, by implication, it might also take the form of a *body.* The burning bush, then, which burns and is not consumed, with its associated imagery of light but no heat (the text makes no reference to warmth or heat), might be taken as a highly paradoxical metaphor of what such a body might be like. (Indeed, the rabbis will take it as one of the chief metaphors for Torah, which forever yields new possibilities of meaning and which stands in the world as a kind of divine body; some of the church fathers will see in the burning bush an incarnational motif.) The body of God in the Old Testament is absent but there is a sense in which the world itself can be taken as being like or akin to the body of God. As we argued above, the world which flows from the divine creative speaking remains in contact with the divine voice, through the motifs of Spirit, breath and voice, just as a text remains the product of its author's voice (which can in some degree be reconstituted from it through an act of interpretation). Indeed, the world can be said to stand to God's creative voice as a text to its author: in an ambiguous relation of alienation and dissemination. Texts, in other words, are like bodies: they bear the voice to places far away but do so only at the price of alienation (the oral and largely private medium of speech between persons becomes the visual and largely public medium of the text, for instance). In each case, a riskful act of interpretation is required by the reader in order to make sense of the text to hand, where "making sense" can be taken to be a process of resolving the text back into the content of its original authorial function.[17]

17. I am here following a hermeneutic closer to Schleiermacher rather than, for instance, Ricoeur.

According to this model, the very creation of the world entails a degree of alienation of the divine voice as it becomes subject to the vagaries of interpretation and misinterpretation. An interpreted world is one in which meaning is lost as frequently as it is gained, and truth, as Pilate observed, is not easily ascertained. The divine will to create a world that would be both truly external to the original divine speaking yet also intimately bound up with it (we recall the role of the Spirit as something that hovers between created and uncreated, inscribed in the world as the world's memory of its provenance in the divine speaking, much as a text "remembers" its author), necessitated the possibility of sin and corruption. The world is a place in which either its true provenance is authentically remembered, which is to say its origin in the divine order, or alternative memories hold sway in narratives of deracination and alienation, leading to the abuse of freedom and power, and practices of violence. Within such a scheme of things, the repair or repristination of the world, which is its retrieval *by the divine speaking* back into the creative ground of its origin and formation, seems a *telos* that is natural to the created order. It is the Spirit again, as the "memory" of the world, who plays a special role in the fulfillment of that end, as we can see in the Spirit-filled prophets who guide Israel towards her true destiny. It is the Spirit who points to the coming eschatological intervention of God in history, and who attends Mary at the Annunciation.

That Jesus bears a different kind of relation to the voice of God is a central theme of the New Testament. Unlike the prophets' voices, his own human voice is not only shaped by the divine speaking but is itself so utterly *conformed* to it that in him the human and divine speaking become one. In Johannine terms, the Father speaks in him and he breathes the Holy Spirit upon the apostles (John 14:8-11 and 20:22). This unity of voice gives at the same time a unity of body; and so we can say that the body of Jesus — as the bearer of the divine voice — is in some sense also the body of God.

The body of Jesus has a unique status, as it is simultaneously the body of God, in whom the voice of the Father is heard, and a material entity that is a natural part of the created order. This entails a deep paradox for, just as we saw with the burning bush in which fire and the combustible bush coexisted in an inexplicable and wholly contradictory way, the — infinite and uncreated — body of God combines with a — finite and created — part of the material world in the person of Jesus. It is this unfathomable paradox which is resolved, or perhaps it is better to say *realized,* in the sacrificial pouring out of the body and blood of Jesus *into* the material elements of the world which is first signalled in the institution of the Lord's Supper and is accomplished in the resurrection and ascension. Jesus" body resurrected and ascended is the unity of the world as text with the authorial voice of God. His sacrifice in and through this "dual" embodiment is the regeneration and repristination of the world. In the vocal terms we are developing here, it is the point at which the words of the text are filled again with the authorial voice, and the text, while remaining text, becomes again wholly transparent to its creator's presence.

That is a process which inevitably entails a healing of all the innumerable acts of misinterpretation, misunderstanding and misappropriation which have marred history and the world as the pristine text of God. It would seem appropriate that it is through silence that that disorder is challenged and re-deemed. Only in this way can the distorted speech of the creation be brought back to its site of originary purity distilled in and from the breath of the living God. That silence is a moment in the speaking relation of the Son with the Fa-ther, and can take place as *molchanie* only there, to return to the Russian terms introduced above. But it is at the same time also the divine cessation of speech in all its cosmic implications. It is also *tishina*, and, as such, a cosmic event which takes place at the root of history and the world. The sacrificial character of that silence resides in the intersection of *molchanie* and *tishina*, and as such is a unique moment in the relation of Trinity and world.[18]

Liturgy, as complex, Spirit-filled speech grounded once in "the silence of the unseen and unknown call of the deity much hymned in the innermost sanctuaries" and again in "another silence that speaks rich in tone," mediates the healing intersection of the two forms of divine silence — the one destruc-tion and the other relation — into the fragmented world. But it does so not through the proclamation or even performance of silence but rather through the liturgical realization of Jesus' own self-performance as the sacrificial body of God. His loving silence before the Father, and his hearing of the divine si-lence which brings the world to an end, within the trinitarian matrix, mani-fest not as soundlessness but as transformed materiality: as the reconfigura-tion of world as divine body.

Silence as Healing and Jewish-Christian Relations

The argument that the collocation of the two types of silence on the cross precipitates in a transformation of Jesus' own body and thus regenerates the

---

18. One of the functions of the Spirit is the mediation of this new speech-silence into the world, through human conformity to the divine self-communication. See in particular John 16:13-15, and the role of the Spirit as creating a new ecclesial speech in the Letter to the Ephesians.

relation of the divine to the world is one which opens up and challenges narrow conceptions of the "liturgical."[19] From this point onwards, the redeeming and sacrificial silence of God which is borne by the Spirit must itself become part of the natural order and thus be available to be appropriated at the level of human religious life and culture. It is just such an appropriation, which is "liturgical" in the extended sense, that I am seeking to sketch in a preliminary way at the close of this paper, and to do so in the area of Jewish-Christian relations (reflecting the character of this volume as a whole).

Daniel Boyarin has argued that Pauline exegesis is grounded in a revaluing of the meaning of certain key words in a way that presupposes a belief in the independence of words and concepts and in the prior existence of concepts with respect to words.[20] This, he holds, is based in a distinctively Platonist and incarnationalist understanding (the Word exists prior to the Incarnation). Against this view, John David Dawson has recently argued that it is *figural* reading which is at work in Paul's exegesis.[21] This means that the primary referent of the relevant texts is a form of divine action in the world. While the advent of Jesus marks a certain distinction with respect to the language and symbolic order of the Old Testament, as a form of divine action in the world the Incarnation represents a continuation of the primary reference of the Old Testament and indeed actually requires it.

In this essay I have argued that silence comes into view in a new way through the Incarnation and the unique speaking relation between the Son and the Father. I have not therefore maintained that an entirely new order of things has come into view with the silence of the cross, since that silence has no meaning without the conceptualities of silence as developed in the Old Testament. The position I have outlined here is therefore one which approximates to Dawson's view of a continuity between Old and New Testament in terms of divine action in history, as the plain sense referent of the sign. It is not action which grounds the continuity between Old and New Testament however in this paper but a polyvalent semiotics which is internal to silence

---

19. See for instance the important work on liturgical phenomenology by Jean-Yves Lacoste, including his *Expérience et Absolu: Questions disputées sur l'humanité de l'homme* (Paris: PUF, 1994).

20. Daniel Boyarin, *A Radical Jew: Paul and the Politics of Identity* (Berkeley: University of California Press, 1994).

21. John David Dawson, *Christian Figural Reading and the Fashioning of Identity* (Berkeley: University of California Press, 2002). For another important contribution to this debate, focusing on the exegetical practices of wisdom, see David F. Ford, "Divine Initiative, Human Response, and Wisdom: Interpreting 1 Corinthians Chapters 1–3," paper delivered to the Society of Biblical Literature, 2002.

and whose polysemy entails no rupture between sign and meaning (as Boyarin sees in Pauline exegesis). "Silence" takes on its different meanings by virtue of the contexts in which it is embedded. The "progression" from Old to New Testament takes place in terms which are internal to the semiotic therefore, and these accordingly have the potential to be reciprocally informing. There is a continuity of polysemy here in which (as we find in Dawson's continuity of action) the new points back to the old, signifying within the old new possibilities of human-divine relation which are neither contrary to the Old Testament nor unthinkable outside the New Testament. Rightly understood, the concept of silence may offer the beginnings of a new way of conceiving the mutuality between Christianity and Judaism therefore grounded in scriptural usage and reciprocal hospitality.

Silence ultimately is a contentless sign. It is a free-floating signifier which draws its meaning from the character of the other signs which provide its context and thus bring it into the semiotic realm. But within a world-system conceived as divine speech, silence has a resonance which is at once cosmic and relational, natural and redemptive. As such, silence is a language shaped around liturgy that we are called as creatures to learn in order that we may speak.

CONCLUSION

Liturgy, Time, and the Politics of Redemption: Concluding Unscientific Postscript

C. C. Pecknold

Jesus says *whoever has shall be given more* (Mark 4:25). At the end of this volume we should be aware that we have received a gift for Jewish-Christian relations. Now it is up to readers to make generous use of this gift, aware that good things can always yield more. What these authors have given us is a much-needed resource for developing a liturgically mapped politics of redemption. The book implicitly argues that doxological praxis is central to the task of "repairing the world." That is not to instrumentalize worship, but to recognize the *pedagogical, political, and redemptive* effects which flow from the liturgical ordering of life, and to consider how liturgical action may be "writ small" into the ways we learn to make political judgments (see the essays in this volume by Ward and Ochs).[1] This signals a return to Scripture and liturgy for political wisdom. In this concluding postscript I will first outline what the implicit argument has been, and then offer a thick theological narrative (basically Augustinian) that lends further political meaning to these liturgical investigations.

One of the implications of this book is that the liturgical transfiguration of Jewish-Christians relations may be critical for modern, western secular history too. In keeping with the aims of the Radical Traditions series, the book extends the argument of Peter Ochs and others that the problems of secularism (the wounds of modernity) can only be solved from within, and

---

1. This corresponds to contemporary debates in political theory about "radical democracy," and a new attentiveness to "micropolitical practices." For a helpful introduction to "radical democracy" by one of its best proponents, reflecting on its origins in the thought of Sheldon Wolin, see William Connolly, "Politics and Vision," in *Democracy and Vision: Sheldon Wolin and the Vicissitudes of the Political*, ed. Aryeh Botwinich and William Connolly (Princeton: Princeton University Press, 2001), pp. 3-24.

that this "within" is to be found in the scriptural roots of modern reasoning itself.[2] By attending to the liturgical mediation of the scriptures in Jewish and Christian communities that have inspired our modern civilization, the essays may be read as advancing a timely conversation about the place of "religious reasoners" in public discourse.[3]

The Implicit Argument

The challenge at the end of this book is to try to make this implicit argument more explicit, and to suggest the ways in which it might advance further. As a "down payment" on future conversations, then, this essay attempts to sketch how manifestations of the Word of God are made legible in history by attending to the mediating and redemptive place of Torah and Christ in the liturgical reasoning of this volume. There are, I believe, three main stages of this book's implicit argument, and each stage of the argument displays an important dimension of liturgical mediation in both Jewish and Christian forms of life.

1. Liturgy Teaches

The fast pace of contemporary political time is radically out of sync with liturgical time.[4] Political decisions are not deliberative or wise, but fast and furious, often based solely upon "market time." The suggestion of "market time" reminds me of the highly ritualized order of the stock markets. The "traders" in their colored vestments perform a priestly rite (at a fever pitch), mediating between individual and group consumers and those corporations who have gone "public." But what is it that these traders of "market time" mediate? The political economy they mediate is hardly redemptive, and it does not offer the political education necessary for any wise "public" body. Indeed, it may be argued that it is actually *apolitical* because it makes consumption a higher good than citizenship.

2. See Peter Ochs, *Peirce, Pragmatism and the Logic of Scripture* (Cambridge: Cambridge University Press, 1998); and my *Transforming Postliberal Theology: George Lindbeck, Pragmatism, and Scripture* (London: T&T Clark, 2005).

3. See Robert Audi and Nicholas Wolterstorff, eds., *Religion in the Public Square: The Place of Religious Convictions in Political Debate* (Lanham, Md.: Rowan & Littlefield, 1997); and Jeffrey Stout, *Democracy and Tradition* (Princeton: Princeton University Press, 2004).

4. Cf. Sheldon Wolin, "What Time Is It?" *Theory & Event* 1:1 (1997).

As well, the "media" is profoundly at odds with liturgical time as it seeks to keep up with the pace of the governing economy. The contemporary irony of the media is that it consistently fails to mediate in ways that could be described as true, good, or beautiful. The "otherworldly" pace, rhythm, and temporality of Jewish and Christian liturgical time educates us against the habits and customs of what might be called the politics of speed and rapid turnover which offers very little political wisdom for the world. Liturgical time provides a different political education, one that forms a people who are capable of "redeeming time" from the tragedy of collapsing at high speed under the weight of "economic benefit." It is liturgical time that is needed to educate a public, not only so that they may deliberate and make wise political decisions, but so they become people capable of reading history in a truly redemptive way.

2. Liturgy Locates the Kingdom of God

The second stage of the argument is that in order to remove those obstacles that hinder us in our ability to love both friends and enemies we must first learn how our liturgies locate the kingdom of God. These liturgies are teaching the people of God how to read the signs of the world through the signs of revelation. This is to suggest a strong relationship between sacred texts, hermeneutics of embodiment, and politics.

We may gain a better understanding of what is hermeneutically at stake by appreciating, with help from Augustine, the "wounds" of history in relation to the Word of God. This stage of the argument concerns how political failures concern our failures to read well. In the terms of this volume, this is to claim (analogically) that Jews and Christians have failed one another in history because they have failed to read one another well (see the essay by Magid and human bodies as *Torah*). And this failure, in Augustinian terms, is a failure of each traditional-self to recognize his or her own order of love before God and neighbor. The argument calls out for each tradition to engage in a rereading of its own narrative of the Word *together* in order that they may each learn from one another how to perform the politics of redemption inscribed in their common narratives of being God's Israel. Locating the Kingdom of God, then, is bound up with learning how to read God's Word. And learning how to read within this Kingdom is inextricably bound up with "saving" and "redeeming time." That is to locate the Kingdom in time, and to discover a political education in Jewish and Christian liturgies that offer an eschatological horizon of hope.

3. Liturgy Performs a Politics of Redemption

The third stage of the argument then turns to the way in which this political education is *redemptive*. The curriculum for this education is the liturgical performance of God's Word, and the question is, how do these liturgies mediate redemption? If they do not mediate in the way of "traders" on the fast floor of the New York Stock Exchange, or if they do not mediate in the way of "journalists" who run over truth as they race toward deadlines, then what sort of "ontology of mediation" can we discern in these liturgies? And do we have two different "ontologies of mediation," one Jewish and one Christian, being performed on this stage of history? Or are there a single "ontology of mediation" and two mediators? In asking such questions, the volume implicitly yearns for a shared politics of redemption. In recognition of this yearning, I reflect on Torah as mediator, and on Jesus Christ as mediator. This is because Torah and Christ mediate between the Word of God and our embodied, liturgical performance of that Word in history. In this mediatorial reflection, the wounds of Torah and the wounds of Christ become sites for thinking about "messianic politics."

In sum, this conclusion merely asks questions about the pedagogical, political, and redemptive aspects of these liturgical mediations. For example, do richly liturgical traditions such as Judaism and Christianity have only prophetic critique to offer modern politics, or might they also perform something constructive, pedagogical, and recognizably redemptive at the same time? Could the political education that these liturgies offer teach against habits which are currently eroding political culture around the world? Can the scriptural wisdom that is performed in these pages help liberal democracies in times of perpetual war, fear, suffering, and trouble? These are just some of the questions that we have asked in direct and often indirect ways.

In what follows, I display an Augustinian response to the implicit argument made through the course of these diverse essays. Augustine is a seminal figure in the history of the Church, and also in the history of Jewish-Christian relations. So it is not entirely accidental to conclude the volume with reflections generated by his complicated place in the conversation. The reflections follow a kind of *itinerarium*, from the finality and self-enclosure of solipsism, to the recognition of "our wounds" as both *aporiai* and *apertures* of grace, and this book climaxes with the importance of learning from our different but often interdependent "ontologies of mediation."

Solipsism as Political Sin

Solipsism as a term, according to the *Oxford English Dictionary,* did not come into use until the nineteenth century. It is associated with ideas about the *ego,* with a view that human knowledge cannot extend beyond the self. It is a way of describing the wholly self-interested state of our human nature. Earlier, in the seventeenth century, Hobbes taught that this selfish state of nature led to violence, and thus he theorized a mortal god which could protect us from ourselves *(Leviathan).* To overcome our "state of nature" we needed, Hobbes thought, "the state." For Hobbes, the state is propaedeutic for an altruistic society. However, that movement, from "the self" to "the state," is too fast. It runs over the idea that there is "something wrong" with our state of nature, and that "the state" can redeem us from this something that is wrong: we are selfish. Trying to identify the "something wrong" in the movement from "the self" to the mediating institution of redemption (the state) is a theological prognosis. As the Lord says to Cain, sin is lurking at your door (Gen 4:7). Call it solipsism, monologism, selfishness, self-interest: it keeps us trapped inside. And it is this sense of being "trapped inside" that Jews and Christians have long called "sin." Coming to some recognition of this requires an honest account of sin as solipsism, of self-love gone wrong. But rather than conceiving of "a mortal god" who can protect us from ourselves, perhaps we need a very different politics, a very different order that is capable of liberating us from this trap.

Augustine might have directed us to what he called the problem of self-love: *cor incurvatum in se ipsum.* That is, solipsism is the problem of the heart turned in on itself. Like the dog chasing its own tail, it is a tendency, *especially in our relation to the other,* to become self-enclosed.[5] In Augustine's terms, this is to disorder the love of God and neighbor from "the inside," from the heart turned inwards, and therefore trapped or enslaved by the solipsistic self. Here sin disfigures love, and places obstacles in the way of our truest selves as we are known through the quality of our relations with God and neighbor. Put differently, *vice* is an ever-present threat from *within* the human practice of *virtue.* To call this vitiated threat "sin" is not to explain it away (for the Augustinian, evil does not have a causative nature and thus cannot be explained), it is to diagnose the problem theologically, and to diagnose the problem theologically is to suggest that it will require a theological cure.

---

5. Jewish-Christian relations can become static for similar reasons: dyadic self-enclosure is a constant threat in relations of interdependency. The presence of a third can potentially break the self-enclosure of the dyadic relation. The "Scriptural Reasoning" movement, closely allied to the aims of this series, is thus inspirational to the work of many of the writers of this volume.

Especially in our relation to one another, Jews and Christians face this problem of being trapped inside: trapped inside our houses, trapped inside our fantasies about "the other," trapped inside our histories, and trapped within the paradox of our identity-difference relation. Both Christian and Jewish identities are now inextricably linked to the drama of our differences being played out on a world-historical stage. But we are only just beginning to learn how to sustain the long-term, transgenerational habits of face-to-face "co-abiding" that would enable us to consistently learn from one another what it means to be *covenant people* who place their stories within God's story. We think that it helps to have learned that anti-Jewish polemics were historically contingent, that they were internecine family fights: and it does help to learn this. We think that it helps to have learned from sociologists how important exclusion has been in the growth of sects. We think that it helps to have learned about the so-called "witness doctrine" of Augustine, which had the paradoxical effect of, on the one hand, infantilizing the very tradition that gave birth to it, and on the other, generating ecclesial policy-decisions which protected Jewish identity and practice well into the eleventh and twelfth centuries.[6] We think of *Nostra Aetate* and *Dabru Emet* as watershed events, and they are. But what is accomplished if we learn all of this and yet, in practice, still remain afraid to open the door to one another? Jewish-Christian co-abiding must begin "learning about our learning" *together.*[7] And yet solipsism is constantly lurking, tempting us to keep our learning and our teaching to ourselves. We should resist the safety of this and learn to continually open the door, not only so that we might face one another in learning what it means to be God's faithful people, but so that we might face God more faithfully as Israel. It is unlikely to be "the state," or any other mortal god, who will protect us from turning in upon ourselves. It is only the God of Israel, and the God of Jesus Christ, who will redeem us from our sin.

Our Wounds as Openings for the World

In his *Confessions,* Augustine writes that "our wounds may be great and numerous" (10.43.69). Augustine has a comprehensive sense of the plural: "our wounds." He means something like the "the wounds of history," or the

6. See Jeremy Cohen, *Living Letters of the Law: Ideas of the Jews in Medieval Christianity* (Berkeley: University of California Press, 1999); and my "Augustine's Hermeneutical Jew, Or What's a Little Supersessionism Between Friends?" *Augustinian Studies* (February 2006).

7. Rowan Williams, *On Christian Theology* (Oxford: Blackwells, 2000), p. 132.

wounds that have always, at all times and in all places, disfigured the order of love "from the inside" of creation. If one considers the wounds of all of history, it is indeed overwhelming ("great and numerous"). But even if we simply take the historical wounds of Jewish-Christian relations, we are faced with a burden too great for us to bear alone. We need help. Whatever the cause of these wounds, God has allowed them, and they are "our wounds." But perhaps the scriptural-liturgical return is a return to the source of the power to heal wounds. It is the post-solipsistic recognition that no "mortal god" will protect us: only God's love can heal soterio-political suffering.

Augustine's response to the presence of "our wounds" is, not surprisingly, to point to Christ's wounded body as the humble physician, the *medicus humilis,* whose humility on the cross is the antidote for the tumor of pride (*en. Ps.* 118.9.2). The death of this physician is true medicine for the people who need healing (*Jo. ev. tr.* 110.7). Christians have this ancient tradition of thinking about wounds as sites and sources of healing and they liturgically order their lives around this crucified Christ because they believe that from those wounds pour salvation and healing, not only for their own private wounds, but for "our wounds, numerous and many," healing for the whole world. We are not used to thinking that redemption will come to us through wounds: and especially not through wounds in our socio-political bodies that have such cosmic significance for us that we call them *holocausts.* Nevertheless, the Christian logic is that the one who is wounded is the one who heals. The witness of St. Thomas placing his fingers in the wounds of the Risen Christ offers Christians a way of facing doubt, disability, pain, suffering, sin, and the wounded body through a body of transformed wounds. And thus Christ himself becomes a way of reading every wound, a way of reading all historical pain, as both an *aporia,* an instigation for doubt, and an *aperture,* an opening into God's own life. Christ's wounded body is an embodied hermeneutic which suggests that God has made his own life into a wounded body that heals.

The Politics of Mediation

Many of the authors of this volume explicitly view the Exodus and Sinai narrative as central to the mediation of redemption (and it is implicit throughout all of them). For Jews the story of revelation and redemption is mediated through Torah, which is not to say simply, the scroll, but God's redemptive logic inscribed there, embodied in Israel, and performed throughout history. For Christians, a hermeneutical shift occurs. The story of revelation and redemption as Israel in the Exodus-Sinai narrative must be read through christological mediation, and it follows that the interpretation of Torah, likewise, is ruled by the embodied hermeneutic: Jesus Christ.

This is potentially problematic: this hermeneutical shift in response to historical particulars can become eschatologically supersessionist rather than mutually supersessionist. It is too easy to say that Jesus Christ has superseded Torah (and St. Paul is always at great pains *not* to say this). The nature of the paradox of identity/difference, that is, the paradox that each of our identities as Jew and Christian is dependent upon our mutual difference, means that we are in some respects bound to a kind of mutual supersessionism. But this should not be projected upon God's future, and the messianic dimension of each tradition resists this projection. What we have to deal with is a powerful narrative that Jews and Christians apparently read very differently. But in this hermeneutical-political difference, Jews and Christians have to constantly face the God of Israel, because it is only in this liturgical facing that we can keep ourselves open to the messianic.

Interestingly, the category of the "messianic" is preserved by both Christian and Jewish writers alike in this volume (see, for example, the essays by Gibbs, Magid, Ward, Kepnes, or Bader-Saye). This category has been opened afresh in the twentieth century through such diverse European thinkers as Walter Benjamin, Theodor Adorno, Emmanuel Lévinas, Franz Rosenzweig, Jacques Derrida, Jacob Taubes, Alain Badiou, and Giorgio Agamben. For all of them, the messianic is a way of resisting the closures of modern binary thinking. It is a category that also resists syncretistic reduction or totalitarian opposition because it literally "holds history open." For the writers of this volume however, the "messianic" describes the way in which Torah and Christ give us access to messianic time. Here the messianic indicates the possibility of a *decisive transformation of history*. Unlike some of the poststructuralist writers, the authors of this volume think that only God can decisively transform history, and so the critical question for them is: how do Jews and Christians participate in these "messianic" politics of redemption? Where is the liturgical opening for our participation in God's politics of redemption? This brings us to the particulars of mediation.

Torah as Mediator

Not surprisingly, Torah is central to all of the essays by Jewish writers. It is probably at its highest pitch conceptually in Gibbs's essay in the section on liturgical scrolling. He writes:

The narrative is built on the portions of Torah read, week by week, that make a year of the scroll. And at the end of the year, the scroll must be re-rolled. The rolling and re-rolling of the Torah is the image of this circle of our reading. Thus rolling the scroll (or if you prefer the computer verb, *scrolling*) is the time that is the performance of eternity. It always begins again, even when it has just finished. A year is the narrating time, just long enough to tell the story of the Torah. The time it takes to read through the scroll is the measure of the year. (p. 133)

This liturgical scrolling is the implanting of eternal life in history. As Oliver Davies reminds us, "Torah . . . forever yields new possibilities for meaning and . . . stands in the world as a kind of divine body" (p. 222). If the Torah stands as a kind of divine body that implants eternal life in history, then it is probably not a coincidence that Gibbs's essay is also an exercise in Jewish messianic thinking — liturgical scrolling embodies "a social memory that awaits its messianic future" (p. 139). This may make the messianic body strange to Christians. It may seem strangest to Christians in Shaul Magid's equally messianic reflections on "human bodies as Torah." Magid argues that

> the midrashic depiction of Sinai as the "wedding" of God and Israel results in the wedding ritual adopting the trappings of that event, e.g. the Torah as the vehicle of the covenant is embodied in the bridegroom and bride and the ritual space of the *chuppah* becomes Sinai. That is, the midrashic correlation is reciprocal: Sinai is a wedding and any common wedding becomes Sinai. (p. 190)

The rabbinic claim that Sinai is a wedding, and by analogy, every wedding may become Sinai warrants Magid's reading of human bodies as Torah, and scriptural interpretation as sex, a process of generating life or, in Rosen-zweigian terms, "implanting" eternal life in history.[8] Here the divine messianic body is the "one flesh" of a married body.

But when weddings give way to marriage, so do rituals give way to reality. Magid argues that "the Sinai event [is] now presented as the preliminary stage in the process of full 'penetration'" (p. 207). The movement from wedding ritual to marital reality mirrors the movement from the reality of the Sinai

8. If readers want to reflect further on the question of hermeneutical difference, this rabbinic figural reading of Sinai might be contrasted with Ben Quash's figural reading of the slain Lamb in the Book of Revelation: namely that the Lamb is wounded, and by analogy, all our wounds may become the wounds of Christ. This comparison of actual figural readings, between texts and bodies, may further illuminate the relation between the maculate Torah and the wounds of Christ.

event to the implanting of this eternal fire in history. The ritual prefigures a "messianic future, projecting an ideal redemptive moment into the mundane and fallen state of human affairs" (p. 192). For Peter Ochs, this reality is apparent by the fact that we are no longer on the mountain, but we are on the way from it, carrying the weight of the Word into the world. But whether the relation to Sinai is understood in terms of marriage or in terms of "carriers of the Word," it is in either case faced with the problem of human sin, and as Magid notes, "sin prevents divine flow and is thus the source of pain" (p. 199). How are we to think of Torah as mediator if we are faced with this problem of human sin? What is it in the Torah itself, in the divine body of Torah, that will heal this problem of human sin?

In one of the first books in this series, Radical Traditions, David Weiss Halivni argues that the school of Ezra and his scribes received a "maculate" Torah that had been compiled, redacted, and woven into a canonical fabric (in the fifth century B.C.E.). The language of maculation is polite; at its weakest it simply means blemished, and at its strongest it means that it has been made impure. The work of Ezra and his scribes involved the restoration of this revelation to the repentant nation of Israel who longed, after the Babylonian exile, "to return to the Torah of Moses."[9] But Ezra and company did not do this by changing the written words of this Torah. They preserved what they received (written Torah), even where passages conflicted or seemed suspect, because the Pentateuchal text was for them inviolable, it reflected the holiness of this revelation to Moses at Sinai. Ezra instituted uniform and coherent practices in the tradition which enabled exegetical work on the Pentateuchal text to be *an unending restoration* of what was revealed at Sinai (Torah).

Rabbi Halivni concludes, "the covenant of Sinai was realized by means of Ezra's canonical Torah; thus Ezra's canon received retroactively a Sinaitic imprimatur. The destiny of the nation began in earnest, and our canonical Torah was born, etched in inviolable holiness — not by fire on tablets of stone, but by faith upon human hearts."[10] It is true, then, Israel received a maculate Torah, replete with all the difficulties critical scholarship points out today — "nevertheless, this text, with all its problems, is evidently the selfsame Torah that was placed before the people of Israel upon their return from exile . . . the written word served as the concrete symbol of revelation — perfect, awe-inspiring, and beyond reproach."[11]

9. David Weiss Halivni, *Revelation Restored* (London: SCM, 2001), p. 76. My comments on Halivni are also to be found in my book *Transforming Postliberal Theology*, pp. 86-87, 96-98.

10. Halivni, *Revelation Restored*, p. 85.

11. Halivni, *Revelation Restored*, p. 45.

It is helpful to think of the maculate Torah as a wounded body that itself has the paradoxical capacity, inscribed through the logic of revelation, for healing. This, of course, is to draw parallels between Torah as a wounded body and Christ as a wounded body. Elsewhere I have written that "for Christians, the Ezra story must be christological in some significant way. The wounds of the 'maculate text' can be read as Christ's wounds, and the 'repair of the world' might be read [through] the agency of Jesus Christ, the immaculate Word of God made maculate in being made human."[12] But equally, for Jews, the story of Jesus Christ may be read as founded on that original event of love, that is, it must be Sinaitic in some significant way. In this way, Christ's wounds can be read as part of the maculation of Torah, *and* part of the process of unending restoration that is bound up with *tikkun olam* in an intimate way, namely *liturgically*. That is, if we understand that Halivni's notion of the maculate Torah is implicit in the liturgical scrolling displayed in the Jewish essays in this volume we are able to see that the repair of the world depends upon Jewish doxological praxis.

Christ as Mediator

Christian contributors also turn to Exodus and Sinai in thinking about redemption in history. Scott Bader-Saye, Oliver Davies, and Sam Wells each reflect in their own ways a similar pattern of thinking about Exodus and Sinai as paradigmatic of the dynamic between ritual and reality that Magid identified, and of the dynamic between the Word of God and Israel. But the central mediator is Jesus Christ. This is clear throughout all of these essays, and in none of them more than in Graham Ward's.

Graham Ward writes that the cross of Christ is a sign which gives grammatical coherence to all Christian action. This draws substantially from Augustine. In *De Doctrina Christiana* Augustine uses Ephesians 3:18 to reason through four dimensions of the cross: with *hands stretched out,* the breadth signifies faith performing good works through love; with *elongated body* fixed down to his *feet,* the length signifies patient perseverance through time; with crown of thorns and *wounded head,* the height of the Cross orients all action towards the city of God; and in *the unseen depths of the Cross* driven deep into the blood-soaked earth of Golgotha, Augustine sees the depths of the Cross signified in the sacraments from which flow untold depths of God's grace. "This sign of the cross encompasses the whole of Christian activity: doing

12. Pecknold, *Transforming Postliberal Theology,* p. 97.

good works in Christ and persevering in adhering to him; hoping for heavenly things, not profaning the sacraments" (*De Doct. Chr.* 2.41.62).

For Augustine, the cross of Christ orders the politics of redemption, and this is a politics which must include God's perseverance with the people he calls to himself as Israel. Those who respond to that call, Jewish and Christian alike, respond first and foremost through praise. It is why, as Ben Quash highlights in his essay, the presentation of the slain yet powerful Lamb in the Book of Revelation is accompanied by the *trisagion,* the "holy, holy, holy" which is the heavenly recognition of the holy seed, the gift given by the God of Israel for the healing of the nations. Quash writes, "the vision of God which Christians have is a vision of a wounded Lamb" (p. 151). As the Book of Revelation has it (itself written as a scroll), it is only this wounded Lamb who can open the scroll, which is not only the scroll of Revelation, or the scrolls of Torah, but the scroll of every particular history, including our own personal histories. "What is finally true," Quash surmises, "is yielded to those who carry wounds" (p. 151). That is because all wounds become figured by the wounded Lamb, whose wounds are openings into Torah, which is to say openings into God, and openings into God's truth for the world.

What is striking in any appreciation of Christ as mediator is the way in which christological mediation originates in a historical, particular body, and teaches us how to read the signs of this crucified and resurrected body. Naming Jesus of Nazareth "the Christ" is already to have made a powerful hermeneutical decision about how to read the signs of Torah. To participate in this christological mediation is to learn how to read well. The church fathers called this liturgical learning "sacrament." Sacrament became a technical word for describing how Christ's body taught us to read signs, and preeminently how Christ's body teaches us to read the signs of Torah, the signs given to us as the Word of God. This thinking reaches patristic maturity at the end of the fourth century through Augustine's work on sign theory. Michael Cameron provides a helpful summary of Augustine's teaching here, which centers on how Christ's body, as Word made flesh, teaches us to read not only the signs of Torah, but all signs:

> The Word made flesh (John 1:14) discloses the capacity of the uncreated and supratemporal to "dwell" in the created and temporal. Because of the symbiotic relationship between Christology and language (*Doc. Chr.* 1.13.12), the incarnation constitutes the basis for a renewed sacramental understanding of signification whereby the sign not only represents but contains and mediates the reality it signifies. . . . [T]he bond of sign and reality is so close that the signifying thing takes the name of the thing signified. . . . [T]he sign

incarnates meaning before it is understood to point the way to meaning. Functionally speaking, for temporal beings image is intrinsic to essence, and medium is elemental to message.[13]

This sacramental semiotics, in which the bond between sign and reality is intimate, is a transformative (and transfiguring) relationship between the body of Christ and linguistic signs. However, the quick leap from Christology to all language is a leap *over* the original, generative insight, that this relationship was between Christ's body and the signs of Torah. That is, sacramental semiotics are born out of reading Christ and Torah as mediators of redemption read in dynamic relation to one another. This means that the road Christians have to travel on with Jews is principally the road of Torah, which may simultaneously be for them the way of Christ. What does this mean for Christians liturgically? Liturgically this means that the practice of the Eucharist is a micropolitical practice, a political education in learning to read Scripture. The Eucharist not only embodies Christian hermeneutics but invites participation in its temporal performance in the world, a performance which replicates the divine, sacramental logic of the incarnation, the Word of God made flesh in history. It liturgically inscribes on human bodies the sign and reality of Christ's body, which is the incarnation of the Word of God. As such, Christians believe that when they consume the "sacraments" of bread and wine, they are in some real way consuming the Word of God made flesh. And in consuming the Word of God, redemption is being mediated to them, and through them. Redemption is being made through them because their wounds are being figured by Christ's wounds, which is simultaneously to be figured by the wounds of Torah, and thus they themselves become wounded healers who liturgically perform God's politics of redemption in the world.

The christological grounding of Jewish-Christian relations displayed in this volume does not compete with but complements the "Torah-logical" grounding for Jewish-Christian relations. The idea of "liturgical scrolling" as the Jewish performance of eternity in time, which "transpires in the reading of Torah," suggests that "the text itself is built on a gap of time, one that is not bridged by the story" (p. 135). This concerns what Halivni calls above the "maculation" of Torah, and what I call the "wounds of Torah," namely the gaps, discontinuities, aporias, and problems which invite us to participate in eternal time through these redemptive openings. Inviting Christians into these openings, through shared interpretation, is to co-abide as Israel in the process

---

13. Michael Cameron, "Signs," in *Augustine through the Ages: An Encyclopedia*, ed. Allan D. Fitzgerald (Grand Rapids: Eerdmans, 1999), p. 795.

of unending restoration of Torah. In complementary Christian terms, what Graham Ward and Oliver Davies suggest, at either end of this liturgical drama, is the symmetry between the Christological and Torah-logical grounding for Jewish-Christian relations. Here it seems to be the case that "Christ's abiding" with God also becomes a model for Jewish-Christian co-abiding with God. And that Christ's wounds, and the wounds of Torah, likewise become curricular for our co-abiding. For Christ's wounds, and the wounds of Torah, are not only a sign of a painful disruption in "the flow of divine love"; they are also an invitation to abide with God in prayer, that index of human needs, and praise, which directs the service of the heart to a process of unending restoration. Perhaps it helps us to understand Ben Quash's interpretation of the slain Lamb, that "what is finally true is yielded to those who carry wounds," as also true of the wounds which mark Jewish-Christian hermeneutical difference. It may also help us to reflect further upon what might make the divine silence, discussed by Davies, redemptive in history.

Rumors of Political Wisdom

Post-enlightenment thinkers such as Comte, Durkheim, Weber, Marx, and Freud were interested in making predictions about religion. Their prediction was that religion was in irreversible decline, and would likely disappear. In the late nineteenth century, and for much of the twentieth, such divinations were omnipresent. After centuries of pushing religion to the political sidelines, there are signs everywhere that "traditional religion" is more politically significant than ever before. In the midst of the 2000 presidential election campaign in the U.S., Peter Beinert, editor of *The New Republic*, predicted that "religion" would "increasingly replace electoral politics as the realm where battles for the national soul are fought."[14] Religion has not faded in importance: for better or for worse, it has been thrust into the political spotlight again.

Such political shifts towards religion at the beginning of the twenty-first century are being recognized not only by political pundits but also by a majority of the citizens in the world's most powerful nation. Gallup polls suggest that two-thirds of Americans believe that "all or most of today's problems" can be solved by religion.[15] The academics have not been far behind. When

14. Cited in Stanley Fish, "One University Under God?" *The Chronicle of Higher Education,* January 7, 2005.

15. Jennifer Harper, "Religion 'Very Important' to Americans," *The Washington Times,* June 25, 2004.

asked by a reporter what will replace the triumvirate of race, class, and gender in the culture wars, the literary theorist Stanley Fish shot back a single word: "religion." Fish writes, "the geopolitical events of the past decade and of the past three years especially have re-alerted us to the fact . . . that hundreds of millions of people in the world do not observe the distinction between the private and the public or between belief and knowledge."[16] Democracy alone may not save us. The virtues of democracy are considerable, but can democracy remain democratic without taking religion seriously? Many people are intuitively returning to religion for political wisdom. That has meant a religious interrogation of modernity, liberalism, and the dominant mediating institution of secular life, namely, the nation-state. How does "the state" fare in the light of this concluding narrative about ontologies of mediation?

It could be that William Cavanaugh gives us the answer. He has argued that the modern state should be understood as "an alternative soteriology to that of the Church," and he might have also added an alternative soteriology to that of Israel.[17] Any modern state, inasmuch as it finds expression in its politicians, would be very quick to deny such a claim. But there is something compelling about this mythology, especially in America, where the flag is treated like the eucharistic host, and heroes are those who give their lives in war to maintain peace for a not-so-just economy. Nationalism, war, the economy — all contribute to a very different liturgical ordering of life in the modern state, and one is left to ponder the degree to which these practices do constitute "false soteriologies" which are incapable of mediating redemption.

Regardless of whether Cavanaugh is right about "the myth of the State as Savior," we nevertheless need those liturgical communities of the Word of God who can perform the public service of an embodied critique, offering micropolitical resistance to the false soteriologies that can arise from a variety of quarters from within contemporary political culture. True democracy requires nothing less. But redemptive words must be added to Cavanaugh's excellent thesis: not only do we offer the resources for the critique of politics, but also the resources for political repair. What this book has suggested is a positive advance of the thesis that "critique" should be followed by "repair." This is to meet false soteriologies with pilgrim soteriologies that are rooted in their doxological response to the revelation of the Word of God in history, and are thus historically capable of staying with problems over much longer periods of time than nation-states. If Jews and Christians can stay with their

---

16. Fish, "One University Under God?"

17. William T. Cavanaugh, *Theopolitical Imagination: Discovering the Liturgy as a Political Act in an Age of Global Consumerism* (London: T&T Clark, 2002), p. 9.

problems for over two thousand years, perhaps they offer a political education for the nations: a vision of co-abiding that may provide new possibilities for collective redemptive action in our world. Both singly and together, Jewish and Christian liturgies display some of the power of God's Kingdom. For in the worship of God, the Lord of the Universe draws near to those who have eyes to see and ears to hear. There are rumors of a deep political wisdom in this worship, and there is a longstanding rumor that the messianic kingdom is very near. The authors of this volume ask Jews and Christians to return to their scriptures and liturgies in order that they might seek first the kingdom of God, and in doing so, receive a political education that is deeply needed in these troubled and disordered days.

Contributors

Scott Bader-Saye is Professor of Theology at the University of Scranton. He is the author of *Church and Israel After Christendom: The Politics of Election* (Westview).

Oliver Davies is Chair in Christian Doctrine at King's College London. He is the author of *A Theology of Compassion* (SCM).

Robert Gibbs is Professor of Philosophy at the University of Toronto. He is the author of *Correlations in Rosenzweig and Lévinas* and *Why Ethics? Signs of Responsibilities* (both Princeton University Press).

Steven Kepnes is the Murray W. and Mildred K. Finard Professor in Jewish Studies in the Department of Philosophy & Religion at Colgate University.

Shaul Magid is the Jay and Jeannie Schottenstein Chair in Jewish Studies at Indiana University. He is the author of *Hasidism on the Margin: Reconciliation, Antinomianism, and Messianism in Izbica and Radzin Hasidism* (University of Wisconsin Press).

Peter Ochs is the Edgar Bronfmann Professor of Modern Judaic Studies at the University of Virginia. He is the author of *Peirce, Pragmatism and the Logic of Scripture* (Cambridge University Press).

C. C. Pecknold is a Research Fellow in the Faculty of Divinity at the University of Cambridge. He is the author of *Transforming Postliberal Theology* (T & T Clark Continuum).

Ben Quash is the Dean of Peterhouse and Convenor of the Cambridge Interfaith Programme, Faculty of Divinity, University of Cambridge. He is the author of *Theology and the Drama of History* (Cambridge University Press).

Randi Rashkover is Associate Professor of Religion at York College of Pennsylvania. She is the author of *Revelation and Theopolitics: Barth, Rosenzweig, and the Politics of Praise* (T & T Clark Continuum).

Graham Ward is Professor of Theology at the University of Manchester. He is the author of *True Religion* (Blackwells) and *Cultural Transformation and Religious Practice* (Cambridge University Press).

Samuel Wells is Dean of the Chapel at Duke University. He is the author of *Improvisation: The Drama of Christian Ethics* (Brazos).

Index

Adorno, Theodor, 236
Agamben, Giorgio, 49, 236
Anderson, Benedict, 95
Aquinas, Thomas, 33
Aristotle: on effect/causality, 44; on ethics and action, 29, 48; on Greek *leitourgia* as service, 29-30; and *kinēsis*, 48, 48n.36; *Nicomachean Ethics*, 29, 48; *Politics*, 29-30
Augustine: on desire, 41; on God's eternity and human temporality, 112, 113; on the sign of the cross, 239-41; on solipsism, 233; and the temporality of Psalms, 113, 120-21, 121n.7, 123; and *vinculum caritatis* (bond of love), 32; on wounds of history, 231, 234-35; *Confessions*, 46, 112, 113, 120-21, 121n.7, 123, 234-35; *De Civitate*, 42; *De Doctrina Christiana*, 239-40

Bader-Saye, Scott, 21, 239. *See also* Providence, doctrine of
Badiou, Alain, 236
Balthasar, Hans Urs von, 39, 155-57, 160; and the Eucharistic *Sanctus*, 162-63; and "theo-logic," 31; on transfiguration, 46
"The Bare Facts of Ritual" (Smith), 191-92

"Barth, Barmen, and the Confessing Church Today" (Hunsinger), 3-4
Barth, Karl: and concrete/worldly behaviors, 19; and divine freedom, 16-17; on history of salvation, 98; and love of neighbor, 18-19; and the Patmos Group, 2-3; on Protestant doctrine of providence, 101, 107; on Sabbath day, 110; and theological realism, 2-3, 9-10, 16-19
Barzofsky, Rabbi Shalom Noah, 207n.53
Bataille, Georges, 19-20
Beinert, Peter, 242
Bell, Catherine, 188
Benjamin, Walter, 93, 236
Beveridge, Albert, 106
Blanchot, Maurice, 41
Bonhoeffer, Dietrich, 2-3
Book of Common Prayer, 43, 141
Bourdieu, Pierre, 19-20
Bouyer, Louis, 161
Boyarin, Daniel, 225
Boyle, Nicholas, 147-48, 150
Buber, Martin, 75-76, 79-80
Bultmann, Rudolf, 35n.18

Cameron, Michael, 240
Caputo, John, 11
Cavanaugh, William, 243

Certeau, Michel de, 182
Church of England, 168, 168n.4
Claudel, Paul, 36
Co-abiding, 32, 34-39, 241-42
Cohen, Hermann, 5, 130
Colossians, Letter to the, 30-31
Comte, Auguste, 242
Confessing Church, 2-4
Confessions (Augustine), 46, 112, 113, 120-
    21, 121n.7, 123, 234-35
Cyril of Jerusalem, 161

Dabru Emet, 234
Damasio, Antonio, 48
Davies, Oliver, 22-23, 237, 239, 242. *See
    also* Silence, liturgy of
Dawson, John David, 100-101, 225
De Civitate (Augustine), 42
De Doctrina Christiana (Augustine), 239-
    40
Deleuze, Gilles, 32-33
De Lubac, Henri, 32
Derrida, Jacques: and the Christian
    liturgical act, 32-33, 33nn.13-15; and
    différance, 33, 33nn.14-15; "How to
    Avoid Speaking," 10-12, 33; nihilism of,
    13-14; on prayer, 10-12, 13-14
Desire: as animator of the ensouled flesh,
    41; and the seven wedding blessings,
    198-99
Dionysius the Areopagite (pseudo-
    Dionysius), 12, 33, 33nn.14-15
Durkheim, Emile, 188, 242

Ehrenberg, Rudolph, 2, 23
Ekklēsia, 37
Enlightenment views of human progress,
    94
Esther and the practices of
    improvisation, 167-87; accepting and
    blocking, 170, 172-74; assessing status/
    status reversals, 170, 174-77; Esther's
    relation to Christian liturgy, 187; and
    festival of Purim, 168; forming habits,
    169-70, 185-87; improvisation and

Christian ethics, 168-71; overaccepting
    gifts, 171, 179-83; and politics of
    redemption, 167-68, 187; questioning
    givens, 170-71, 177-79; reincorporation,
    171, 183-85; and six aspects of
    improvisation, 169-71
Eternity and history, 127-40; the
    construction of social temporality, 128-
    30; and historiography as messianic
    activity, 136-39; the hour and temporal
    repetition, 128-30; and the Jewish year,
    131-35; and the physical scroll, 132-33;
    and the practice of *haftarah*, 137-39;
    and the practice of rolling the scroll,
    133-35; and Rosenzweig's *The Star of
    Redemption*, 127-40; and the scholarly
    study of liturgical practice, 139-40;
    speech-thinking and communal
    liturgy, 128; the Torah as recounted
    history, 135-36; and universal
    redemption, 130-31; the week, 130-31
Eucharist: as liturgical enactment of
    divine provision, 110-11; as
    micropolitical practice/mediation, 241;
    as overaccepting, 182-83. See also
    Trisagion (the *Sanctus*) and the
    Eucharistic prayer
Eusebius, 100
Exodus, Book of, 96-97
Ezra, Book of, 238-39, 241

Faust (Goethe), 46
Festivals, Jewish: Esther and festival of
    Purim, 168; history told in, 120; as
    markers of time, 114-15; and revelation
    of the Torah at Sinai, 120
Figuration, 99-101, 102-3
Fish, Stanley, 40, 243
Foucault, Michel, 32-33
Fox, Michael V., 173n.10, 174n.13, 175n.15,
    177n.18, 186n.32
Frei, Hans, 99
French Revolution, 96
Freud, Sigmund, 188, 242

Geertz, Clifford, 188

Genesis: creation narrative, 220-21; and time, 113-15; and Word of God theology, 14-16

Gibbs, Robert, 4-5, 21, 236-37. *See also* Eternity and history

Gospels, synoptic, 218-19

Gregory of Nyssa, 36, 36n.21, 41, 42, 47-48

Gruenwald, Ithamar, 189

Haftarah, 137-39

Halivni, David Weiss, 238, 241

Hallel service, 120, 121-23

Hampshire, Stuart, 47

Hannah, petitionary prayer of, 7-8, 7n.16, 14

Hegel, G. W. F., 79-80

Heschel, Abraham, 59

Hobbes, Thomas, 233

"How to Avoid Speaking" (Derrida), 10-12, 33

Hunsinger, George, 3-4

Improvisation and Christian ethics, 168-71. *See also* Esther and the practices of improvisation

Intersubjectivity, 39, 78-80

Isaac of Acre, Rabbi, 202n.40

Isaiah, Book of, 149, 152-60, 153n.12; and commodification of time, 158-59; and the enjoyment of God's time, 159; and the image of burning, 155; military destruction and emptying of the land, 154-55; and moral uncleanness, 153-54, 153n.13; and the *Sanctus,* 152-60, 161-62; time and God's action toward his people, 157-59; time and worship in, 159-60; and "woe," 154, 154n.14

James, William, 72

Jenson, Robert, 94n.12

Jewish-Christian relations and the politics of redemption, 229-44; Augustinian response to the implicit arguments, 232-35; the category of the "messianic," 236; Christ as mediator, 239-42; and co-abiding, 241-42; hermeneutical-political differences, 236; the historical wounds of Jewish-Christian relations, 234-35; liturgical action and political judgments, 229; and the liturgy of silence, 224-26; and modern secularism, 229-30; political economy and political time, 230-31; and the politics of mediation, 235-42; and religion in the political spotlight, 242-44; and sacramental semiotics, 240-41; and solipsism, 233-34; and Torah as mediator, 236-39

Jewish marriage ritual, 188-211; and the bride as object, 198-203; the bride as stopgap/seal, 200-202; and the bridegroom's statement of intent, 190-91; and the bride's silencing, 208-9; and discrepancies between ritual and reality, 189-92, 202-5, 211; and human bodies as Torah, 193-98, 237-38; legal and quasi-legal components, 189; and liturgical incongruities, 194-95, 198-99; and male desire *(zimzum),* 198-99; men/women and written/oral law, 195-97; as metaphor for Sinai/*chuppah,* 190, 193-95, 207, 210-11; motif of procreation/the sex act, 193, 195; and real relationships, 201-2, 203-7, 210-11; the seven blessings, 189n.5, 190n.7, 192-95, 198-200, 206, 211; seventh blessing, 206, 211; sixth blessing, 206; and transgendering/gender reversals, 194n.15, 196-98; Zalman's Hasidic/kabbalistic interpretation, 191, 192-211

John, Gospel of, 32, 34-35, 218-19

John Damascene, St., 48

Kant, Immanuel, 60

Kepnes, Steven, 21. *See also* Rosenzweig's hermeneutics of liturgical practice

Kreisau Circle, 3

Lash, Nicholas, 148

Lévinas, Emmanuel, 56, 67, 75, 137, 236
Lévi-Strauss, Claude, 188
Liturgical acts *(leitourgia)*, 29-49; the
  agent of, 31-39; the agent's selfhood/
  identity, 32-33; the agent's surrender/
  sacrifice, 32; and Aristotle, 29-30, 48,
  48n.36; as an offering, 43-44; and
  Christ-likeness, 34; and co-abiding in
  Christ, 32, 34-39; cultic use of
  leitourgia, 30, 30n.6; defining, 31, 48-49;
  Derrida and *différance,* 32-33, 33nn.13-
  15; dispositions and affections, 47-48;
  effect and mode of causation, 44-46;
  the effect of the act, 44-47; and ethics,
  29, 48; evaluation of, 41-43; and the
  faith community, 37-38; and the
  individual human body, 35-37; and
  kinēsis, 48, 48n.36; and life hidden
  within Christ, 30-31; naming and
  judging, 41-43; the nature of the
  action, 39-41; the object of, 43-44; and
  Paul, 30-31; rational judgments and
  striving for apatheia, 47-48; reason-
  action connection, 47-48; as service,
  29-30; six key elements of, 31; and
  social encounters/interrelationality, 38-
  39; and "theo-logic," 31; and
  transfiguration, 46-47; as utopic
  moment, 41
Liturgical calendar. *See* Rosenzweig's
  hermeneutics of liturgical practice
Liturgical performance. *See* Esther and
  the practices of improvisation
Liturgical practice. *See* Rosenzweig's
  hermeneutics of liturgical practice
Locke, John, 73
Luther, Martin, 168
Lyotard, Jean-François, 94

MacIntyre, Alasdair, 94
Magid, Shaul, 22. *See also* Jewish
  marriage ritual
Maimonides, Moses, 6
Mark, Gospel of, 216, 216n.2

Marketplace: contemporary idolatrous
  praise of, 147-51; and providence, 105
Marx, Karl, 148, 242
Matthew, Gospel of, 216, 216n.2
Maximus the Confessor, 215
Mead, Margaret, 188
Media, 231
Mediation, liturgical: Christ as mediator,
  239-42; the Eucharist as, 241;
  pedagogical aspects of, 230-31; political
  aspects of, 231; the politics of, 235-42;
  redemptive aspects of, 232; Torah as
  mediator, 236-39
Milbank, John, 19, 78n.13, 104
Morning prayer, 50-87; the Amidah, 84;
  Barchi nafshi et YHVH, 60-61; *Baruch
  she amar,* 64-65; and binarism of the
  modern West, 86-87; and binary
  character of the modern "I think," 85;
  and covenantal Israel, 78, 85, 85n.17;
  and creation, 75-76; criteria for
  verification of judgments, 77; and daily
  renewal of creation, 64-65; dimensions
  of reflection/inspective and judgment,
  76-77; and ennobling/humbling, 77; as
  exercise in logic of making judgments,
  66-74; and expansion/contraction, 76;
  God's "great love" and gift of
  knowledge, 83; *Hineni mitatef . . . k'de
  l'kayem mitsvat bor'i kakatuv b'torah,*
  61-62; and the hypothetical character
  of our judgments, 77; the identity of
  the worshiper (the "I"), 62, 62n.9, 63,
  74; and imagination, 82; as implicating
  worshipper and community, 74-87;
  implications for how we see/think, 85-
  86; and intersubjectivity, 78-80; and
  Jewish Evening Prayer, 52-53, 69-70;
  judging the world with/without
  Morning Prayer, 65-66; judgments
  made after Morning Prayer, 67; and
  logic of relations, 57, 69-74, 75, 77;
  Modeh ani lefanekha, 58-59; and
  modern socialization, 50-51; the
  morning blessings *(Birchot*

Hashachar), 58-62; and Moses' call, 83-84; night to day judgments, 54; and physical action of the body, 61-62; and propositional model of making judgments, 55-57, 63-64, 66-69; reading the stages of, 57-87; and reflections on redeeming judgment, 63-64; and the relational character of our being, 77-87, 78n.13; *Reshit chokhma yirat YHVH*, 59-60; and the soul's images and perceptions, 62; and transformation of the "I" into "We," 64-66, 78-81; the verses of praise *(Pesuke D'zimra)*, 64-66

Moses: and burning bush, 221-22; call of, 83-84; and creaturely "I," 85; and Mosaic dialogue, 218

Murder in the Cathedral (Eliot), 91, 93, 95, 98, 104, 107

Mystagogical Catecheses (Cyril of Jerusalem), 161

Nation-states, 95-97, 243

Nazi regime, 2-3

New Testament: on God's providential care, 107-8; liturgy of silence and continuity with Old Testament, 225-26; synoptic Gospels, 218-19

Nicomachean Ethics (Aristotle), 29, 48

Niebuhr, H. Richard, 108-10

Niebuhr, Reinhold, 108-10

Nostra Aetate, 234

Novak, David, 14

Ochs, Peter, 20, 229, 238. *See also* Morning prayer

Old Testament: creation narrative and subject/object divide, 220-21; divine voice and body of God, 221-22; Exodus, 96-97; Genesis, 14-16, 113-15, 220-21; and liturgy of silence, 225-26

Parashah Ha-Shavuah, 117-18

Passover Haggadah, 116

Patmos Group, 2-3

Paul, St., 30-31, 46

Pecknold, C. C. *See* Jewish-Christian relations and the politics of redemption

Peirce, Charles, 69-74, 75, 77, 84n.16, 85n.17

Pennington, Chad, 121n.7

Philippians, Letter to the, 30

Pickstock, Catherine, 19

Pliny, 146-47

Politics: and doctrine of providence, 103-4, 106-11; perceptions of time and, 95-97

Politics (Aristotle), 29-30

Postmodern views of progress, 94-95, 94n.12

Prayer: in the Anglican tradition, 182; *halakha* and petitionary prayer, 8-9; Soloveitchik on, 6-9; and Word of God theology, 6-14. *See also* Morning Prayer

Providence, doctrine of, 91-111; and the Church in the postmodern world, 98; and critical historical scholarship, 93-94; divine providence, 101-2, 107-10; and effect on community, 95-97; and Eucharist celebration, 110-11; and figuration, 99-101, 102-3; liturgical practice and patient waiting, 110-11; and "manifest destiny" rhetoric, 106; and the marketplace, 105; modernity and the disfiguring of, 104-6; as narration/narrative, 99; and the nation-state, 95-97; and natural/social science, 105; needed shifts in discourse about, 99-104; New Testament on, 107-8; Niebuhrs' discussion of eschatology and, 108-10; perceptions of time and politics, 95-97; and the political economy, 104-6; and postmodern views of progress, 94-95, 94n.12; as practical doctrine of action, 103-4; the practice and politics of, 103-4, 106-11; and shift from language of control to affirmations of redemption, 101-3;

threefold good news of, 98-99; and time, 91-104

Psalms: and Augustine's *Confessions*, 113, 120-21, 121n.7, 123; the Hallel service and communal chanting of, 120, 121-23; Psalm 105 and intersubjectivity, 79

Pseudo-Dionysius (the Areopagite), 12, 33, 33nn.14-15

Purim festival, 168, 186

Quash, Ben, 21-22, 237n.8, 240, 242. See also *Trisagion* (the *Sanctus*) and the Eucharistic prayer

Rahner, Karl, 36n.19, 143-44

Rashi, 207n.53

Rashkover, Randi. *See* Word of God theology

Reagan, Ronald, 100

Reasoning, liturgical, 47-48

"Redemption, Prayer, and Talmud Torah" (Soloveitchik), 5-9

Revelation, Book of, 39; early Christians and subversiveness of, 146-47, 150-51; and the sacrifice of the Lamb, 151-52, 240, 242; on sovereignty, 146; the *Trisagion* and the vision of, 145-52

Ritual studies: in contemporary study of religion, 188-90; and the Finnish hunting ritual, 191-92, 202-3, 205, 211. *See also* Jewish marriage ritual

Romans, Letter to the, 46

Rose, Gillian, 7

Rosenstock-Huessy, Eugen, 2-3, 23-25

Rosenzweig, Franz, 115-16, 128, 236; correspondence with Rosenstock-Huessy, 23-25; and the Jewish year, 131-32; and the Patmos Group, 2-3; on the physical scroll in the liturgy, 132-33; view of Jews and world history, 136; and Word of God theology, 2-3; *The Star of Redemption (Der Stern der Erlösung)*, 112-13, 115-16, 127-40

Rosenzweig's hermeneutics of liturgical practice, 112-23; the annual cycle of Torah reading, 118; Augustine and recitation of Psalms, 120-21, 121n.7, 123; Augustine on temporality, 112, 113; Garden of Eden and time of exile/time of history, 114; Genesis 1 and time, 113-15; and the Hallel service, 120, 121-23; and issues of temporality in Torah, 113-15; and Jewish seasonal festivals, 114-15, 120; the liturgical calendar and holy time, 117-23; the *Parashah Ha-Shavuah*, 117-18; Passover Haggadah liturgy, 116; recitation of Psalms and eternal time, 120-23; secular time and the modern world, 115; Shabbat and celebration of natural creation and bodily needs, 119; Shabbat and liturgical time, 117-19; temporality/sacred time in Jewish liturgy, 115-16

Ruach (breath), 217

Sanctus. See *Trisagion* (the *Sanctus*) and the Eucharistic prayer

Scharlemann, Robert, 34

Secularism: and Jewish-Christian relations, 229-30; secular time and the modern world, 115

"*La Sensation du Divin*" (Claudel), 36

Sermon on the Mount, 107

Seven wedding blessings. See Jewish marriage ritual

Shabbat: as celebration of natural creation, 119; domestic/liturgical preparations before, 118-19; and the liturgical calendar, 117-23; and liturgical time, 117-19; morning service and rolling the scroll, 133-34; and reading of Torah, 117-18; as separation between profane and sacred, 114

Siewerth, Gustav, 155

Silence, liturgy of, 215-26; and the body of Christ, 219-24; and continuity of Old and New Testaments, 225-26; cosmic and relational contexts, 219-24; divine conversation between Father and Son, 218-19; divine silence and human silence, 215; divine silence and liturgy, 215-16; divine silence from cosmic perspective, 216-18; divine voice and body of God, 222; and Jesus, 216, 218-19, 223-24; and Jewish-Christian relations, 224-26; Moses and burning bush, 221-22; Old Testament, 220-22, 225-26; and paradox of the Incarnation, 221; private and public speech, 219; and *ruach* (breath), 217; and silence of the cross, 219-21; and subjective/objective divide, 220-21; two types of silence, 219-20; voice and world, 221-23

Skopos of the church, 37

Smith, Adam, 104, 105

Smith, Jonathan Z., 188, 191-92, 202-3, 205, 211

Solipsism, 233-34

Soloveitchik, Joseph, 5-9, 14

Song of Songs, 207-8, 207n.53, 208n.59

Spinoza, Baruch, 32

The Star of Redemption (Der Stern der Erlösung) (Rosenzweig), 112-13, 115-16, 127-40

Sydney, Sir Philip, 49

Taubes, Jacob, 236

tefillah, 7, 10

Theological realism. *See* Word of God theology

Time: commodification of, 91-92, 158-59; and the disfiguring of providence, 104-6; and doctrine of providence, 91-92, 95-97, 97-104; and Genesis, 113-15; history and simultaneity, 95-97; history as additive, 93; and Jewish festivals, 114-15; and politics, 95-97; and rise of nation-state, 95-97; Shabbat and liturgical time, 117-19; and transition between Middle Ages and modernity, 93

Torah: bodies as, 193-98, 237-38; Ezra and the maculate Torah, 238-39, 241; the Jewish year and reading of, 131-32; as

mediator, 236-39; and revelation at Sinai, 120; Shabbat reading of the *Parashah Ha-Shavuah*, 117-18. *See also* Torah scrolling

Torah scrolling: and practice of *haftarah*, 137-39; and the Shabbat morning service, 133-34; and two blessings recited, 133-35; the year and the physical scroll in the liturgy, 132-33

Trisagion (the *Sanctus*) and the Eucharistic prayer, 141-63; Balthasar on, 162-63; and Book of Revelation, 145-52; as calling for temporal openness, 162; and call to sing a "new song," 149; and challenge to Christians, 150-51; and early Christians, 160-61; economic dimensions, 163; and the ends of the Earth/natural world, 143-45; the eucharistic prayer itself, 141-42; and global economic market, 147-51; and holiness in time-taking, 151-52; and Isaiah 6, 152-60, 153n.12, 161-62; and isolationism, 150; and moral pluralism, 149-50; placement within the prayer, 141-42; political implications of, 145, 146-47; and sacrifice of the Lamb in Revelation, 151-52, 240, 242; and the sanctifying power of the divine presence, 160-63; and seeds of new growth, 162

Troeltsch, Ernst, 93-94

Turner, Victor, 116, 188

Vriezen, T. C., 153n.12

Wallace, David Foster, 92

Ward, Graham, 20, 239-40, 242. *See also* Liturgical acts *(leitourgia)*

Weber, Max, 242

Webster, John, 10

Wedding blessings, Jewish. *See* Jewish marriage ritual

Wells, Sam, 20, 22, 158-59, 239. *See also* Esther and the practices of improvisation

Williams, Rowan, 121n.7

Wittgenstein, Ludwig, 70

Wolfson, Elliot, 201n.36, 202n.42, 204

Word of God theology, 2-25; applied to political resistance, 2-3; and Barth's theological realism, 2-3, 9-10, 16-19; and concrete/worldly behaviors, 19; and contemporary philosophical challenges, 5; correspondence of Rosenstock-Huessy and Rosenzweig, 23-25; and Derrida, 10-12, 13-14; and discourse of prayer, 6-9, 10-12, 13-14; and divine freedom, 16-18; and the God of Genesis, 14-16; and the Jewish-Christian exchange, 24-25; and language of redemption/language of human need, 5-6; and "liturgy" (*leitourgia*), 10; and love of neighbor, 18-19; need for recovery of, 4-9; and Rosenzweig's *Star of Redemption*, 4-5; and Soloveitchik on petitionary prayer, 6-9, 14; and *"tefillah,"* 7, 10; and the theo-logic of Prayer, 10-19

Yoder, John Howard, 173n.9

Zalman, Rabbi Schneur, 191, 192-211. *See also* Jewish marriage ritual